Born to
SHOP

L O N D O N

Second Edition

D0818451

Born to SHOP

LONDON

Second Edition

SUZY GERSHMAN
and
JUDITH THOMAS

With an Introduction by
MICHAELJOHN

BANTAM BOOKS

TORONTO • NEW YORK • LONDON
SYDNEY • AUCKLAND

BORN TO SHOP: LONDON
A Bantam Book / May 1986
Bantam Second Edition / April 1987

Cover art by David Calver.
Book design by Lynne Arany.
Maps by Judith Thomas and Lauren Dong.

Library of Congress Cataloging-in-Publication Data
(Revised for vol. 2)
Gershman, Suzy.
  Born to shop.

  Rev. ed. of: Born to shop / Susan Schneider Thomas.
1986–
  Includes index.
  Contents: [1] France—[2] Italy—[3] London.
  1. Shopping—Directories.   I. Thomas, Judith Evans.
II. Thomas, Susan Schneider. Born to shop.   III. Title.
TX335.T45 1987   381.1'.1'025   86-32093
ISBN 0-553-34439-0

Published simultaneously in the United States and Canada

Bantam Books are published by Bantam Books, Inc. Its trade-
mark, consisting of the words "Bantam Books" and the por-
trayal of a rooster, is Registered in U.S. Patent and Trademark
Office and in other countries. Marca Registrada. Bantam Books,
Inc., 666 Fifth Avenue, New York, New York 10103.

PRINTED IN THE UNITED STATES OF AMERICA

FG   0 9 8 7 6 5 4 3 2 1

The BORN TO SHOP Team:

reported by:
Suzy Kalter Gershman
Michael Gershman
Judith Evans Thomas
London correspondent:
Debra C. Kalter, M.D.
original reporters of first edition:
Suszette Gallant
Suzy Gershman
Carolyn Schneider
Judith Thomas
editor: Jill Parsons
executive editor: Toni Burbank
assistant to executive editor: Andrew Zega
cover design: Krystyna Skalski
cover art: David Calver
book design: Lynne Arany
copy editor: William D. Drennan
maps by: Judith Evans Thomas and Lauren Dong

TO OUR MOTHERS

Acknowledgments

Well, here it is friends, you asked for it, you got it—revised, updated, and reorganized *Born to Shop: London.* You'll see the latest news on your old friends, some new friends, and a new special section—we've added the shopping low-down on Bath and Stoke-on-Trent, two day trips that are very much worth doing.

We want to thank Bantam for allowing us to rewrite this book . . . and the entire *Born to Shop* gang of ours for their help and hard work. Thanks also to Georgetta Lordi, Mytro Cutler, and Patrick Board at Inter•Continental Hotels. We certainly have to thank the front desk staff at the Mayfair Inter•Continental who did not smirk at us, even once, when we ordered up from Pizzaland those few nights. (Really! Is there anything better? A jacuzzi in your room and a pizza place downstairs that delivers?)

Even though Pan Am charged us double bags, two for one of our allowance on the suitcase that weighed sixty pounds because it was filled with books, we still want to thank them for getting us over and back safe and sound. They don't know we fly them all the time, so we have to give them a hand and also applaud their in-flight shopping service. Did you know you can buy an Hermès scarf on a Pan Am flight for the cheapest price in the entire world?

We do have a correspondent in London this year—the shopping doctor, Dr. Debbie, who has now worked for us in Hong Kong, Rio, São Paulo, and Minas. She's busy healing the sick but takes time out to watch for new stores so we can check them out when we visit her. We bring her homebaked cookies and let her play with the remote control on our TV set at the Mayfair.

Oh, yes, special thanks also to Aaron Gershman, who did some of the reporting in this book. He visited Hamley's every day to check the quality of the store and has been to every toy museum in London. He also endorses Pizzaland, the tube, and Starlight Express.

CONTENTS

Editorial Note

Although every effort was made to ensure the accuracy of prices appearing in this book, it should be kept in mind that with inflation and a fluctuating rate of exchange, prices will vary. Dollar estimations of prices were made based on the following rate of exchange: one English pound = $1.50 U.S.

Introduction

Born to shop? Absolutely. If anyone was ever born under the shopping star—it's Suzy Gershman and her friend Judith Thomas. I should know. I've been listening to her chatter on about her finds and her bargains for over ten years now.

Mrs. Gershman was one of the first people I met when I moved from London to Beverly Hills. She came in and said she wanted to be my first client because she knew the salon was the rage of the royals in London and she just had to be the first in town to try us out. She explained that trying new shops and finding the latest finds was her business. I thought this was a polite way of saying that if she didn't like her haircut, she'd be moving on.

We must have done something right, because she's kept coming back. And she brought in her friend and partner Mrs. Thomas. I don't know if it's because we let her sit around and read all the British fashion magazines and eavesdrop on the celebrity chitchat—but whatever it is—they keep popping in. And whenever they do, they tell *us* their latest finds. A lot goes round in a beauty salon, but everyone here gets a big kick out of testing the tips we hear from their lips.

Especially me. Being "bi-coastal" (as they say in L.A.), I shuttle back and forth to London a lot. A lot of people here think L.A.–N.Y. is bi-coastal. To me, the L.A.–London commute provides it all. My lifestyle has me working on a movie set one day, working in the salon another, on an airplane or doing a store promotion the next day and all the while having to be up on the latest in both Beverly Hills and London. My customers all keep me posted, of course, and we always have our eyes to the future—feeling out new trends and new fashion directions. But just before I go to London, I like to browse through *Born to Shop: London* to pick up odds and ends and hot tips that might otherwise escape me. And I'm always amazed that I, a Londoner, can learn something new.

I've been trusting Mrs. Gershman and Mrs. Thomas for several years now and find they have a good eye and a good sense of humor. We've been passing information around, back and forth for so long now that I've come to count on them for at least one tidbit every six weeks.

Since it's unlikely you'll be dropping by the salon on the same day as Mrs. Thomas (Mrs. Gershman moved to Connecticut, so she's not so regular), I heartily recommend this book as a great start for your next British shopping spree.

John of MICHAELJOHN
London and Beverly Hills

Preface

It all started out as a joke.

Four ladies who lunch, all wearing silk blouses, diamond earrings, and—for God's sake—hats. We were celebrating the thirty-ninth birthday of one Judith Evans Thomas, dear to each of the other women at the table.

Birthday discussion was minimal. You do understand the situation. Instead, we talked about what women always talk about when they get together over lunch—childbirth, day care, husbands, and shopping.

Okay, we talked mostly about shopping.

Okay, we began to trade shopping secrets.

By the end of lunch, we walked away three pounds heavier and all business partners. It still was a joke.

We sold the books immediately and laughed all the way around the world. All of us were devoted bargain shoppers par excellence. One woman stayed in Beverly Hills to run the control group; the other three continued shopping and updating our secrets. Europe never was the same.

The dollar rose and fell, terrorism came and went. But the notion of a guide to shopping began to catch on.

There are two partners now—we gave up just about everything else to continue shopping. It's a dirty job, but someone has to do it.

The original three books (on France, Italy, and London) have now all been totally rewritten and updated and revised and restructured and fixed. New books have joined the ranks. Domestic books (on New York! Los Angeles!) are being added to the series. The series evolves, but one thing is constant: We are having the time of our lives.

But we now are also running a business, and since so many people ask us how this works, here goes:

▼ No store can purchase a listing in this book, or any other book we write.

▼ Most stores (let's call that 99%) of the stores we visit do not ever know we have visited them as reporters.

▼ We visit each shop at least twice, usually more than that.

▼ We visit each city at least three times and often over a period of years before we write one word.

▼ We visit each store again for a revision.

▼ All opinions expressed are solely our own—we are highly opinionated and make no bones about what we like or don't like.

▼ We make no attempt to visit every store in a city or an area.

▼ We do not use about 40% of the material we have; likewise, about 40% of the stores we visit do not qualify.

▼ These books are being updated and revised on an annual basis, but if you catch a change before we do, we would appreciate a card or note to:

Born to Shop
Bantam Books
666 Fifth Avenue, 25th Floor
New York, NY 10103

▼ We do try to answer our mail personally, but please understand that we are out of town a lot. We feel terrible about the woman who wrote us three weeks before her vacation, asking for some information about Paris—we didn't even get her letter until after we returned from South America . . . and she was long gone.

Born to Shop is no longer a joke to us—it's our business. We're laughing with joy that the books are selling and that you're writing such nice letters. Someday we hope to be laughing all the way to the bank—to pay our American Express bill!

Suzy Gershman and Judith Thomas
Spring 1987

I ▾ THE SHOPPING EXPERIENCE

King George's Revenge

Shopping in England has always been different from shopping on the Continent. First, we all speak the same language. Everything is easier in your own language. Second, there are two established types of English fashion—the traditional English look, and the wild and crazy stuff. We know what we will find when we go there, and we are never disappointed. This is much different psychologically from shopping in another part of the world where you don't know what to expect.

Besides sharing the language, we share a basic understanding of value. The English insist on quality, on items that will wear and wear and wear. America has evolved into a wash-and-wear country, but our essential values are British. For those who are opposed to throwaway fashion, shopping in England offers a slight price break in terms of dollars but a bigger savings in the long run—British-made merchandise is made to last. Shopping in Britain means investment shopping.

Shopping in Britain also offers a unique crossroad to European merchandise. If you are not going to the Continent, you can still save some money on most European designers. When you browse and spend in London you always have choices, and one of those choices is to buy big-name European-designer goods at competitive prices. No, they won't be as inexpensive as in France or Italy, or their country of origin. But they will be less expensive than in the United States (usually!). And—get this—much high-style European merchandise

1

cannot be sold to locals who prefer traditional Anglophile looks. Therefore the sales are incredible.

So pack up your brolly and your Wellies. Who cares if it rains or shines on you? London is a shopper's paradise.

Take Back Your Culture (Unless You're Speaking of Pearls)

E ven the most stingy of tour directors lets his group free in a foreign city for a few hours of shopping. Tour directors regularly push culture, scenery, and historical references, but they do know enough to let their wards have a few hours to themselves to shop. For the most part, tour directors just don't understand the true shopper. Instead, they are big on museums, statues, ruins, and dead saints.

We have nothing against any of these things. We believe that especially for a first trip to Europe, one should combine a little of everything to get the most enriching experience possible.

On return trips, however, we ask you to remember:

▼ Hampton Court has a remarkable maze, but if you really want to get lost, wouldn't you rather do it in a department store?

▼ The Victoria and Albert Museum has one of the world's best costume collections; perhaps your own could use some work on it.

▼ Big Ben is a very nice clock, but wouldn't you prefer something in a wristwatch?

On your trip to England, you will see many churches, cathedrals, ruins, fountains, national treasures, and restful, street-side cafes. You will drink strong tea, eat flaky scones, and gain weight on salt and vinegar crisps. But you may never again see stores like the ones you are about to see. Travel has never been more comfortable, or rewarding. (You can even accrue a ton of mileage for your flight bonus club while you save money and have a good time!) Designer merchandise has never been more popular. The so-called elite names of fashions and furnishings have become more and more available to the middle class. At last there is designer gear at a price that is accessible to those who have the price of a round-trip ticket to Europe and a moderate spending allowance.

Shoppers Unanimous

O f course, not everyone wants to go to London to shop. There are shoppers and there are *shoppers*. We all buy a few things. The amount you buy may be governed by finances, storing limitations, or whatever. But the enthusiasm with which you pursue your purchase separates the *shopper* from the mere shopper.

This book is for the *shopper*. This book is for the person, male or female, who considers a good shopping experience to be equal to a stimulating religious or sexual experience . . . possibly better. That doesn't mean that he or she got a bargain, or even bought anything. The experience was psychologically exciting, invigorating, uplifting, and creative. The true *shopper* may be exhausted physically after a hard day on the pavement but will be mentally exhilarated.

The shopping experience should satisfy all

the senses—there will be interesting and often beautiful things to look at, touch, smell; new pieces of information to learn, bits of history, sociology, marketing, and behavioral science all wrapped up together (with a bow, if that's no extra charge). The experience is topped only if something of value to the shopper can be purchased, and purchased well within budget.

Some shopping is done for the glory of seeing what is available; some shopping is done to see what beautiful and wondrous things can be acquired within means; some shopping is taken on as a challenge, kind of a can-you-top-this need deep within the bosom that only Monty Hall or your best friend would understand.

To many, the thrill of the chase is to bring home a prized item at a low price. After all, anyone with the money to do so can walk into a Fifth Avenue, Rodeo Drive, or even Old Bond Street shop, lay out some cash, and walk away with an item of taste and beauty. It's easy. What isn't so easy is finding the same item in a less obvious place but getting a big discount on it. Some shoppers do not enjoy their splurges unless they shop the top of the line. There are people who hate crowds, big stores, sales, and public transportation. To them, a quiet specialty store where they are known and will get the most intimate service is worth any price. (We love good service, but we are not that kind of person.)

To us, shopping is both a sport and an art. We value our time, so we would not spend a day to save $10. We do, however, take serious pride in saving money, in going two for one, or in coming home with a 50% saving. For the same money our friend spent in the fancy shop, we like to have gone to the discounter and bought *two* of the item (or have saved *half* the money). We believe in mixing merchandise so that we look like a million without having spent it. And we always quit shopping when it ceases to be fun.

We call ourselves (unofficially, of course) shoppers unanimous. Unanimously, shopping is our first choice. Our feelings about shopping are akin to those others have about liquor, cigarettes, maybe even drugs. (Haven't you found that a really good bargain gives you an incredible high?!!) We are addicted not only to spending a portion of our income but also to spending it in the ways that amuse and satisfy us the most.

The Moscow Rule of Shopping

T he Moscow Rule of Shopping is one of our most basic shopping rules and has nothing to do with shopping in Moscow, so please pay attention. Now: The average shopper, in his or her pursuit of the ideal bargain, does not buy an item he wants when he first sees it because he's not convinced that he won't find it elsewhere for less money. He wants to see everything available, then return for the purchase of choice. This is a rather normal thought process. If you live in an Iron Curtain country, however, you know that you must buy something the minute you see it because if you hesitate, it will be gone. Hence the title of our international law: the Moscow Rule of Shopping.

When you are on a trip, you probably will not have the time to compare prices and then return to a certain shop; you will never be able to backtrack cities, and if you could, the item might be gone by the time you got back, anyway. What to do? The same thing they do in Moscow: Buy it when you see it, with the understanding that you may never see it again. But since you are not shopping in Moscow and you may see it again, weigh these questions carefully before you go ahead:

1. Is this a touristy type of item that I am bound to find all over town?

2. Is this an item I can't live without, even if I am overpaying?

3. Is this a reputable shop, and can I trust what they tell me about the availability of such items?

4. Is the quality of this particular item so spectacular that it is unlikely it could be matched at this price?

If you have good reason to buy it when you see it, do so. If you get taken, you can always tell the tale as you sit in your rocking chair in front of the Shoppers Unanimous Old Age Home, where no one tells of war heroics and everyone exchanges shopping stories.

Caveat: The Moscow Rule of Shopping breaks down if you are an antiques or bric-a-brac shopper, since you never know if you can find another of an old or used item, if it's in the same condition, or if the price will be higher or lower. It's very hard to price collectibles, so consider doing a lot of shopping for an item before you buy anything. This is easy in London, where there are a zillion markets that sell much the same type of merchandise in the collectibles area. At a certain point, you just have to buy what you love and not worry about the price or the Moscow Rule of Shopping.

▼ Always buy a designer on sale when it's marked down to half, fits you, and is a good color. Amen.

The British Sale Philosophy

The British are largely responsible for teaching the Americans to appreciate a good buy. As a result of their belief in thrift, the Brits are famous for doing their shopping in two distinct patterns: What has to be bought is bought when needed; everything else is bought on sale at either Christmas or midsummer. The British believe that a good sale is their due for surviving without the item until it has been marked down. It is socially acceptable to shop the sales, and many women boast of their bargains. If you have bought a luxury item, you are considered "daft" if you pay full retail price. Brits pride themselves on being smart shoppers.

Many Americans are now cashing in on the big British sales. If the dollar is very strong and the pound weak, you may hear comments about how nice it must be for you to come over and get "their" bargains; if the pound is strong against the dollar, you are more welcome because then you are putting extra money into the Queen's coffers. Because sales are intensely important to the locals, be prepared for some stiff competition for the more practical items. We find we do best on designer goods that the British consider too frivolous to begin with—especially French and Italian designers who may be too expensive for the average London lady but at a marked-down price are *much* cheaper than in the United States.

Royal Warrants

S peaking of the Queen, you may wonder where she shops. She doesn't. Things are "sent round" to Buckingham Palace for her to consider. Money and price tags never touch her hands. However, she asks only certain stores and factories to send round goods—these stores have the royal seal of approval, which is called a royal warrant. We firmly believe that if Her Majesty were to set foot in Toys-"Я"-Us while on a buying spree for Prince Harry, she would award the first American royal warrant, but the Queen has only been to Bloomie's lately. Oh, well . . .

Holding a royal warrant demands total discretion. The warrantholder may not talk about the royals in any way—especially to the press or public—or he will lose his warrant. So if you walk into Turnbull & Asser and ask them what size pj's Prince Charles wears, you will be met by an icy stare and stony silence. Royal warrants are allowed to display the royal coat of arms and to use the words "by appointment." Since there is more than one royal family in Europe, and there are several members of the Windsor (or Mountbatten) family, you may also see several coats of arms in any given store—appointments from various royals.

A warrant is good for ten years and then must be renewed. If you are dropped you sort of get a royal pink slip without any redress. Every year about twenty to thirty new warrants are issued and the same number of pink slips are passed out.

There are warrants on everything from royal laundry detergent (Procter & Gamble) to royal china, and there can be several warrants in the same category. For china, HRH has as much trouble getting it down to one pattern as we do—there are warrants at Royal Worcester,

Spode, and Doulton; the Queen Mother gets her bone china from Royal Crown Derby.

Royals are billed for what they buy; it is not clear if they pay wholesale or merely get a discount. It's unlikely that they pay the full retail price.

A complete list of current royal warrants is published in the United States by William Morrow & Company, Inc. Remember, royals do not issue warrants to jobbers, bargain basements, or factory outlets. Drat!

Savile Row

Women do a lot of the guiding behind a man's wardrobe. If Savile Row is on your mind, you can go with your man, or send him on his own.

If he wants to look like a prince, with or without a royal warrant, he probably wants to wear custom-made, or bespoke, suits, made at a Savile Row tailor. Not every bespoke tailor is on Savile Row, but the name has become a generic for quality and good fit in men's clothing. More than half of the clients are American businessmen who think it the ultimate in sartorial pleasure to have a custom-made English suit.

While most of Savile Row's custom suits still are custom-made, if you are quoted an unreasonably cheap price (under $500), ask questions. Some tailors keep stock patterns with a nearby factory and have your suit run up there, with the cuffs adjusted to your measurements by hand. You may get a very fine suit this way, but not for bespoke prices. Know what you are buying. Other tailors have come to specialize in this business and take pride in selling you an almost custom suit for about $250. Not a bad deal at all, if you are an almost rack size.

For true custom work, expect two fittings, perhaps a third. If your man has weird habits—he likes to play golf in a three-piece business suit—mention it to the tailor so he can recommend fabric or tailoring that will provide the proper give. The well-made suit is like a good piece of camouflage: It makes the body appear to be "perfect" and still moves with the man.

The price of a bespoke suit ranges from tailor to tailor and depends slightly on the fabric you choose. (Winter suits always cost more than summer suits because of the fabric, but once you're choosing a fine wool there usually is very little price difference between two fabrics.) Expect to pay at least $700; you may pay as high as $1,200. You will get a VAT discount. The average suit is two-piece; you must request a vest—called a waistcoat—and will pay about $75 more for it. The tailor will not volunteer to make two pairs of pants to interchange with the jacket, but you can push him to it. A bespoke suit is a formal business suit and will not wear evenly if the jacket is worn with two pairs of trousers. Savile Row tailors think the practice of getting an extra pair of trousers is very "Hong Kong."

Savile Row tailors expect their suits to last twenty years, which makes them a bargain for the man who plans to wear them for twenty years. And, yes, a good Savile Row tailor will make a woman's suit. It will be very traditional, but of the usual quality.

A few names for starters:

HAWES & CURTISS, 2 Burlington Gardens. Even though Sir Alistair Cooke has become an American, he epitomizes British fashion. Don't you just want to start humming the theme to *Masterpiece Theatre* right now? His tailor is Hawes & Curtiss.

KILGOUR, FRENCH, & STANBURY, 8 Savile Row. KFS is a famous name to any well-dressed or well-heeled American businessman—their ready-to-wear suits are made and sold in the United States. Their bespoke suits, however, are available only in London.

ANDERSON & SHEPPARD, 30 Savile Row. These are the guys to take you by the hand and guide you through the whole thing—comforting for the nervous or the ambivalent. Warning: The armholes usually are cut high, in the European fashion. Make sure your man can move. (If he's thin, he'll love this fit!)

HENRY POOLE, 15 Savile Row. Expensive, but very well known to those who know. Poole offers a more military fit in a suit and also makes bespoke uniforms if your true love is needing a little something for a reunion of the Cold Stream Guards.

GIEVES & HAWKES, 1 Savile Row. This one is one of our faves, just for atmosphere. If you happen to have an American-size husband (ours look like football players . . .), this may be one of the better choices—the many tailors here are used to American bodies.

POULSEN & SKONE, 53 Jermyn Street. Poulsen & Skone is a shoemaker located above a shirtmaker—that is very convenient after you've ordered your suits. (Keep swatches!) Bespoke shoes are rather an extravagance but are not the most expensive shoes in town. If your man is used to paying $150 for simple loafers, he'll love it here. It takes about a half hour to be measured, but it may take six months to receive your shoes.

For the gentlemen, we have two other sources that provide Savile Row benefits without being on Savile Row.

THOMAS PINK, 2 Donovan Court, SW10; 16 Cullum Street, EC3. If he wants to try something a little more exciting than a Turnbull & Asser shirt but still be in the pink, he may want to ring up Thomas Pink—who is very "in" at the moment and famous for his quality men's shirts. Mr. Pink's shirts have their own logo, a pink square of fabric, sewn into the shirt tail. Proper Etonians have been known to drop trousers just to show off their pink.

MANLEY LAIRD (no office), 870-2409. If your man needs a custom-fitted suit but can't get out of his business meetings to make it to the tailor, ring up Manley Laird, who has an office on wheels. You will be fitted at your convenience—hotel or office—for a *veeery* proper Savile Row–style suit. It takes a week to get your garment.

Sloane Rangers

I f your man is expected to wear Savile Row, you just may classify yourself as a Sloane Ranger. Sloane Rangers emerged shortly after the world discovered Princess Diana and her friends—and their favorite shops, all in the Sloane Street area. At the same time, *The Preppy Handbook* was a best seller in the United States, and the Sloane Ranger became known as the British version of the preppy. Actually, the Sloane Ranger spends a good bit more money than the preppy and never wears anything that's bright green with little blue whales on it.

Sloane Rangers were among the first to try Giorgio at Harvey Nichols. They inherit a good bit of their furniture and make the rest of it look like it's inherited. They never get tired of those cute little Laura Ashley prints. Since they think that wearing their family jewels is tacky, they buy paste at Fior or Butler & Wilson (they go more for the deco than the glitz here), which they know enough not to wear with their pearls or cashmere sweater sets.

Hot Young Things

I f you want to go from the ridiculous to the sublime, just look all around London. Savile Row on one hand, Hyper-Hyper on the other.

Hyper-Hyper is a relatively new market where design students and hot young things come to be turned into Cinderella while selling the latest in fashion and nonsense from their tiny stalls. A few have made it. Karl Lagerfeld discovered a milliner (Kirstin Woodward) here and whisked her right off to Paris. Many other big designers and their assistants are on the prowl here, for new talent and new ideas to steal.

Whether you like avant-garde fashion or not, this is like a trip to a museum of visual delight on Mars. Take teens and adolescents with you . . . and your camera. Street fashion is blooming in London and is rapidly being absorbed into the American culture and the mainstream. The big New York department stores estimate that over 50% of their merchandise comes from London now. Designers like Betty Jackson were virtual unknowns a year ago and now are getting full-page newspaper ads in American newspapers as stores bring in more and more new talent. The best place to take advantage of the dollar-pound exchange is with new names.

The best buys in London are on unknown designer goods. Many of these unknowns sell their work for $500 a pop—so not everything is a steal. But if you are the kind of person who seeks a unique design before a well-known brand name, check out some of these up-and-coming stars and also get yourself over to Hyper-Hyper:

Charlie Allen
Ratchel Auburn
Alistair Blair

Melissa Caplan
Joe Casely-Hayford
Chimel
Jasper Conran
Crolla
Wendy Dagworthy
Barbara Devries
Graham Fraser
Georgina Godley
Katharine Hamnet
Betty Jackson
Stephen Jones
Anthony Kwok
John McIntyre
Rifat Ozbek
Chris Parry
Arabella Pollen
John Rocha
Richmond-Cornejo
Stevie Stewart (Body Map)
Joseph Tricot
Georgina von Etzdorf
Vivienne Westwood
Kirstin Woodward

HYPER-HYPER, 26–40 Kensington High Street, W8; hours: Monday to Saturday, 10:00 A.M. to 6:00 P.M., Thursday night until 7:00 P.M.

2 ▼ THE BUSINESS OF BUSINESS

The Importance of Imports

We aren't very political and we don't understand everything in the paper about the balance of trade, but we do know that importing is a very important part of this country's appetite. Aside from the Boston Tea Party, we can't think of a time in American history when folks at home weren't happy to get packages from friends, family, or retail sources based overseas—especially in the Old World.

Naturally, we understand that imports cost more in the United States because you have to pay for transportation and usually you have to pay duty (duties are highest on goods that compete with United States–manufactured goods—such as clothes—and lowest on items not made in the United States). We expect to get a bargain when we buy from the source. While some international manufacturers raise and lower their prices on a per-market basis to compete with local talent, most English-made goods are something of a bargain in England. Of course, the bargain depends on the strength of the dollar, but generally speaking, goods should be 20 to 40% cheaper in England than in the United States.

How the System Works

We do not have a big enough book to tell you all the secrets of retailing life right here, right now; but here's an oversimplified version of how retailing and manufacturing and importing and exporting work so you can understand the steps and the structure of the process of buying, selling, making, and moving goods. Once you know how the system works, you'll better understand how and where to look for the best buys.

The selling of goods involves two sets of middlemen:

▼ manufacturers

▼ retailers

Let's talk about the sweater business. We own the Hop Sing Mills, as you may recall. We are located in Hong Kong, New York, Manchester, and Biella (Italy). While we own some very nice mills, we do not own the sheep that produce the wool we need to make our wool sweaters. (We don't own our own polyesters, either.) We make many grades of sweaters, so we use various wools from different parts of the world. We get our wool from suppliers all over the world, on a contract basis. For special colors, blends, and textures, we even use an internationally famous distributor (in Switzerland!) who supplies us with "fancies" and who takes special orders for color baths.

Of course, very often our clients—designers—come to us and ask us to produce the colors they want. Other designers look at our sample card and choose the colors they want. Our design department works a full six months ahead of fashion designers, so we are ready with our choices and can influence their choices.

One of the reasons our mill does so well is that we work the international fabric and yarngoods markets and provide the latest fashion colors for designers.

To provide more services, we design some sweaters ourselves. Some are what we call bread and butter—very traditional crews, V-necks, turtlenecks; you get the picture. Then we do some fashion work, snazzier stuff—oversize sweaters, sweatshirt looks. And for a few special customers, we do one or two high-fashion sweaters—these are very sophisticated sweaters that may or may not influence a designer. Perhaps we'll modify a Chanel design or copy a Lagerfeld sweater (excuse us—we'll *adapt* a Lagerfeld sweater). When a favorite designer or big-spending customer comes in, we'll casually show him what we've come up with. Maybe we'll write an order, maybe we'll modify this design to the designer's specifications, maybe we'll eat it. No matter. It's just a sample.

Besides designers, we also work directly with buyers. Big department-store buyers are very much like designers (they just don't get paid for it) and are expected to create something special for their store. So the Bloomingdale's sweater buyer comes to us and says, "It's going to be a big year for Chanel sweaters, but I want to do something a little bit different." Since we're so good at what we do, and since we already know it's going to be a big year for Chanel sweaters, we give the buyer a cup of tea and show her the samples and the color charts we have already prepared just for this meeting. After all, this one buyer can order ten thousand units of one sweater from us. That's a very hefty order.

Then we say, "We've got just what you need (sweetheart), we bought just enough of this yarn for you so you'll have this sweater on an exclusive basis, no one in the world can match these goods. . . . What do you think of the body of the sweater in this pink color, with the collar and cuffs in this black and a little of this aubergine here and there with these old French Air Force gold-tone buttons we found from a little dealer in Mougins?"

It's our job to make suggestions to the buyer to try to convince her that we can deliver something special. It's her job to make sure that whatever we agree on will be delivered on time and will sell through or knock 'em dead, as we say in the business. If delivery is late, we may lose Bloomingdale's business. If we convince the buyer to take the pink and black and aubergine Chanel sweater and it's a bomb, she may never trust us again.

Life is hard.

A Minilesson in Manufacturing

Hop Sing is quite an operation and we have a lot of equipment—we make polo shirts in several gauge knits and in several fabrics (cotton and blends), and we make sweaters (wool, blends, cashmere, and acrylic) of many different styles and weights. We do very good work at very competitive prices. As a result, we have a lot of clients: All of your favorite big-name American designers and department stores, as well as many you have never heard of, come to us. In Europe we also have a big business with locals. We make exactly the same thing for a lot of them but put different labels into the merchandise. Or we make what they ask for.

When we ship our merchandise to our clients, it must be perfect. To deliver 1,000 perfect sweaters, we make 1,200 sweaters. The sweaters that come out less than perfect are called damages or seconds or irregulars. The defect may or may not be readily noticeable, but for one reason or another some of the merchandise does not make it past our eagle-eyed inspectors. We sell these damages to a jobber, who pays us a little bit of cash for our mistakes. Something is better than nothing. After we have 1,000 perfect sweaters and, say, 50 damaged sweaters, we still have an extra 150 perfect sweaters. These are overruns. We can do a very handsome business with overruns because they are perfect. In the old days—up to two or three years ago—we would put our own label into these overruns and sell them in Hong Kong in Stanley Market. But times are changing, and in the United States the factory outlet business is booming. Now, our client—Mr. So-and-So, the hotshot designer—wants those 150 extra sweaters and wants them with his label on them so he can sell them at his factory outlet in Flemington, New Jersey! He has purposely opened a factory outlet to unload these overruns and to reach a new segment of the market that he couldn't reach before. Since he pays us for this merchandise, we can't complain too loudly. Ah, to be in England when sweaters were king.

A Minilesson in Retailing

The retailers are our partners: We at Hop Sing make the goods; the retailers sell them. We could never reach the public the way they do, so we need them and they need us. We do not sell directly to the public.

Technically speaking, anyone can be the retailer—if you give a tag sale, you're the retailer. The retailer is the last link of the distribution chain in bringing goods to the public.

People know to go to a retailer to buy what they want, be it the old-fashioned general store that sold everything you ever needed (or dreamed of needing—when life was that simple), or the specialty retailer who sells merchandise for left-handed people only. Just as there are all kind of merchandise and all kinds of methods of distribution, so there are all kinds of retailers.

Traditional retailing works very simply:

▼ The store hires buyers who specialize. They know their market.

▼ The buyer finds the resources (vendors) and buys in bulk (by the dozen or gross) at a wholesale price. Wholesale generally is considered to be cost plus 20%. So the buyer comes to visit Hop Sing Mills and we work hand in hand on that level. Big-time buyers shop all over the world, which is one of the reasons why we have so many international offices. We do this primarily for distribution purposes, of course, but we also want to compete and let buyers know that we are in the markets where they are. Our wholesale prices are based on pickup at the warehouse, or are FOB (freight on board) New York—we'll pay to ship it to New York, but the retailer pays to get it from New York to his store in Dayton, Ohio, or Milan, Italy. We don't care where the goods go, just so they get there on time.

▼ The goods arrive at the store or the store's warehouse. Clerks inventory the merchandise and tag it with codes and the retail price. The retail price usually is double the wholesale price. The tagged merchandise goes on the floor to be sold to the public.

▼ After the merchandise has been on the floor for some time (probably two months, at least in the United States), it is marked down to move it out and make room for new merchandise. The sale merchandise may be displayed less prominently than the new merchandise.

▼ As the season ends and the clothes become obsolete, they will be marked down a second time. The retailer may or may not receive "markdown money" from the vendor; the retailer may or may not be able to return the unsold, end-of-season goods to the vendor. These two points are negotiable but also vary from line to line and category of merchandise.

Okay, that's traditional retailing. But a lot of fortunes, and fun, have been made with nontraditional retailing (see page 31).

Retailers, Designers, and Manufacturers Meet

Because we at Hop Sing Mills are manufacturers and do not put Hop Sing labels into our merchandise, the general public does not know about us. The public thinks that the name on the label owns the machines and knits the sweaters. In some cases, yes, the manufacturer does own his own mills, and this is a vertical operation. He may even own his own sheep. In other cases, many of the steps in the process are contracted out. Hop Sing is contracted to designers and department stores; the wool supplies and distributors are contracted to us. The name on the label is considered the manufacturer. Naturally, we can put a retailer's name on the label as well.

The name on the label may be a designer's name, such as Calvin Klein or Bill Blass. These designers set up corporations using their own names and are forced to separate their personal liabilities from those of their businesses. In many cases the designer whose name is on the label does not even own the company, or the rights to his own name. But that's another story.

If the name on the label is not a person's

name, it may be a company name—like Crazy Horse. No one related to Chief Crazy Horse owns that business. It simply is a company name that has employed several designers over the year and has continued to do a strong enough business to make itself a staple in the industry. Some years are better than others, some designers are better than others, but mostly the designers are anonymous. They may move on to their own labels or they may stay anonymous for life.

Occasionally a designer comes out from the shadows and gets so much press or has such impressive sales figures that he can demand his name go on the label. Thus you may see Louis dell Ollio for Anne Klein on the label. Even though Mrs. Klein has been dead for over ten years, Anne Klein is the name of the business, and Mr. dell Ollio has won the right to have his name on the label. It is also possible for a designer to establish his name for someone else's line and then start his own company, as did Donna Karan.

Licensing

Once you understand that a designer may design an item but that it may not be made by his own little hands, or even in his own (or borrowed) little factory, you begin to get the basis of licensing. Licensing is the selling of a person's name or likeness to another company for the production of goods made in association with the licensor. The licensor usually is a designer, but it can be a retailer. The licensee always is the manufacturer and usually is a company you have never heard of. Licensing is such a big business these days that anyone or anything famous can license something. Notoriety is the name of the game, however.

Thus the television show *Dallas* has spun off products under the Southfork label that include a dress line (very nice dresses—sold only in London, however); an outdoor grill ($1,400, ya'll), and pieces of soap with Pamela Ewing's likeness in living color. When you buy designer fragrance, underwear, lingerie, or chocolates, you are not buying anything the designer actually made himself. His deal is to lend his name to the product. End of story. He may have been involved in the creation of the product, he may have had approval of the product, he may have insisted on total participation from sketch to test, or he may simply have gone to the bank. It is impossible to know.

Licensing now is such an international business that many products are available in countries other than the home country of the designer or the maker—such as the Southfork dresses that are sold only in London, or the Norma Kamali that is made in Japan. Likewise, you'll find that André Courréges is in far more stores and has far more licenses in Tokyo than he is in Paris. It is possible to buy European designer goods in the Orient that you will never see in New York, or to buy in New York products that you have not seen at their home in Europe. This also accounts for the fact that merchandise you may see in Europe and in the United States at the same time of year (especially in department stores) sometimes is not the same.

A designer will make his name but not his fortune in couture. (He may lose money in couture, actually.) But once the designer has enough press to make him famous, he has something very salable—his name. The designer can then sell his name to various manufacturers who will produce God knows what and will use their own distribution base to make sure these goods get into the stores. Pierre Cardin is the king of the license, with hundreds of different products for sale bearing his name. The American license king probably is Calvin Klein or Ralph Lauren. In some cases the licensor and the licensee have a falling out and separate; another manufacturer may be called in to produce the same (or similar) merchandise, and the public never knows a switch has taken place except maybe they will notice an improvement in quality. In even rarer cases, the licensor has made so much money from playing the game properly that he buys the licensee outright—factory, elastic, and everything.

Licensed goods may be made anyplace in the world, wherever the licensor has his factories. Thus a sketch may go from Christian Dior (who happens to be very dead) in Paris to a manufacturer in New York who sends it to his contractor in Brazil. If the designer holds a tight rein, he will make sure that nothing is ever made that does not follow through with his design concept and quality standard. However, the bigger designers often devote themselves to their couture collections and let assistants handle everything else. Their attorneys and business managers often handle the license business, and many times products are made that are not in keeping with the previously established image of the designer. Ask Yves Saint Laurent why he's in the cigarette business.

We at Hop Sing are makers for firms that hold licenses—in other words, they contract their work to us and act as middlemen to collect royalties and distribute merchandise. All we do is make the designer sweaters and sew in the designer labels, as we were hired to do. We have no profit sharing and we pay royalty only to those designers we have direct contracts with.

Private Label

Because we are a big firm, we also do a private-label business. Private labels are the opposite of designer labels—this is a business of direct contracting rather than indirect contracting. With a private label there is no middleman or designer name taking the credit or the blame for the design. The consumer has no idea who really designed the goods because the label is a house brand. (Very often the private-label designer is a once famous designer—he's sort of a ghostwriter and is well paid to keep mum about it.) Usually the private brand is the actual name of the store; sometimes the store creates a label or merchandises a fictional name for its house brand. Thus Neiman-Marcus has private-label merchandise that says "Neiman-Marcus" on the label, or even "made especially for Neiman-Marcus," and it also has a brand called Red River, which is the house brand. A&P (yes, the supermarket) has the Ann Paige label; Barney's has the Basco label. Galeries Lafayette has a big private-label business. Stores come directly to us and ask us to make whatever they want with their own label in it.

The vendor who holds a license has to charge a higher price for designer goods so he can pay a royalty to the designer. (The designer usually gets 5 to 8%.) The vendor can make the exact same merchandise, without the designer label, and sell it to stores for less so that it retails for less. With private labels the consumer gets more quality for less money and, as Grandpa Sy used to say, "How many different ways can they make aspirin?"

More and more department stores are going into the private label business, connecting their fine reputations with the quality of the merchandise they have contracted for. When you see a sweater with the Lord & Taylor label you are supposed to know that the Lord & Taylor buyers would choose nothing but the best for you and therefore you are getting a deal. Private labels come with the psychological edge that is called trust. Hop Sing does not mean trust to much of anyone.

The most famous private label in the world is Marks & Spencer, in London. Their standards have become *de rigueur* for quality private labels, so consider that your purchase must have:

▼ the best ingredients in foodstuffs, with freshness dates on the goods

▼ care tags on all garments

▼ dye lots that match

▼ polyfilament thread, since this is the strongest type available

▼ exact color match on zipper

▼ no puckering in stitches; all stitches of consistent size

Franchises

A franchise is a type of license on the retailing side of the equation. It has nothing to do with manufacturing, so we at Hop Sing don't get very involved. But it works like this: Just as a designer, or a retailer, can sell his name or likeness to a manufacturer, so he may also sell the right to be represented in the retail business. Yves Saint Laurent does not own all those Rive Gauche boutiques you see all over the world, and Ralph Lauren does not own all those Polo shops you see all over the world. Wealthy businesspeople become agents for a designer, or buy the rights to a shop in a certain location. It is not uncommon for one person to own several designer shops or even several different designer shops—many of those tony shops on Madison Avenue are owned not by big-name designers but by entrepreneurs. These stores are franchises.

The merchandise in a franchise is supplied by the designer, but the store policies are supplied by the owner; thus sale periods and the extent of the markdowns are determined on an individual basis. If you are a big spender who comes into town to patronize certain big-name designers, it never hurts to ask for the owner or to get chummy with him. You will get phone calls about sales, some special service, and maybe even some discounts.

A franchise owner shops a designer line, just like a buyer from a department store. The franchise owner sees the show each season and places an order. The house usually sets a minimum, but the rest is up to the owner. Thus you will see some crossover merchandise from one designer shop to another and between a designer boutique and a department-store designer boutique, and you will see some apparently exclusive merchandise. Pricing usually is similar from shop to shop because the wholesale prices are rigged by the designer, as is the variation of the currency—a design house may arbitrarily fix the bank rate to allow for currency fluctuations, so if the dollar gains or falls against the pound it is unlikely that the prices at Rive Gauche or Sonia Rykiel will change.

A designer boutique in a department store is not a franchise. Some designers own some (even all) of their shops in retail establishments. They train the sales help and may pay their salaries.

Sales

Needless to say, we at Hop Sing never want to see our sweaters again after we ship them. They are solely the retailers' responsibility. Although some makers accept returns, we do not. Good-bye and good riddance.

The retailer must walk the very precarious line between buying enough sweaters to have stock for all his customers and eating a lot of extra sweaters. An experienced buyer prides himself on being able to estimate the right number to order. But every season, he is surprised. Something he didn't count on selling so well goes nuts—then he may or may not be able to get enough merchandise to meet demand. Another item that he bought in depth turns out to be a turkey (the Nehru jacket) and nothing will convince people to buy it. Between these two extremes is the more middle-of-the-road situation: A certain amount of merchandise in a particular style moves out on its own legs, and about 25% of it doesn't move. But when it goes on sale, it walks right out the door.

Since Europeans are such big fans of the big sale event, stores in Europe hold all their markdowns for one or two sale periods. Department stores often offer promotional events outside these two big sale periods, which is something they learned from Americans and they think helps move merchandise or promote traffic in the store.

Conversely, certain merchandise will be its most expensive in traditional retailing outlets at very specific times of the year:

▼ Fall merchandise costs most in August and September.

▼ Furs cost most in the fall.

▼ Resort merchandise costs most in November and December.

▼ Spring merchandise costs most in March and April.

American Sale Prices vs. European Prices

As a rule of thumb, the American sale price on a garment equals a 20 to 25% markdown. The second markdown is 40 to 50% of the originally ticketed price, which puts you basically at the wholesale price. With European-made merchandise, the first markdown covers shipping and duties, and the second markdown brings you to the landed price; anything less is below the European retail price but above the European wholesale price. As a result, you often can buy European designer merchandise in the United States for the same as—or less than—in a retail store in Europe.

Not every European-made garment is cheaper in Europe than in the United States in the first place, and not every European-designed garment is actually *made* in Europe. Not every European-designer retail outlet carries the same merchandise. The field is wide open to bargains. The general rule of thumb is simply this: If you are shopping at the beginning of the season for the very latest in fashions, the European price will be better. If you are deep into the season, you may do better in the United States. If the season is over and you can go to Europe for the big closeout sale (European shops have only one or two sales a year), you will get the best price there.

One of the best tricks to remember when shopping for European bargains in the United

States is that the U.S. boutique owner does not want to pay to ship his end-of-season merchandise back to the country of origin. He will do whatever he has to do to get rid of that merchandise and recover some amount of cash. So very often you can find a final reduction of 75%. High-fashion clothes have a very short life-span. Usually the shopowner would rather sell the clothes at a fraction of their value than store them or sell them to a jobber. He may give them to charity for a tax deduction, or he may have one hell of a sale. Ask to get on the mailing list; ask for sale dates. Don't be embarrassed to be a "sale only" customer—store managers value such customers and seek their patronage when the store has merchandise to move out. Sales are a normal part of the business cycle. Thank God.

3 ▼ THE BUSINESS OF BARGAINS

Nontraditional Retailing

Nontraditional retailing happens to be a much older practice than traditional retailing. Money and even stores, for that matter, are relative newcomers in the age-old practice of swapping goods and services. And certainly, once there was one store with posted prices, there was a hungrier merchant who was ready to deal. The business of dealing has become a big business as more and more shoppers become interested in getting the most for their money.

Getting the most for our money happens to be an old American trait. Our country was founded by people who left the old way of doing things in favor of something a little bit different. The search for value has been passed on to us so that no matter how wealthy we may become, few of us feel good about throwing money away needlessly. You don't have to be cheap to be smart. In recent years, value has taken on an added dimension for the baby boomers, who have watched inflation erode their standard of living and who have sadly discovered that their parents are richer than they are. To our dismay, we are discovering that the simple things we took for granted in our childhoods may now be out of reach. The quality items we thought we were entitled to, that we never questioned would be available for our children, often are priced out of reach. The only way we can get the value we crave is through careful shopping—discounting, couponing, bartering, comparison shopping, catalogue pricing, and using whatever helpful sources and inside information come our way to pave the way to a better bargain.

Foreign visitors find themselves thrilled, amused, and perplexed by the differences between traditional and nontraditional retailing but flock to this country partly for the new and nontraditional methodology—they know that prices on many goods are cheaper in their home countries, but they find many old designer friends from home at competitive prices in the United States and adore the American bargains they find at discounters and off-price stores. We know many a visitor who has gone home filled with stories not of motherhood or of apple pie but of K-Mart and the Secaucus (New Jersey) warehouse outlets.

American retailing has changed drastically in the past ten years and continues to shift as old patterns fall flat of expectations and new ideas catch on. Off-price, discount, and outlet shopping are booming. Entire villages of shopping complexes are being born. Warehouse-hopping has become downright chic. People are shopping first for the bargains and second for the entertainment and amusement of it. We are in the midst of a new American revolution. English retailing is not as new a business. England is an older country, and is much slower to adapt to hot new ideas. But retail business has been hurt in England recently also, and too many people have been to America—the world of retailing is changing. The sale shop still is the Brits' favorite way to clear out merchandise, but factory outlets are booming in Stoke-on-Trent, and the trend may spread to London.

Discount Stores

A new breed of department store has begun to flourish in the United States—the discount store. Here, traditional merchandise is 20% off. In London, you get this same 20% off at a duty-free. Or you can shop at the big, mass merchandisers such as Marks & Spencer, C&A, or Littlewoods, where prices are less expensive. These stores are comparable to Penney's or Sears in America and obviously don't have too much of the same merchandise that Harrods or Harvey Nichols has.

The discounter sells some branded merchandise and some private-label merchandise at a 20 to 25% discount from department stores but does so in a self-service, department store atmosphere. No jazzy displays, no room sets, no mannequins with pink hair and wearing sunglasses imported from Italy—but the stores are large, clean, and well lighted.

Discounters do not sell at wholesale prices, despite the fact that they may advertise that they do. Discounters do sell current, seasonal merchandise at less than traditional retail prices. They may not have dressing rooms, they do not have a large sales force, you may have to wait for twenty to thirty minutes in line at a cash register, but you will save money.

Off-Price Shops

Off-price shops also sell current, seasonal merchandise but at prices less than 20% off. These stores can be smaller than discounters and less fancy, or they may be as big as a warehouse and very nicely decorated. Usually they specialize in certain categories of merchandise, such as women's or children's clothes.

Seconds

Since we all make mistakes, it's easy enough to understand that when manufacturers make mistakes they end up with imperfect merchandise that cannot be sold through traditional retailing channels. Yet the manufacturer is loathe to throw out the baby with the bath water. Instead, he collects his imperfects and sells them to a store or a jobber who likes damaged merchandise because he's got customers who are careful shoppers and who realize that the imperfection may be insignificant but the saving is not.

In the fashion industry, this imperfect merchandise is called seconds, irregulars, imperfects, or damages. The stores that sell this merchandise fall into several categories:

▼ Some are owned by the manufacturer himself.

▼ Some department stores have the means to buy up this merchandise and sell it to their regular customers on an "as is" basis—Filene's of Boston is a traditional department store that uses its double basement space as one of the country's most exciting bargain basements. While the merchandise elsewhere in the store is absolutely perfect, Filene's Basement is a treasure trove of seconds, irregulars, markdowns, write-offs, and orphaned pieces of clothing.

▼ Sometimes the damages are sold to little stores that specialize in buying up this kind of stuff.

▼ Seconds or imperfects also are unloaded on small-time businessmen who may sell through their own outlets, or sell on street corners, at flea markets, in tube stations, or any other place they can get away with it.

Depending on the brand, the imperfect merchandise may not be very imperfect. Some brands, especially high-priced designer brands, have such strict quality control that a reject is virtually perfect. We once saw a reject at the Pratesi outlet in Pistoia that had been rejected because the lace border wasn't thick enough. Picky, picky. This was a $400 sheet that was sold for $50 because it was "damaged." The finest merchandise in the world has the strictest of quality controls.

Damaged merchandise also may be fixable. Say you buy a suit at your favorite department store. In your rush to get into the outfit, you don't notice that the zipper is jammed. You take the suit back to the store and tell them that you have bought defective merchandise and want either a refund or a new suit. Any good department store will give you either. The department store then sends the suit back to the manufacturer and gets a credit for the damage. The manufacturer doesn't have time to replace the zipper and get the item back into a store before the season ends. So he will release it—probably unfixed—with all his other damages to a jobber or seconds store. You will be able to buy this perfectly wonderful skirt for a fraction of its value price and $2.80 for a new zipper.

Whether the item became a damage in the factory or in a department store, by the time it gets to a nontraditional retailer, you must watch for these possible problems:

▼ dye lots that do not match

▼ bubbles in plastic or glass

▼ chips in enamel or finish

▼ uneven finish

▼ nonmatched pattern at seams

▼ off-register prints

▼ misstitched logo

▼ zipper that is poorly inset, or broken zipper

▼ stitching that is missing in a section or is uneven

▼ belt loops that do not match or are not all present

▼ belt loops that are perfect but belt is non-existent

▼ broken belt

▼ buttons or fasteners that are broken or missing

▼ knits that have snagged, puckered, or stretched

▼ holes

Since seconds are considered inferior to firsts, it is not uncommon for seconds to be sold without labels. Ask the retailer to identify the goods for you. Occasionally a really prestigious maker will deny that he has seconds at all. Undoubtedly his nose will grow long, like Pinocchio's.

Remember, seconds are not sale merchandise that has not sold; they are stepchildren. When you inquire after them, don't be upset if a shopkeeper gives you a less than friendly answer. Also understand that the help in seconds stores may be less than perfect—just like the merchandise they sell.

Jobbers

Jobbers are middlemen. Usually they are small manufacturers who fulfill contracts for bigger manufacturers or stores or designers. For example, a designer sketches his fur designs but doesn't own the fur operation that makes them; a jobber may take care of the order. The jobber may have a few extra coats made to sell to his private clients, or he may sell them to another jobber with a retail outlet.

Depending on the condition of the goods, the jobber's price will be anywhere from wholesale to 20% above or below wholesale. (The price goes down if he's got something he's trying to dump; it goes up if he has the overhead of a retail shop or has incredible merchandise.)

The jobber may or may not want your business. He may take street business on one day because he feels like it and reject it on three other days—because he feels like it. Sometimes a personal introduction makes a difference. Regardless, there are two things to remember:

▼ Just because the merchandise is less expensive than in a department store doesn't mean that it is of any particular quality. There are jobbers at all ends of the retail spectrum. While you may want to spend your vacation going from jobber to jobber, we don't think you do. It can be a frustrating business, and you may not end up with anything special.

▼ Jobbers who have retail outlets often buy from jobbers who do not, so they may be running a little general store in seconds and overruns. Always ask how old the merchandise is and look for damages. Try on if you can; sizes may not be as marked.

When you buy from jobbers, do not expect fancy conditions. The stores will be less than posh, and the help may even yell at you. There may not be a dressing room, or the dressing room may be the communal type. Jobbers may sell only in bulk, by a minimum order, or by multiple units. Jobbers rarely have a full size range; usually they cannot order something for you. They do not consider themselves in a service business; they may not take checks or credit cards.

Sale Shops

The British have perfected a most untraditional piece of retailing to move out their sale merchandise, a method that is particularly popular with big-name designer shops and seems unbelievable to an American. Designer shops will hoard their unsold sale merchandise and put it away until once or twice a year, when they will rent space and open up a sale shop. This sale shop will sell only markdowns. The shops are open for a matter of months and then close. Word of mouth spreads among locals and good customers, the clothes are sold, and the shop closes—only to resurface again in another location a year later.

All the big names do it—including Saint Laurent, Cecil Gee, The Beauchamp Place Shop, etc. We went to a store where we had found great bargains only months before and discovered it was a major-name-designer boutique of another sort. The space had been leased to a new tenant who was decidedly not in the sale business.

Sale shops go into empty storefronts and then leave—like magic. The best times to find them are around the Christmas holidays and toward the end of summer. It's not rude to ask a designer if he will be opening a sale shop in the future; after all, you're an American—you can say anything.

Auctions

We think that auctions are a tremendous amount of fun and should be considered for pure entertainment's sake. In London, however, there are certain auctions that are quite serious and important and while fun, are at the extreme opposite end of your basic country auction. If you attend a big auction at a prestigious house, ask around about proper wardrobe. Evening auctions can be black-tie events—they are seldom white-tie. Viewings are almost always during the day, as are the majority of auctions. Proper business clothes are essential—even if one isn't bidding.

As in all major cities, London has an auction season: October to May. Country auctions and the like often are held in the summer, but fancy auctions are held only at auction houses in the city during the season. Occasionally auctions are closed to the public—like the fur auctions in Leningrad, where pelts are sold to furriers in lots—but usually you can be admitted to an auction by catalogue or free. Weekly auction programs are published in the *Times* on Tuesdays and in the *Daily Telegraph* on Mondays. Some houses sell certain types of works on specific days of the week, like china on Monday and European oil paintings on Friday—or something like that. In season, there will be about a hundred auctions a month in London alone.

It would be a mistake to assume that everything you buy in an auction is a bargain. Various auctions have various functions in their respective fields; often that is to set the prices for the rest of the world. On the other hand, you should not be intimidated. You may indeed get a real "steal," or you may be shopping in a country where the market price for an item you are interested in is considerably less than in the United States.

Do be wary of fakes at auctions, particularly from the less famous houses. If you buy an item because you love it, and if it doesn't matter whether it's real or not, that's one thing. But if you are buying for investment, name-dropping, or status-seeking purposes, use a house expert, or better yet, a private expert as a consultant. The better houses will not intentionally sell you a forgery or a fake; small-time auctioneers may not care what's in the lots as long as they move them out. A house may even admit they don't know if a piece is authentic. Sotheby's uses the full name of an artist when they know the work is authentic but uses only the initials of the artist (in the catalogue listing) if they have some doubt as to the provenance of the work.

The most famous auction houses in London are Sotheby's and Christie's, but don't underestimate Phillips Son & Neale or Harmer's. And, of course, Bonham's has been around since 1793—they probably know quite a bit. Some London auction houses are:

BONHAM's: 65–69 Lots Road, SW10; Montpelier Street, SW7

CHRISTIE's: 8 King Street, SW1*

CHRISTIE's: South Kensington, 85 Old Brompton Road, SW7

HARMER's: 41 New Bond Street, W1

HARRODS AUCTION GALLERIES: Arundel Terrace, Barnes, SW13

HARVEY'S AUCTIONS: 14–18 Neal Street, WC2

PHILLIPS SON & NEALE: 7 Blenheim Street, W1*

SOTHEBY PARKE BERNET: 34–35 New
Bond Street, W1*

(*This denotes the Big Three—very fancy
houses that may be intimidating to the inex-
perienced.)

There are also stamp and coin auctions. Call
the London Philatelic Association (01-283-7968)
for specific information, or ask your hotel
concierge.

Don't forget country auctions that you may
find on a weekend outing and that usually are
charming—but if they had something truly
important to sell, it would have gone to a big
house in a major city to command a big price.
So enjoy. At a country auction, expect to pay
cash for your purchase. There is no VAT on
antiques. Be prepared to have to make your
own shipping arrangements. (See page 75).

When you shop at an auction of any kind,
remember:

▼ The house is not responsible for the authenticity of the article.

▼ There is a house commission (8 to 10%)
charged the seller, but the buyer will have to
pay taxes. Some houses also commission the
buyer—ask, as this can raise the price of your
item by another 10%.

▼ You are entitled to know the price a similar
item went for in previous years and the price
the house expects the item to go for at the
current auction. Often these prices are posted
at the viewing or may be published in the
catalogue.

▼ Find out before you bid what currency you
must pay in. International houses often accept
many currencies, and you may do better with
your dollar converting to one rather than another. This can pay off with a large purchase.
There is a trend now in the serious antiques
furniture and art market for items over $5,000

to be quoted in U.S. dollar prices. If a price is quoted to you in "dollars," verify that you are both talking U.S. dollars.

▼ Keep a calculator in your hand during the bidding to know what the prices are; remember to do your figure at the current American Express rate of exchange rather than the bank rate. The bank rate will be more favorable than the one you will actually be paying, so don't cheat yourself from an accurate conversion of what you will truly be paying.

▼ Expect to pay tax on the item when you call for it. Find out the tax ahead of time. VAT is not paid on antiques.

▼ The auction house may pack and ship your purchase for you, but it may be cheaper to do it yourself or ask your hotel concierge to handle it for you.

▼ Make sure that the item you are about to buy may leave the country! Some countries won't let you out with what they consider to be items of their heritage. Conversely, make sure you can get it into the United States. You will not be reimbursed if the government confiscates any of your property. If the item is an antique, get the papers that verify its age. (According to Customs, an antique is a hundred years old—or more.)

And speaking of those wonderful folks of the Customs Service, do remember that they, too, hold auctions. Auctions are held quarterly on unclaimed or seized merchandise and are held at the Customs office at certain ports of entry. The government does not keep mailing lists for auctions but does set their auction dates at least a year ahead of time so you can make plans.

Before the actual auction you may view the merchandise and register to buy. Call your local Customs office for more information.

To Market, to Market

One of the difficulties in shopping in London is deciding which markets to visit and which to pass up. Unlike most other cities that usually have one or two good markets, London is crawling with good markets. There are actually dozens of them, and it's impossible to get to them all unless you spend a month doing little else. Our best tip on markets is to fly into London on a Thursday, so you have jet lag and wake up at 5:00 A.M. on Friday morning—wide awake. That's when you get up, get dressed, and go to the Bermondsey Market, which is one of our faves. Don't forget to bring a "torch" (flashlight), because it's dark at six o'clock in the morning. A few markets are sort of fancy, like Grays, but for the most part we consider them fun and don't like to be overdressed there.

Remember:

▼ Dress simply; the richer you look, the higher the price. If you wear an engagement ring, or have one of those wedding bands that spells out RICH AMERICAN in pavé diamonds, leave them in the hotel safe. We like to wear blue jeans and try to fit into the mode of the country as best we can.

▼ Check with your hotel concierge about the market's neighborhood. It may not be considered safe for a woman to go there alone, or after dark. (Petticoat Lane makes us a bit wary.) We don't want to be either chauvinists or paranoid, but crime in market areas—especially outdoor markets—can be higher than in tourist areas.

▼ Have a lot of change with you. It's difficult to bargain and then offer a large bill and ask for change. As a bargaining point, be able to say you have only so much cash on hand.

▼ If you look like a tourist, the price may start out higher; if you don't know much about what you are buying, the price may also start higher. You do not need to speak any specific language, however, to make a good deal. Bargaining is an international language of emotion, hand signs, facial expressions, etc. If you feel like you are being taken, walk away.

▼ Branded merchandise sold on the street can be hot or counterfeit.

▼ Go early if you expect the best selection. Go late if you want to make the best deals pricewise.

▼ Never trust anyone (except a qualified shipping agent) to mail anything for you.

▼ Make sure you are buying something you can legally bring back to the States (see page 85). Don't buy those tortoiseshell boxes at Bermondsey because those beauties will be turned away by U.S. Customs.

In London, many market areas are so famous that they have no specific street address. It's usually enough to name the market to a cabbie, but ask your concierge if you need more in the way of directions. Buses usually service market areas, as may the tube.

Outdoor Markets

BERMONDSEY MARKET (also called New Caledonian Market): Bermondsey Square south of Tower Bridge, 6:00 A.M. to 2:00 P.M., Friday only; this market dries up around lunchtime

BOND STREET ANTIQUES CENTER: 124 New Bond Street, W1; 10:00 A.M. to 5:30 P.M., Monday to Saturday; closed Sunday

CHURCH STREET MARKET: daily

CAMDEN PASSAGE: Upper Street, Islington, N1; Wednesday and Saturday—best; Thursday and Friday—books and prints

COVENT GARDEN: stalls are in the square between the shops; daily

LEATHER LANE: EC1; daily

PETTICOAT LANE: off Middlesex Street but on several different streets; we like Cutler Street—Sunday morning only—and Brick Lane, also only open on Sunday; 8:00 A.M. to 2:00 P.M. Sunday

PORTOBELLO ROAD: off Westbourne Park, W11; open to the public 9:00 A.M. to 5:00 P.M. Saturday, to the design trade during the week

SHEPHERD MARKET: Shepherds Bush, W12; 9:30 A.M. to 3:00 P.M.; closed Sunday

Indoor Markets

ANTIQUARIUS: 135 Kings Road, SW3; closed Sunday

ANTIQUE SUPERMARKET: daily

CHELSEA ANTIQUES MARKET: 253 Kings Road, SW3; 8:00 A.M. daily; closed Sunday

GRAYS MARKET: Davies Street and Davies Mews, W1; closed Sunday

JUBILEE MARKET: Covent Garden, WC2; Tuesday and Friday, crafts; Saturday and Sunday, antiques; 9:00 A.M. to 4:00 P.M.

KENSINGTON MARKET: Kensington High Street, W8; 10:00 A.M. to 4:00 P.M.; closed Sunday

KNIGHTSBRIDGE PAVILION: closed Sunday

MAYFAIR ANTIQUES MARKET: daily

4 ▾ DETAILS

When a Buy Is a Good-bye

A true-blue shopper has been known to lose her head now and again. Don't tell us this hasn't happened to you, especially when it comes to a so-called bargain. We've made so many mistakes, in fact, that we've had to have a long and careful talk with ourselves to come up with an out-of-town shopping philosophy that lays down the ground rules.

Shopping in a foreign country is much more romantic than shopping at home, there's no question about it. Even nonshoppers admit that they prefer to shop when away from home (be it another city or another country). If you make a mistake in another American city, you can usually return the merchandise and get a credit with just a small amount of hassle. On a foreign trip, returns can be a major problem and usually aren't worth the effort. So to keep mistakes to a minimum, we have our own rules of the game:

▼ Take a careful and thorough survey of your closet (including china and linen) and your children's closets before you leave town. Know what you've got so you can know what you need. While you don't have to need something in order to buy it, knowing that you need it (and will be saving money by buying it abroad) will help your conscience a lot.

▼ If you *need* an item of clothing to complete an ensemble, bring a piece of the outfit with you. (At the very least, very carefully cut a small swatch of fabric from the inside of the hem or a seam.) We don't need to tell you about the gorgeous black and turquoise Yves Saint Laurent silk blouse we bought (cheap, too) to go with last year's turquoise silk suit that didn't match. All of us have had that happen so many times it's painful. Don't get caught again. When you go through the closets, write down the holes you may want to fill in on a foreign trip. Organization will help keep you from a costly error.

▼ Make a list of what you are allowed; limit your serious shopping to these areas to avoid heartbreak and temptation.

▼ Figure the price accurately. Carry a calculator and do your figuring at the American Express rate, not the bank rate. (See page 42.)

▼ When money fluctuates wildly, keep checking with banks or hotels. We know a man who left his hotel in Italy at 9:00 A.M. and got 1,950 lire per U.S. dollar. When he returned at lunchtime, he got 1,700 lire per U.S. dollar. The pound does fluctuate—it is more stable than the lira, but the little lira story is not just for those going on to Italy.

▼ Figure in the duty. Each person is allowed $400 duty-free (see page 85). If you are traveling with your family, figure out your family total. Children, even infants, still get the $400 allowance. If you have more than $400 worth of merchandise, you can pay a flat 10% on the next $1,000; after that you pay a duty rate accordingly. Sometimes the duties equal the VAT, so you come out even. Is the bargain still a bargain?

▼ Will you have to schlep the item all over the world with you? If it takes up a lot of suitcase room, if it's heavy, if it's cumbersome, if it's breakable and at risk every time you pack and unpack or check your suitcase, if it has to be hand-held (don't laugh—we once hand-carried a primitive ceramic sculpture from Fortaleza to Bahia to Rio to Miami and then to L.A.; it arrived intact but wasn't worth it), estimate your time, trouble, and level of tolerance per the item. Sure it may be an inexpensive item, but if it's an ordeal to bring it home, is it really a good buy?

▼ Likewise, if you have to insure and ship it, is it still a bargain? How will you feel if the item never makes it to your door?

▼ Do your research on prices at home first. We spent several hours choosing and shipping china from a British discount source only to discover an American discounter who, once the price of the shipping was taken into account, had the same price. The English china experience proved a waste of time more than of money, but both are precious—especially on foreign soil.

▼ We are ambivalent about the value of counterfeit merchandise and cannot advise you to buy it or to walk away from it. If you suspect an item to be a fake, you must evaluate if this is a good buy or a good-bye. Remember that fakes most certainly do not have the quality of craftsmanship that the originals have. You may also be asked to forfeit the item at U.S. Customs or to pay duty on the value of the real object. We also admit that we rarely find fake anything in London (although there are serious forgeries found in the art world, that's big potatoes; we're thinking more about imitation Vuitton, etc.).

▼ Our rule of thumb on a good buy is that 50% (or more) off the U.S. price is a valuable saving. We think that a saving of less than 20% is marginal, is not worth the effort (of course, it depends on the item and how it will come back into the country with you, etc.), and usually is not a good buy. If the saving is 20 to 50%, we judge according to personal desire and the ratio of the points above. If the

saving is 50% or better, we usually buy several
and whoop with joy. That's a good buy!

Be Prepared

We thought we left homework the day
we graduated. But the bargains go to
the shopper who is ready to recognize them, and that means doing some
homework.

▼ If you have favorite designers or targets of
acquisition for your trip, shop the major department stores and United States–based boutiques (if in your city) for comparison prices.
Don't assume you will get a bargain on a
European purchase.

▼ If you do not live in a city that has a lot of
European merchandise, do some shopping
through *Vogue* and *Harper's & Queen*. In the
ads for the designer boutiques, you'll find phone
numbers. Call and ask about prices and sales.
Don't be afraid to explain that you are con-
templating a shopping trip to Europe and are
doing some comparison pricing.

▼ Read English magazines to get familiar with
looks, shops, and life-styles. While they cost a
fortune (sometimes $14 a magazine), many li-
braries have these magazines. We go to Michaeljohn, our British hairstylist, sometimes
just to read the magazines.

▼ Or go in with several friends on a foreign
magazine co-op. You may want to get a subscription to the British *Vogue* and share it
among four other friends.

▼ Understand the licensing process (see page
22). Two men's suits may bear the identical

label of a well-known French designer but will fit entirely differently because they are made entirely differently.

▼ French cosmetics and fragrances can be extraordinarily less expensive in France but marginally less in England; sometimes it doesn't pay to schlep them home. You'll save 20% on Chanel makeup but only 10% on Lancôme. Homework will pay off here.

▼ The best buys in London are on British designer merchandise on sale and that cost enough to qualify for the VAT and fit into your suitcase and into your U.S. Customs allowance; once over your $1,400 Customs allowance, you will pay 33% duty on those bargains. The other good buys are china, crystal, and collectibles.

If you shopped in the United Kingdom in the dollar's glory days, you may be shocked at the current high price of merchandise. Everything is expensive, even cheap merchandise. You may do enough homework to consider a splurge in a major American city at the designer sales rather than the cost of air fare and hotels. Don't go expecting bargains without understanding where the bargains are. Know your stuff before you go!

Negotiating and Bargaining

Just as shopping is an art, negotiating and bargaining also are an art. Unfortunately, they are a different art—many shoppers absolutely fall apart when it gets to the finer points of the deal. As we've traveled, we've found a sort of *Passages* of emotions that we want to share because chances are you will have some of the same feelings at one time or another:

Ages 15 to 25: The Bargain Years. We could walk away from a sale easily; we thought haggling was fun; we were worried about being "taken" and overpaying; we thought half was the only price to pay; we knew it all and acted like it.

Ages 25 to 35: The Sophisticated Years. We felt a bit uncomfortable bargaining, a bit too refined, perhaps. Or we restricted our negotiations to the obvious places—outdoor flea markets, souks, and bazaars. We took a friend when we shopped for a new car, lest we be embarrassed to ask if we had to pay the sticker price. We just didn't like the degrading experience of the whole thing.

Ages 35 to 40: The "Who Cares?" Years. We began to settle into such comfort with ourselves that we didn't care what anyone else thought. We bargained voraciously when it seemed appropriate; we paid the first price when that seemed appropriate (yes, even at flea markets). We came to understand the difference between haggling and true negotiating; we were finally free.

After all, the experts tell us that anything is negotiable. When you bought your house, you went through a period of offers and counteroffers, didn't you? When you bought your car, did you ask the dealer to throw in a few goodies, or lower the price if you took it off his hands immediately? Have you ever bought items by the dozen or even the gross to get a price break? All these maneuvers are a form of negotiating. To have the best possible negotiations in a foreign country, remember these rules:

▼ Each country has a different cultural assessment of bargaining. Germans are insulted if you bargain. Moroccans are insulted if you don't. The Brits expect you to bargain slightly in a market atmosphere, but not in shops. Feel out the situation before you get embarrassed. Remember that the British wait for the sale and then buy in huge lots; they don't have to bargain.

▼ Even in fancy stores, where bargaining would be unheard of, sometimes there can be some fancy negotiating. Is the store about to mark down this item? Will they hold it for you until it is marked down? Will they charge your credit card and mail the item? (We tried this at Porthault in Paris once—it didn't work!) This garment is damaged and it's the end of the season—could they lower the price a notch? If you are polite, well dressed, and know exactly what you want, feel free to ask for it. (We did have the price of a toy marked down because the package was open and they didn't have another at Prisunic in Paris.) We've also seen some master maneuvering by society *grande dames* who bought a lot of merchandise, had a very royal manner about them, and announced firmly that they expected to deal. For example, in London we once overheard this conversation between an American cosmetics magnate and the manager of the shop, a very nice (in fact, famous) shop that sells quality china in the West End:

MANAGER: "And how will you be paying for this, madame?"

MADAME: "Credit card."

(She then wandered the shop while he wrote up the bill. She returned to sign the credit slip.)

MADAME: "Oh, my! This is really quite high. I've bought over a thousand dollars' worth of merchandise from you. I believe that's a rather sizable order. Can't you do a little better for me?"

MANAGER: "Uh, why, yes, madame, of course. We will ship the items to your home free of charge."

MADAME: "Oh, how very kind of you!" (Madame got herself the equivalent of a 30% saving because the freight on all that china would have been very high.)

We've also seen and overheard similar transactions on the Rue Paradis in Paris, where a discount actually is given with a remark like, "Well, since you're a friend of so-and-so's, I'll take off another ten percent. I'm not really supposed to do this, but don't tell anyone. You're such a good customer, I'm sure it will be okay."

At a big-name-designer shop in Milan, we asked for a discount and got an inexpensive gift instead.

You've heard that the rich get richer? Well, the rich get the discounts, too. If you buy a lot, it doesn't hurt to ask or to negotiate for a special price. All they can do is say "no."

When shopping in markets, remember:

▼ Never involve yourself in a serious negotiation with elaborate ceremonies (tea- or coffee-drinking, toasting the children, showing of family snapshots, etc.) if you aren't serious. Walk away if your price isn't met, of course, but don't be rude. On the other hand, don't let the vendor make you feel obligated to buy. Once we saw some hand-embroidered sheets. On careful examination, we didn't like the quality of the sheets.

"You like my sheets?"

"No, thank you."

"You buy my sheets?"

"No, thank you."

"You make offer. I think about any offer."

Mistake: "Well, I don't know."

Then we offered what we thought was an insulting price, hoping to make the man leave us alone. He accepted! Well, we did think it was a steal, and we did make someone very happy with what we considered to be the cheapest house gift we've ever given, but still, we bought because we felt obligated, because we did not know how to get out of the situation. The moral of the story: If you decide not to play the game, *don't play.*

▼ Do your homework; know the fair price for an item. If you still go by the old "half of what's asked probably is fair" rule of thumb in flea markets in London, you will buy very little. There is a markup on the actual selling price, but not a big one.

▼ Because American English and British English are such similar languages, you will not get cheated in a language or "foreigner" negotiation. An outsiders' tax is added to the price of most market goods in many countries, but not for Americans in London.

▼ If you are buying collectibles and aren't a museum expert, have some books or materials with you to help you check on the quality of the item you are inspecting. This will frighten the frauds and make friends with true collectors who may have hidden special pieces for the people who truly care about this kind of item.

▼ Always be polite. No *Ugly American*-type scenes, please.

Mail Order

Whether you've been to Europe several times and have your own set of contacts and favorite shops, or whether you've never been to Europe and aren't sure when you'll get there, you can take advantage of lower prices at the point of manufacture by doing some armchair shopping via mail order. We keep track of mail order for the very important reason of comparison shopping. Aside from the time (and the fun) spent combing a foreign city for a bargain, it's annoying to discover that you could have gotten a better price through a catalogue or by doing business with a tried-and-true source through the mails.

You are allowed to bring in up to $250 worth of goods through parcel post (you pay duty, of course, but you don't need a custom-house broker) without making a "formal" declaration. This makes mail order a breeze.

Most mail-order companies have their own catalogues, as do big department stores. You may automatically go on the list if you make a purchase, or you may have to ask to be sent a catalogue. Sometimes you will be charged, or the price of the catalogue will be deducted from your first purchase.

If you or a friend have done business with a firm abroad, you may just want to call, telex, or write them directly for more of what you bought, or something you saw in the shop. Our rule on this is that it's relatively safe to call a shop where you've been recently and where you speak the same language as the shopkeeper. Anything more complicated than this should be handled by telex or letter. Keep copies of all correspondence. Do not put a credit-card number on the telex, however (you may give it on the phone). Once you leave the country, however, the shop may no longer wish to do business with you. We know a woman named Alix who went wild for the fabrics and the prices at Souleiado in Paris. Her husband did not have the patience to wait for her to pick out everything she wanted. He suggested that Alix take swatches or style numbers and call the store from the United States to make the actual arrangements. Alix was then advised that Souleiado would not do mail-order or telephone business with the United States because their goods are sold in various Pierre Deux shops there. Not to be outsmarted, Alix tried Souleiado in London (no luck) and finally bought off-the-bolt at Brother Sun in London. (She's also been known to call the Irish Linen Shop in Bermuda for a telephone order put on her credit card.)

Shops in the Virgin Islands and in Bermuda do a tremendous amount of mail order and telephone orders. There are often GSP breaks (see page 87) on duty, and the shopkeepers always speak English. More adventurous shoppers we know have a control store in Hong Kong that does mail order. Before a big trip or a major purchase, they check the Hong Kong prices with the European prices. We often find Hong Kong prices are cheaper than London prices for some rather traditional British-type goods; you may want to investigate this further.

When doing mail-order business, we lean more toward British and British colonial mail order because you never have a language problem. We also keep in mind:

▼ Foreign catalogues are easiest paid for by credit card. You can get an international money order (post office, bank, or Deak-Perera), but this takes extra organization on your part. Firms that have done business with you probably will take your personal check. We never send cash in the mail and suggest you don't, either. Long live plastic.

▼ To continue getting a catalogue after the first order, you must usually buy something during a twelve-month period. The continuing catalogues are free.

▼ Some British big-name catalogues are for sale in the magazine rack of a bookstore or newsstand—look for Harrods at Christmastime and Laura Ashley for spring and fall. Conran's has a New York branch store that handles mail order as any other U.S. store—it's not worth the time or trouble on an ordinary item to mail-order from Conran's in London.

▼ If you are buying clothes, make sure you have the size right. Exchanges are going to be a real hassle. Goods imported into London will have the size system of the country of origin, so know what you are ordering and what size you wear from that designer.

▼ Know a little British vocabulary—a sweater is called a jumper in England, so don't think you're getting a little navy apron dress when you order a navy blue jumper. A boot is the trunk of an automobile, not something for your feet.

▼ The VAT usually is deducted at the time of purchase for mail-order goods. Some stores deduct a portion of the VAT if your purchase is under $100 or whatever store minimum they have for full value. Hamley's does this.

▼ Always specify the shipping arrangements you want. Items shipped between November and December always take longer to get here. Santa is very busy these days, as is Father Christmas in England.

▼ If you are ordering several small gift items each under $50 in value, ask the store to ship them in different packages to different friends of yours. There is no duty on unsolicited gifts each under $50 in retail value.

▼ If you are doing gift buying, write out your gift cards and send them with your order. If the store knows you, they will attach your cards and send the gifts to the recipients—making your life much easier for you. We know a woman who likes to give lavish gifts to her friends but doesn't like to pay a lot of money for them. Every year she buys one dozen identical boxes from Halcyon Days in London. She writes out one dozen of the same cards but does not address the cards. She sends her order, her credit-card number, and the gift notes to Halcyon Days along with one dozen names and addresses. They gift-wrap and ship for her. She has saved herself $40 on the price of each box and the time and trouble of mailing and wrapping gifts during the busy holiday season.

▼ When you are in London, make a contact with a salesperson and ask about future mail-order purchases. Ask if he will handle your orders personally.

▼ We, being the most cautious snobs in the world, limit our mail-order business, on adventures beyond $25, to firms that we have visited while in London. Perhaps this is being overly cautious, but you may take it as a warning. Of course, we've been in just about every shop in London, so it's easy for us to make this rule.

▼ Use your catalogues to help you find the best bargains. Mail-order china is as competitively priced as in-store china. Yes, Gered does mail order—but their prices are higher than those of the Reject China Shop, which also does mail order.

Here are a few of our regulars:

CHINA CRAFT: 130 New Bond Street, London W1, England; free catalogue

GERED: 173–74 Piccadilly, London W1, England; free catalogue

HALCYON DAYS: 14 Brook Street, London W1, England; free catalogue; catalogues come four times a year free after first purchase

HARRODS: 87–135 Brompton Road, London SW1, England; free catalogue after purchase; $5.00 in United States at newsstands

LIBERTY's: 210 Regent Street, London SW1, England; free catalogue

N. PEAL: 37 Burlington Arcade; free catalogue after purchase or upon request in London

REJECT CHINA SHOP: 13 Silver Road, Wood Lane, London W12, England; $3.00 catalogue when bought by mail, $1.25 when bought in person

English Prices vs. Other European Prices

Base prices on English goods have been rising steadily. Those items that American tourists have been flying over in droves to buy have become more and more costly as each month passes. Some stores actually work out what percentage of their business is tourist vs. native; if the business is mostly tourist, the prices are going *up*.

Then there is the Paris scam. There is a major con going on now in London, where many tourists are told that the European designer clothes are cheaper in London than elsewhere in the world. We have not found this to be particularly true. While we're not calling anyone a liar, we've found that the biggest problem is not if Paris is cheaper than London but if New York is cheaper than London!

The bargains in London are on antiques, collectibles, and young designer fashions (and some toys, you're right), not necessarily on high-fashion items. French and Italian designer clothes usually are more expensive than in Europe though less expensive than in the United States.

Export Tax Scheme (VAT)

Most European countries levy a tax on retail goods that can be refunded, or partially refunded, if the goods are taken out of the country. To show you just how serious they are on this point, you must prove that you have taken the goods out to get your refund.

While each country has its own name for the tax and their refund system, the Brits call it VAT—Value-Added Tax (the French call it detaxé).

The VAT is a 15% tax that is levied on all goods, just like a sales tax in the United States. Brits pay it automatically. Tourists can get a refund on it.

The basic Value-Added Tax system works pretty much like this:

▼ You are shopping in a store with prices marked on the merchandise. This is the true price of the item, which any tourist or any national must pay. (We're assuming you are in a department store with fixed prices, not a flea market.) If you are a national, you pay the price without thinking twice. If you are a tourist who plans to leave the country within six months, you ask a salesperson, "What is the minimum expenditure in this store for the export refund?" The rate varies from shop to shop—usually touristy neighborhoods have a higher quota. In most London shops, the qualifying price usually is $75.

▼ All stores have a minimum-purchase requirement before they will grant you the discount. Let's say you buy piecemeal—a $40 sweater one day and return to the store a week later and buy a $10 mascara, two $6 pairs of pantyhose, and some underwear for $22. Then you dash back in a day later for a birthday present for your sister—a silk blouse for $60. You will have paid a total of $144 for the three-day shopping excursion. Had you done some heavy-duty shopping all at once, you could have gotten the discount. BUT if you save your receipts, you can run them all together to get the VAT.

▼ Once you know the minimum, judge accordingly if you will make a smaller purchase, or come back another time for a big haul. Only you know how much time your schedule will permit for shopping. Remember that on a $10 purchase, the 15% saving is too minimal to make the VAT meaningful. Keep the discount in perspective.

▼ Judge for yourself if you are certain the store you are about to do business with will actually give you the refund after the paperwork is done. If you are dealing with a famous department store or a reputable boutique, there never should be a problem. If you are dealing with Uncle Sabib's Cash & Carry Discount & Friendly Tourist Trading Company, you may want to reconsider. It is possible that your refund will not come through. We bought a sweater from one of the world's most famous designers in his London boutique and are still waiting for the refund—three years later (but we haven't given up hope).

▼ If you are going to another European country, consider the VAT or detaxé policy there. For perfume, you'll get better discounts in France. You won't get small refunds in Italy.

▼ If you go for the VAT, budget your time to allow for the paperwork before you leave the country. It takes about five minutes to fill out each form, and you must have them filled in when you present them on exiting the country. The new form is a simple one, but you must prepare it properly.

▼ Along with the VAT forms you will be given an envelope. Sometimes the envelope has a stamp on it, sometimes it is blank (you must provide the postage stamp before you leave the country); sometimes it has a special government frank that serves as a stamp. If you don't understand what's on your envelope, ask.

▼ When you are leaving the country, go to the Customs official who serves the VAT papers. DO THIS BEFORE YOU CLEAR REGULAR CUSTOMS OR SEND OFF YOUR LUGGAGE. The Customs officer has the right to ask you to show him (or her) the merchandise you bought and are taking out of the country. Whether the officer sees your purchases or not, he or she will stamp the papers, keeping a set (which will be processed) and giving you another set, in the envelope. The officer may even lick the envelope for you. You then mail the envelope (which usually is preprinted with the shop's name and address, or will have been addressed by the shop for you). There is a mailbox next to the officer's desk at Heathrow.

A few stern words of warning: The Customs officials in both London airports are very tough people. They probably spent their early careers in one of those tiny wooden shacks in front of Buckingham Palace wearing a three-foot-high beaver hat with a very tight chinstrap. You will not get the VAT unless you show these guys exactly what they want to see. And forget it if you've already sent off your luggage prior to Customs inspection.

▼ When the papers get back to the shop and the government has notified the shop that their set of papers has been registered, the store will then grant you the discount through a refund. This can be done on your credit card, of which they made a dual pressing, or through a personal check, which will come to you in the mail, usually three months later. (It will be in a foreign currency—your bank may charge you to change it into dollars.)

Okay, that's how the system works. Now here are the fine points:

The way in which you get your discount is somewhat negotiable!

State on your forms what form the refund should take: cash, check, or credit card. Credit card is the most simple.

1. The retailer sells you the merchandise at the cheapest price possible, including the discount,

and therefore actually takes a loss on income until the government reimburses him. For example: The bottle of fragrance you want costs $50.00. The discount is $7.50. The best possible deal you could ever get is for the retailer to charge you $42.50 flat, give you the VAT papers, and explain to you that he will not get the rest of his money unless you process the papers properly. Being as honorable as you are, of course you process the papers properly. This is a very unusual and rare occurrence (it does involve trust) but is by far the simplest for you.

2. The most simple is the credit-card refund. You pay for the purchase at the regular retail price with a major credit card. Then your plate is restamped for a refund slip, marked for the amount of the VAT. You sign both slips at the time of the purchase. When the papers come back to the retailer, the shop puts through the credit slip. The credit may appear on the same monthly statement as the original bill or on a subsequent bill. Just remember to check for the credits.

3. This is the most widely used method: You pay the regular retail price, with cash, travelers check, or credit card. You are given the forms, you go through the refund process, you get on your plane, and you go home. Several months later (usually about three) you get a check in the mail made out for the refund. This check is in the currency of the country from which you made the purchase and will have to be converted to dollars and cents, a process for which your bank may charge you a percentage or a fee. Or you can go to Deak-Perera or another currency broker and get the money in the currency of origin to save for your next trip to that country.

   If your refund never appears, you can decide if you want to fight or not.

Just about the only time you will not get a refund—when you qualify for one—is when you shop in alternative resource outlets. If you buy seconds, designer samples, factory rejects, or used merchandise, there is a good chance that you will pay the marked price and not get back any change. There is no Value-Added Tax on antiques in Britain in the first place, so everyone gets a break in that category. Otherwise, it doesn't hurt to ask, but don't be surprised if discounters and outlets don't give refunds.

Shopping Hours

Shopping hours are downright unorganized in London, so try to pay attention to what day of the week you are shopping. Wednesdays may have later openings in the morning and later closings in the evening.

The good news: Stores generally open early in London—this is 9:00 A.M. We're always chomping at the bit and hate cities where the stores don't open until 10:00 A.M. Warning: A few of the big-name shops don't open until 10:00 A.M. All department stores open between 9:00 and 9:30 A.M.

The bad news: Stores close early in London. They do not know the meaning of late. To a British store, a late night means they are open until 7:00 P.M. or possibly 8:00 P.M. No one, but *no one,* stays open until 9:00 P.M. One of the reasons we like the Brent Cross shopping mall (it certainly isn't the ambience) is that it's open until 8:00 P.M. every day.

There is a rule on late closings, but it's a difficult one, so ask. Some stores stay open late on Wednesday nights; some stay open late on Thursday nights, which is decided on by location. In other words, all the shops in a certain neighborhood will be open late that particular night, but you have to match the night to the neighborhood. All we've ever been able to figure out regarding late closings is:

▼ West End: Wednesday

▼ Knightsbridge: Thursday

Very few stores close for lunch, but some do. Department stores do not.

Getting Around

G etting around London is easy. First of all, you speak the language, so you can get reasonable help as soon as you get lost. But more importantly, the underground system is excellent. You can get a free underground map from your concierge; there is also one printed on the back of your trusty "A to Zed." (We never go anywhere in London without an "A to Zed"; we have the color version—it's worth the extra $1.50.) The underground is amazingly deep—it really is underground. Connections may take a while in a few stations if you change lines, but this happens in all big cities with fancy subway systems.

Speaking of subways, the underground is not a subway in Britain. In the Queen's English, a subway is an underground foot passage to get you from one side of the street to another without getting squooshed by traffic. The underground is called the "tube."

There are all-day, all-week, and more extended ticket packages you can buy. If you take three trips on the underground, you have paid the price of the all-day pass. We go for the all-day pass unless we are in Mayfair, where we walk and walk and shop and shop and then crawl back to our hotel (conveniently in the midst of all this walking and shopping) and then walk and shop some more. We like the all-day pass because of its unlimited nature; we find ourselves taking the tube for just one stop—which we wouldn't do if we were paying.

Besides the tube, there is an excellent bus system—those famous double-decker buses your kids are dying to ride on. You can get a bus route map, free. (The all-day pass is good on underground or bus, by the way.) If you are paying as you go, get on the bus and take your seat—a meter maid (or man) will ask for your fare or pass.

While you can rent a car in London for relatively little money (about $25 a day), you don't want to be driving in the city for a shopping spree. If you want a car and driver, your concierge can help you, or you can call Carey International at 800-336-4646 while you still are in the States and make arrangements.

Tube Shopping

Since the tube and the train (Brit Rail) are so well developed in London, the retailing system that goes with them has been raised to a fine art. Some chains, such as the Sock Shop, show up in every major station. But you can always count on there being at least one good bookstore, lots of fast-food places, and sometimes an entire network of stores.

At the Bond Street station there is an entire shopping center, complete with about two dozen shops and many cafes, that begins in the station and builds upward about three or four levels.

A few train stations, such as Victoria, have tourist information centers.

Museum Shopping

U ncle Lennie once gave us the challenge of the day: Come up with some kind of really good shopping adventure for a Sunday in London.

"Petticoat Lane," we replied immediately.

Uncle Lennie just laughed. "Not our style," he said politely. We gave it some thought. Here's Uncle Lennie and Aunt LaRue, staying in their deluxe Mayfair hotel, with very discriminating taste and enough money to be comfortable and have a nice time. They certainly do not want to go to Petticoat Lane and look at the junk and fear for their lives. They want elegance. They want chic. They still want to go shopping.

Pat us on the head, Uncle Lennie. We've figured it out. Sunday is the best day to go museum shopping.

Almost all the museums have at least one gift shop, and all these shops are open on Sunday.

We think the best upscale Sunday you can spend in London is very simply:

▼ Brunch at the Mayfair Hotel (the only deluxe West End hotel that serves American brunch, mind you).

▼ Browse the Victoria and Albert. (The costume collection! Be still, our hearts!)

▼ Shop the Victoria and Albert.

▼ Have tea at Brown's Hotel.

Souvenir Shopping

I f you need to bring a lot of souvenirs back home, you may want to go to a souvenir shop. London has a chain of them called Cerex. There is a Cerex Souvenirs at every major tourist thoroughfare you can imagine— Oxford Circus, Bond Street Station, etc. They make airport souvenir shops look tony.

We think one of the best souvenir shops in town is in Selfridge's.

We vote the single best tourist gift: one of the modern art T-shirts with bold versions of traditional sights; the Big Ben T-shirt is real art. (We are not being sarcastic.) The T-shirts are $7.50, which makes them a fair price in the international T-shirt wars.

Royal commemoratives also make good souvenirs, but be warned that some of these things become collector's items. At the time of a royal event (like a wedding or a coronation), the commemoratives seem to be a dime a dozen, but once they dry up they are gone forever and become collector's items.

Royal souvenirs always are available. At any of several stands on Middlesex Lane in the Petticoat Lane market area you can get a key chain for about $1.00 with a picture of Chuck and Di and the kids set in plastic.

Shopping Centers

I f you consider the market as the original shopping center and the covered market as the original mall, then London is loaded with shopping centers. If you're thinking of the American version of a shopping center, you'll find very little to remind you of back home. The one "American-type" shopping center we've found is called Brent Cross, and it's very much a real-people kind of place. On a short trip to London (any stay less than thirty days) we find Brent Cross a little too boring. But there are many things in its favor:

▼ It's easy to get to on public transportation.

▼ There's free parking if you happen to have a car.

▼ Shops are open late every night—until 8:00 P.M. every weeknight, which is late by standards in London, where everything closes by 5:00 P.M., with one late night a week—until 7:00 P.M. (On Saturday the shops close at 6:00 P.M.)

If you're living in London or want to leave your children in the play park while you take in a few of your favorites (Laura Ashley, Mothercare, Cecil Gee, Wallis, Bally, Marks & Sparks and Boots, among others), this may be a practical solution to your shopping needs.

The building is air conditioned in summer and much resembles a modern American mall, with escalators, potted palms, and all that. This is very much a family place, much like what you have at home.

There is a much smaller shopping center over the Bond Street tube station.

Shopping Neighborhoods

London, because of its architecture, is much more of a neighborhood town than most American cities; thus shopping neighborhoods rather than shopping centers have evolved, and many of these neighborhoods have different personalities. Others are sections

LONDON NEIGHBORHOODS

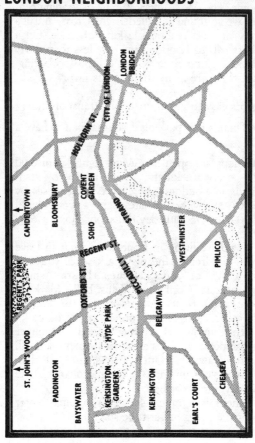

of a greater whole and have no borderlines—
shop "The West End," "Mayfair," and "Piccadilly" and you will be in the same area seeing
the same shops.

The West End

The West End is the name for a large portion
of real estate designated with the letter W and
a number after it. A W1 address is very chic—
for a store or a residence. As a shopping district, the West End is the first stop we make
once we've checked into the hotel. (We stay
at the Mayfair so we can roll out the front
door and be within walking distance of all our
West End resources. When we check in, we
don't even go to the room, we just send up the
luggage and hit the lobby for coffee and the
streets for adventure.)

The big shopping streets in the West End
are Oxford Street, Regent Street, Bond Street
(Old and New), and then Piccadilly. Several
little streets weave between Oxford and Piccadilly in this area, and all of them are dandy for
browsing.

We can't even begin to name our faves in
this area; look at "The Big Names" listings
later in this book, since most of the big names
have their shops here. There's also a ton of big
department stores and British institutions (of
the shopping kind), such as Burberry's, Aquascutum, and Hamley's.

Knightsbridge

Fashionable and "with it"—Knightsbridge's two
most important streets are Brompton Road and
Fulham Road. You'll find some important, established fashion boutiques and shops as well
as two world-class department stores. The famous Sloane Rangers (see page 12) hang out
in Knightsbridge in the area between Sloane

Street and Harrods. You may want to catch some of the big names in branch boutiques here, so look out for YSL, Laura Ashley, Souleiado (Pierre Deux), Butler & Wilson, Paper Chase, Caroline Charles, Ken Lane, and Jaeger.

Chelsea

Chelsea and Knightsbridge back up on each other, but the big shopping street in Chelsea is Kings Road, with its blend of outrageousness and old-fashioned fashion. There're restaurants, antiques, and expensive and inexpensive shopping thrills on both sides of the street. We adore The Reject Shop (not to be confused with Reject China), which we always visit when we're here, along with others such as Habitat, Edwina and Lena, Designer's Guild, Antiquarius, and Manolo Blahnik. Chelsea is not the hot place it once was.

Kensington

Kensington High Street is all you need to know to see the latest in punk looks and new-wave fashion. There's a lot of used-clothing shops around here, and Hyper-Hyper is here. The underground is the heart of the neighborhood and has its very own shopping arcade. This is a good place to catch a Marks & Sparks if you miss the Oxford Street main store. Don't forget Barkers, Grandma Mary's favorite department store in London. Our favorite is the Kensington Market. Don't miss Kensington Church Street while you're in the neighborhood; check out—among others—La Cicogna, Benetton, British Home Stores, Woolworth (good for souvenirs), Bally for children, and good old Crabtree & Evelyn. Koko and Monsoon give you a good look at the two aspects—independent and special, and chain-store chic.

Covent Garden

We're not sure if Londoners call this area Covent Garden, or if there's anything official about this designation, but everyone will know where you are talking about. The entire area around Covent Garden is filled with fabulous little shops (and pubs), which makes the whole place a super shopping area. Include the two buildings of Covent Garden with all their shops in your neighborhood tour, the three markets more or less attached to Covent Garden (between the two buildings; out the back building; to the side of the two buildings), and all the fun and funky shops circling around. Don't miss Patricia Roberts if you know how to knit . . . or purl; Berties for shoes, Laura Ashley, Key Largo for sweaters you've ogled on Princess you-know-who. Walk to Leicester Square via New Row for even more cute shops.

Customhouse Brokers

If you are bringing into the U.S. more than $250 worth of goods, or will not be home and have no one to accept your packages for you, you will probably need a customhouse broker to help you. If you live in a port of entry (New York, Charleston, New Orleans, Galveston, Los Angeles, San Francisco, Seattle, etc.), there will be a bounty of them listed in the yellow pages. Most customhouse brokers deal with businesses, so you may have to shop around a bit to find one that will take a personal shipment.

To make life even more convenient, many customhouse brokers are also associated with freight companies, shippers, and express package delivery services.

The customhouse broker may charge a flat fee, a percentage, or both, depending on what you are bringing in and for what purposes. Expect to pay a $30 flat fee to an express package delivery service and $50 to $100 for a broker who must go to Customs to retrieve your package. However, the fee may already be written into the price of the shipment. Ask.

If your shipment is being sent to you through a customhouse broker, ask the company you contract about the correct way to send the package. Usually it is addressed to them rather than to you; then they deliver it for you. They do not like to store your packages. If the broker asks for power of attorney, find out why.

Mostly, customs brokers are for professionals. You can probably get along fine without one.

Packers and Craters

There is another service business that shoppers should know about that may be provided through your shipper or contracted for separately—the actual pickup, packing, and crating of your many purchases. You can go around town waving your charge cards like magic wands and then have everything picked up for you, packed, and sent home. You never even return to your hotel with so much as a shopping bag. Or you can schlep everything to your hotel and leave it there to be picked up, packed, crated, and then delivered to your shipper or sent air freight. Ask the concierge about these services, or check the yellow pages. The bigger shippers (see page 81) have packing services.

Make sure you have insurance—this usually is a separate transaction and another price.

Insurance rarely is included in the price of packing!

If you are arranging shipping, ask specifically if packing is included in the charge or is billed separately. For antiques, breakables, and serious works of art, the actual packaging can be quite involved.

Insurance

nsurance usually is sold by the package by your shipper. Do not assume that it is included in the price of delivery, because it isn't. There are several different types of insurance and deductibles or all-risk (with no deductible), so you'll have to make a personal choice based on the value of what you are shipping. Remember when figuring the value of the item for insurance purposes to include the price of the shipping. If you bought a desk for $1,000 and it costs $500 to ship it home, the value for insurance purposes is $1,500. If you have the replacement-cost type of insurance, you should probably double the price, since that is approximately what it would cost you to replace the item in the United States.

Shipping

t all began with the *Mayflower* and has been evolving steadily ever since. The *Mayflower* may have come with a handful of Pilgrims and their Bibles, but ever since, Americans have been bringing back treasures and family heirlooms from the mother country—first by sail, then by freighter, and now by plane. It's all very sophisticated now and surprisingly not very expensive.

The good news: You've just found the most wonderful, gorgeous, fabulous, chic, and inexpensive sideboard. You've longed for one for years, know it will be the envy of all who see it. Surely Princess Michael could not have chosen better; your sister-in-law will pass out when she sees it.

The bad news: It certainly won't fit into your suitcase.

Whether the item is as cumbersome as a sideboard, as small as a few bottles of perfume, or as fragile as dinner plates, you can arrange to ship it home. All it takes is a little time and a little more money.

If you anticipate buying an item that needs shipping, do your homework before you leave the United States. You may need a family member to claim the item at Customs if you still will be out of the country, or you may even need a Customs agent (see page 73). You also will want to know enough about shipping costs to be able to make a smart decision about the added cost of your purchase. To make shipping pay, the item—with the additional cost of shipping, duty, and insurance (and Customs agent, etc., if need be)—still should cost *less* than it would at home, or be so totally unavailable at home that any price makes it a worthwhile purchase. If it's truly unavailable (and isn't an antique or a one-of-a-kind art item) at home, ask yourself why. There may be a good reason—such as it's illegal to bring such an item into the country! If you are indeed looking for a certain type of thing, be very familiar with American prices. If it's an item of furniture, even an antique, can a decorator get it for you with a 20% rather than a 40% markup? Have you checked out all the savings angles first?

There are basically two types of shipping: surface and air. Air can be broken down to two ways: unaccompanied baggage and regular air freight.

Surface mail (usually by ship in a transatlantic transaction) is the cheaper. Surface mail may mean through the regular mail channels—i.e., a small package of perfume would be sent through parcel post—or it may require your filling an entire shipping container or at least paying the price for use of an entire container. Many people make the mistake of assuming that the weight of an item will matter in the shipping. While weight matters, there may be a five-hundred-pound difference per price bracket! A piano may weigh more than two Queen Anne chairs, but they may cost the same to ship. Surface mail may take three months, but we've had delivery in three weeks. Allow three months, to be safe; longer if so advised by the dealer. Don't invite anyone to dinner at your new table until the table actually arrives.

We've done enough shipping to know that there is one broker we find far superior to others; furthermore, this broker has offices in the United States and all over Europe. If you care enough to buy an especially fine piece (or two or ten) and want to make sure it's well treated and arrives at your home intact, call Michael Davis Shippers. Michael Davis Shippers has just adjusted their price downward (can you believe it?), but check with their offices for an accurate price quote before you do any big business with them. Generally speaking, their rate is per cubic foot and includes:

▼ picking up the purchase

▼ packing the goods

▼ handling export documents

▼ sea-freight charges

▼ Customs clearance on the U.S. end

▼ delivery to your door

If you want to save even more money, ask about groupage services. Your goods will be held until a shipping container is filled. The container will then go to the United States, to only one of four ports of entry (Los Angeles, New York, San Francisco, or New Orleans), where you can meet the container at the dock, be there when your items are unpacked, and then pay the duties due. A full container is 1,100 cubic feet of space (or 8 feet, 6 inches by 8 feet, 6 inches by 20 feet long—or big enough for about 100 pieces of furniture) and will not be delivered to your door (no matter how much you smile). Expect use of a full container to cost you about $4,000 total (without insurance)—the price will be in pounds sterling, so the rate of exchange very much affects your shipping power. Packing usually is priced apart from shipping, so if you are not shipping chairs and need lots of packing, use of the container could cost you $7,500.

Air freight is several more times expensive than surface but has the assurance of quick delivery. We can't think of anything that would have to be flown to us in the States; if it were so delicate and so important to need to be flown, it may indeed need an international courier, who is a person who hand-carries the item for you. (This is often done with pieces of art or valuable papers.) There is also an overnight air package service (much like Federal Express) that delivers within a day or two. This area is growing just the way overnight U.S. services expanded in the past three years, so check out the latest possibilities.

Here's a sampling of some airline air freight prices to give you an idea of what you're in for:

British Airways cargo: under 100 pounds, $3.90 per pound; over 100 pounds, $3.04 per pound; over 220 pounds, $2.47 per pound; over 660 pounds, $1.60 per pound.

Air France cargo and unaccompanied baggage: minimum charge, $41.00; under 100 pounds, $5.68 per kilo (2.2 pounds); 100 to 200 pounds, $4.18 per kilo. Obviously your expenses will fluctuate with the dollar's exchange rate.

TWA cargo: minimum charge, $147.23 for 10 pounds; first 220 pounds, $4.67 per pound. Insurance is $1.00 per $100,00; your items must be boxed or crated and delivered to TWA at the airport.

Unaccompanied baggage may be sent home whenever you want—you take it with your luggage to the airline desk and make the arrangements there. It often goes on the same flight you do but is cheaper than being checked as an extra piece of luggage. Of course, if the baggage is going home and you're going on to Cairo, it will not be on the same plane as you. If your returning baggage has no new possessions in it, tag it "Returning American Goods" so the Customs people know what it is. (They still will open it if they want to.)

Shipping Wrecks

O ur friend Larissa told us a most unsettling story. Larissa was living in London for six months while her husband completed a business deal. She discovered she was pregnant after she arrived and in short order needed a new wardrobe. She bought maternity clothes in London and shipped home her old American-purchased garments, along with a couple of other items she had purchased for the baby. In doing her research at the London end, she was assured by DHL (a Federal Express–type operation) that the box would be delivered to her mother's home. In daily contact with her mother, Larissa was concerned when the overnight package had not been delivered after seven days. After many phone calls it was discovered that U.S. Customs was holding her box and was charging her duty on her American-bought clothes (many were from European designers) and the new purchases—at the American retail price. Larissa's mom had to drive all the way to the airport (not nearby), pay $750 in duties to get the box, which, of course, was worth more than $750 so she didn't just leave it there (though she considered it).

Then there was Mr. and Mrs. O. (as in Ordinary, not Onassis), who had no previous dealings with shipping. They decided to go to London to buy furnishings for their home and spent a very harried two and a half weeks combing London and the surrounding areas for the most elegant pieces at the best prices. At the time of their first purchase, the shopkeeper recommended a "reputable" shipper that she had dealt with in the past. She assured the O's that they could afford the shipping fees. She made all the arrangements, down to a comparison pricing with Michael Davis Shippers. The O's were shocked at the discrepancy. They continued to shop the London area, contacting their new find—the shipping company—and left England with total confidence. After four months of waiting, their purchases arrived and the crates were unpacked. Each crate offered up a new heartbreak—shelves, moldings, cornices, and hunks of wood were missing from each piece and were found lying discreetly at the bottom of the crate. A call to London revealed that little could be done—the shipper had not insured the crates or advised the client of the need to do so. The O's had assumed insurance was included. They spent double the shipping savings with a furniture restorer.

Just to make you feel a tad better, we'll include the story of our friend Susannah, who went to Harrods and bought her china. It took about an hour because she chose lots of it, and seemed to take another hour for the salesgirl to write it up. Finally Susannah said, "Look, I'm a tourist and my time is precious. Can I just sign the American Express slip and let you take care of this?" She allowed them to finish up, to ship, charge her credit card, and make all the arrangements, and she went on her merrie olde way. Her packages arrived, all in perfect shape, two weeks later. Everything was done aboveboard, and there were no math mistakes or overcharges. Harrods made her life better.

To avoid your own shipping wreck, check our several shippers and ask friends for their experiences. Do not try to make a cheap deal; go for reputation. The yellow pages list zillions of shippers, your hotel concierge will help you find one, and even guidebooks often list their favorites. We haven't done tons of shipping of large pieces from London, but our own past experience has made us devoted to Michael Davis Shippers. You pay for what you get.

Michael Davis Shippers: 111 Mortlake Road, Kew, Richmond, Surrey TW9

We found these names in *The New York Times:*

C. R. Fenton Company: Beachy Road, Old Ford, London E3 (U.S. office: fine art and antiques service, New York City, 212-696-4148)

James Bourlet Sons: 3 Space Waye, Feltenham, Middlesex TW14

Gander & White Shipping: 21 Lillie Road, London SW6

Shop Ships and More

I f you have an item shipped from a shop (a reputable shop, of course), have the VAT papers filled out at the same time. You are entitled to the export refund if you meet the store's minimum-purchase requirement. Ask about the shop's shipping policies before you decide to ship—some stores will charge you for their trouble (a flat fee), then the actual shipping rate, and then an insurance fee. Try to pay for the purchase with a credit card; that way if it never arrives you'll have an easier time getting a credit or a refund. Be sure to ask when the store will be able to ship the goods. We planned to send home some perfume so as not to have to lug it around for a month's worth of touring; the shopkeeper told us she was so backed up on her shipping that it would take her at least six weeks to mail our order. Then it would take several weeks or months for the package to arrive by surface mail. (We took it with us.)

If you want to save a little money and if the item is of a manageable size, consider shipping it yourself. Get the materials from a stationery store and go to the local post office. Make sure you meet local requirements—they may not allow certain kinds of tape, etc. We suggest twine and filament packing tape. Handprint the labels on the package itself, so if they separate you still have a chance to get the package. Be advised that some countries do not insure international packages, or insure only up to a certain rate. (Don't ship a David Emanuel original that's worth $15,000 because you won't get that much insurance through the regular post office! Besides, if you've got the money for the gown, don't cut corners by shipping it yourself.) The U.S. Postal Service automatically sends all incoming foreign-mail shipments to Customs for examination. If no duty is being charged, the package goes back to the post office and will be delivered to you. If duty is required, the Customs official attaches a yellow slip to your package, and your mailman will collect the moneys due when the package is delivered to you. If you feel the duty charge is inappropriate, you may file a protest, or you don't have to accept the package. If you don't accept it, you have thirty days to file your objection so the shipment can be detained until the matter is settled.

If you are caught between these two methods, ask your concierge to ship it for you. He will bill your room for the actual postage and supplies, and you are expected to tip him for his trouble. (This still will be less expensive than the shop route, probably.) Also, we're suspicious snobs and trust only concierges at first-rate deluxe hotels. We advise you to do the same.

Be sure to keep all paperwork. If you use a freight office, keep the bill of lading. If the shop sends your package, keep all receipts.

Ask about the policy for breakage from any shop that ships for you.

Excess Baggage

I f you are merely burdened with the delights of a successful shopping venture, you probably don't need a container but still could use a friend. The British Tourist Authority came up with what looks like a winner to us:

▼

THE CARGOSHOP LTD.: This is a small business that specializes in all sorts of baggage problems, even large ones. Thoughtfully located right off Regent Street, The Cargoshop specializes in over-the-counter baggage or special-purchase portage to all worldwide destinations. Your best bet is to stop in and see them personally, on your first day in London. You can also phone (629-0308), but we suggest an in-office visit—they have many services that will make your shopping much more pleasant for you. For example:

▼ *Collections.* For a price (of course) they will pick up your purchases at the various stores where you bought them and then ship the whole lot of them straight to you. You needn't walk around all day loaded down like the forty-mule train.

▼ *Packing.* Remember that this is a separate service and is charged as such, but it's good to have someone do it when needed. (Most china and crystal firms will pack for you free, by the way.) Antiques and collectibles are another story.

▼ *Insurance.* This is another service, but one you need; The Cargoshop can take care of it for you.

▼ *Storage.* If you are on an extended buying trip, you may need a firm to pick up and store for you, especially if you buy big pieces at auction. The Cargoshop has free storage (auction houses charge).

In working with The Cargoshop, make sure you understand the different types of forwarding—air cargo is much more expensive than shipping. Get all the price possibilities before you decide. Expect to pay a handling charge that takes care of the paperwork, truckage to the airport, U.K. Customs, security checking, and other little details that have to be paid for. Some firms charge for these items on an individual basis. The Cargoshop charges a flat fee of $30. The Cargoshop's hours are: Monday to Friday, 9:00 A.M. to 6:00 P.M.; Saturday, 9:00 A.M. to 2:00 P.M. The tube stop is Oxford Circus.

THE CARGOSHOP LTD., 5 Maddox Street, W1

U.S. Customs and Duties

Have you ever noticed that when you get off the plane in a foreign city, you more or less breeze through Customs? Yet when you return to the United States, you may go through a rather involved system that may or may not include inspection of your luggage and a barrage of questions, some of them personal or even insulting? Well, if it makes you feel any better, all nationals go through more or less the same procedures when they return to their own countries. In fact, in recent years, the United States has been changing its welcoming ceremonies to the red light/green light system that is an imitation of the European system that has been in operation for years.

To make your reentry into the United States as smooth as possible, follow these tips:

▼ Know the rules and stick to them!

▼ Don't try to smuggle anything.

▼ Be polite and cooperative (up until the point when they ask you to strip, anyway . . .).

Remember:

▼ You are currently allowed to bring in $400 worth of merchandise per person, duty-free. Before you leave the United States, verify this amount with one of the U.S. Customs offices (see the list on page 91). This amount does change (recently it was raised from $300), and if you miss the news item in the paper, you may be cheating yourself out of a good deal. Each member of the family is entitled to the deduction; this includes infants.

▼ You pay a flat 10% duty on the next $1,000 worth of merchandise. This is extremely simple and is worth doing. We're talking about the very small sum of $100 to make life easy—and crime-free.

▼ Duties thereafter are based on a product-type basis; see the list on pages 89–91 for more specific information. They vary tremendously per item, so check out the list before you do your shopping! (Look at the hefty levies on hand embroidery!)

▼ The head of the family can make a joint declaration for all family members. The "head of the family" need not be male. Whoever is the head of the family, however, should take the responsibility for answering any questions the Customs officers may ask. Answer questions honestly, firmly, and politely. Have receipts ready, and make sure they match the information on the landing card. Don't be forced into a story that won't wash under questioning. If you tell a little lie, you'll be labeled as a fibber and they'll tear your luggage apart.

▼ You count into your $400 per person everything you obtain while abroad—this includes toothpaste (if you bring the unfinished tube back with you), gifts, items bought in duty-free shops, gifts for others, the items that other people asked you to bring home for them, and—get this—even alterations.

▼ Have the Customs registration slips for your personally owned goods in your wallet or easily available. If you wear a Cartier watch, for example, whether it was bought in the United States, or in Europe ten years ago, should you be questioned about it, produce the registration slip. If you cannot prove that you took a foreign-made item out of the country with you, you may be forced to pay duty on it!

▼ The unsolicited gifts you mailed from abroad do not count in the $400-per-person rate. If the value of the gift is more than $50, you pay duty when the package comes into the country. Remember, it's only one unsolicited gift per person, and you cannot mail them to yourself.

▼ Do not attempt to bring in any illegal food items—dairy products, meats, fruits, or vegetables (coffee is okay). Generally speaking, if it's alive, it's *verboten*.

▼ We don't need to tell you it's tacky to bring in drugs and narcotics.

▼ Antiques must be a hundred years old to be duty-free. Provenance papers will help (so will permission actually to export the antiquity, since it could be an item of national cultural significance).

▼ Dress for success. People who look like "hippies" get stopped at Customs more than average folks. Women who look like a million dollars, who are dragging their fur coats, have first-class baggage tags on their luggage, and carry Gucci handbags but declare they have bought nothing are equally suspicious.

▼ Any bona fide work of art is duty-free whether it was painted fifty years ago or just yesterday; the artist need not be famous.

▼ Other items may be duty-free; check out our listing on pages 89–91 and talk to the Customs office about the Generalized System of Preferences (GSP), which allows many items (some quite surprising) to be admitted to this country duty-free to help the economy of the nation from which they come. While these usually are Third World countries, you'll marvel at the gems that can come in duty-free ... such as gems, for instance (unset stones are duty-free). To the GSP even a country such as Bermuda is termed developing. This is why we can get some French goods in Bermuda for less than we can get them at the factory in France. Check it out.

▼ The amount of cigarettes and liquor you can bring back duty-free is a federal regulation. Usually if you arrive by common carrier, you may bring in duty-free one liter of alcoholic beverage. You may bring in an additional five liters on which you must pay duty. The IRS taxes you at $10.50 per gallon on distilled spirits—so obviously you don't want to go over your allowance unless you are carrying some invaluable wine or champagne. If you drive across borders, the regulations may vary, but it's unlikely you will drive home from Europe. (If you do, please write and tell all.)

Alcoholic beverages, cigars, cigarettes, and perfume made in certain Caribbean and Central American countries are admitted to the United States duty-free with a big thank you to the Caribbean Basin Recovery Act. So if you know anyone doing covert CIA activities, do ask him (or her) to bring you back some perfume.... You may also bring back a hundred cigars and one carton of cigarettes without import duty, but there will be state and local taxes on the smokes. You cannot trade your cigar-cigarette-liquor quota against your $400 personal allowance, so that even if all you bought while abroad was ten gallons of champagne (to bathe in, no doubt), you probably will not have paid $400, but you still will have to pay duty and taxes. Also please note that you must be twenty-one or over to get the liquor allowance, but you may be any age for the puffables—thus an infant gets the same tobacco allowance as an adult.

▼ Some no-nos are governed on a statewide basis, so check your Customs officials at your planned port of entry. A few tips:

1. Asian elephant ivory is not allowed in the United States, but African elephant ivory in souvenir form is okay if accompanied by a permit. Now, then, if you did not make an A in fifth-grade science you will need to know: You can tell the difference between an African elephant and an Asian elephant by the size of the ears (an African elephant has larger ears). Don't buy ivory doodads from markets unless the dealer can certify it is an antique.

2. Tortoiseshell is a no-no—no matter where it comes from (unless, that is, it comes from a plastic tortoise).

▼ If you are planning on taking your personal computer with you (to keep track of your budget, perhaps), make sure you register it before taking it out of the country. If you buy a computer abroad, you must declare it when you come in.

The Department of the Treasury was kind enough to give us their latest list of duty rates, which we are passing on to you in case you want to memorize it. Do read it carefully, since the variables are rather amazing. You pay this tariff after your personal exemption and after the flat 10% on an additional $1,000 worth of goods. We don't know just how much of Europe you're planning on buying, but here goes, just in case you need to know the tariffs:

Antiques: over a hundred years old (prior to entry) admitted duty-free; have proof of antiquity from seller
Automobiles: passenger, 2.7%
Bags: hand, leather: 6.5 to 10%
Beads: imitation of precious and semiprecious, 4.7 to 9.1%; real ivory (when allowed), 6.3%

Binoculars, opera glasses, and field glasses: free

Books: free

Cameras: motion picture over $50 each, 5.1%; still, over $10 each, 4.7%; cases, leather, 8.8%; lenses, mounted, 8.8%

Chess sets: 5.92%

China (other than tableware): bone, 8.8%; nonbone, 2.3 to 14.1%

China tableware: bone, 11.6%; nonbone, valued not over $56 per set, 30.7%; nonbone, valued at over $56 per set, 11.9%

Cigarette lighters: pocket, 10.1 to 15.6%; table, 7.5%

Clocks: valued over $5 but not over $10 each, 46 cents plus 10%; valued over $10 each, 70 cents plus 10%

Dolls: stuffed, free during 1985–86—check for extension; other, 14.1%

Drawings: by hand, free

Figurines: china, 14.1%; if by professional sculptor, 3.4%

Film: exposed, free; unexposed, 4.2%

Fur: wearing apparel, 6.5 to 11.6%; other, 3.4 to 7.4%

Furniture: wooden chairs, 5.3 to 6.5%; other than wooden chairs, 3.4%; Bentwood, 8.8%

Gloves: fur, 6.2%; horsehide or cowhide, 15%

Handkerchiefs: linen, hemmed, 7.3%

Jade: cut but not set, suitable for jewelry, 2.3%; other articles, 21%

Jewelry: silver chief value, valued not over $18 per dozen, 27.5%; other, 8.6%

Leather: flat goods, wallets, 5.6% to 8%; other, 2.7 to 7.4%

Music boxes: 5%

Paintings: by hand, free

Pearls, loose or temporarily strung without clasp: natural, free; cultured, 2.3%; imitation, 12.5%; permanently strung or temporary but with clasp, 8.6 to 17.2%

Perfume: $3 per pound plus 5.9%

Postage stamps: free

Printed matter: free to 6%

Radios: solid-state radio receivers, 7.7 to 9.2%

Shavers: electric, 5.2%

Shell arts: 3.4%

Skis and ski equipment: 5.2 to 6.8%

Stones (cut but not set): diamonds, free; others, free to 2.3%

Sweaters: wool over $5 per pound, 19 cents per pound plus 18.5%

Tape recorders: 4.5%

Toys: 10.9%

Watches: mechanical type, $2 to $5.37 (depending on jewels) plus 10% on value of gold case and 22% on value of gold bracelet; digital type, 4.9%

Wearing Apparel: embroidered or ornamented (includes beaded), 12 to 38.8%; not embroidered or ornamented; cotton but not knit, 8 to 21%; cotton knit, 14.5 to 21%; linen but not knit, 5.3%; silk but not knit, 11.8%; wool knit, 19 cents per pound plus 11.5 to 23 cents per pound plus 25.1%; wool but not knit, 13 cents per pound plus 19% to 31 cents per pound plus 21%

Wood Carvings: 6.2%

District Custom Offices

Anchorage, Alas.: 907-271-4043
Baltimore, Md.: 301-962-2666
Boston, Mass.: 617-223-6598
Bridgeport, Conn.: 203-579-4606
Buffalo, N.Y.: 716-842-5901
Charleston, S.C.: 803-724-4312
Chicago, Ill.: 312-353-6100
Cleveland, Ohio: 216-522-4284
Dallas/Forth Worth, Tex.: 214-574-2170
Detroit, Mich.: 313-226-3177
Duluth, Minn.: 218-727-6692
El Paso, Tex.: 915-543-7435
Galveston, Tex.: 713-763-1211
Great Falls, Mont.: 406-453-7631

Honolulu, Hawaii: 808-546-3115
Houston, Tex.: 713-226-4316
Laredo, Tex.: 512-723-2956
Los Angeles, Calif.: 213-548-2441
Miami, Fla.: 305-350-4806
New York, N.Y.: 212-466-5550
Nogales, Ariz.: 602-287-4955
Norfolk, Va.: 804-441-6546
Ogdensburg, N.Y.: 315-393-0660
Pembina, N.D.: 701-825-6201
Port Arthur, Tex.: 713-982-2831
Portland, Me.: 207-780-3326
Portland, Oreg.: 503-221-2865
Providence, R.I.: 401-528-4383
St. Albans, Vt.: 802-524-6527
St. Louis, Mo.: 314-425-3134
St. Thomas, V.I.: 809-774-2530
San Diego, Calif.: 714-293-5360
San Francisco, Calif.: 415-556-4340
San Juan, P.R.: 809-723-2091
Savannah, Ga.: 912-232-4321
Seattle, Wash.: 206-442-5491
Tampa, Fla.: 813-228-2381
Washington, D.C.: 202-566-8511
Wilmington, N.C.: 919-343-4601

5 ▾ MONEY MATTERS

Paying Up

Whether you use cash, travelers check, or credit card, you are probably paying for your purchase in a different currency than American dollars.

For the most part, we recommend using a credit card—especially in fancy stores. Plastic is the safest to use, provides you with a record of your purchases (for Customs as well as for your books), and makes returns a lot easier. Credit-card companies, because they are often associated with banks, may give the best exchange rates. We even know of people who have "made money" by charging on a credit card. That's because the price you pay as posted in dollars is translated on the day your credit slip clears the credit-card company (or bank) office, not the day of your purchase. Say the pound is trading at 1.54. Your hotel may charge only $1.60 per pound when you convert your money. American Express probably will give you a higher rate of exchange.

The bad news about credit cards is that you can overspend easily, and you may come home to a stack of bills. The one extra benefit about a credit card is that you often get delayed billing, so that you may have a month or two to raise some petty cash.

A thought about credit cards: We have been shocked at the lack of enthusiasm recently for the American Express card abroad. Visa seems to be most popular, then Diners Club, then MasterCard, and then, finally, American Express. Major hotels and shops will always take American Express, although they may ask you if you have another type of credit card. Smaller shops may outright refuse to accept American Express. Do not think you can buy everything you want with an American Express card—even if you've got one of those new fancy platinum ones. Another thought along the same lines: If you go to a shop that does not honor any of the cards you hold but does have a display of cards in the window, ask them to pull out their card forms to find the names (and pictures) of their reciprocal bank cards. Chances are you can make a match. Access, a common European credit card, happens to be the same as MasterCard—yet this is rarely advertised.

If you happen to be given a book of discount coupons by your hotel or tour guide, you will also notice that you get a 10% discount for cash but only a 5% discount when you use credit cards. Storekeepers much prefer you to pay in cash. Remember this also when you are bargaining in the markets. A credit-card transaction costs the retailer 2 to 5%. If you pay cash, you should be able to get that discount.

Travelers checks are a must—for safety's sake. Shop around a bit, compare the various companies that issue checks, and make sure your checks are insured against theft or loss. While we like and use American Express travelers checks, they are not the only safe game in town; don't be swayed by their clever advertising. Ask around. With check competition what it is currently, you should be able to get your American Express checks without charge. Ask the bank you do business with to extend this service to you.

BankAmerica provides travelers checks in various currencies and for $5 more gives you an insurance package that is wonderful. Thomas Cook provides travelers checks free and in foreign currencies. American Express can provide travelers checks in pounds, but you most definitely will pay for this privilege. This is a big plus when changing checks at hotels or shops, because you will have a guaranteed rate of exchange. *However,* you must buy the checks through a bank, Deak-Perera, or another currency broker, who may not give you the same rate of exchange as the American Express office abroad. For example, say you want $1,000 in pounds in travelers checks. You go to a Deak-Perera office (or another currency-exchange office) in your city with your $1,000 in cash (they usually do not take personal checks for over $300). They will give you the closest thing to the $1,000 in pounds at the rate of exchange for which they are buying or selling, which is posted daily. You may gain or lose on this deal.

Cash and Carry

I f you must carry cash with you, use a money belt or some safety device. We use Sport Sac zipper bags that are large enough to hold passport, travelers checks, and cash. We won't tell you where we secure them, but our valuables are not in our handbags, which can be rather easily stolen, or around our waists—since this can be uncomfortable. We've heard of extra-large brassieres, under-the-arm contraptions, and all sorts of more personal and private inventions. You're on your own here—but do remember to take care.

Currency Exchange

A s we've already mentioned, currency exchange rates vary tremendously. The rate announced in the paper (it's in the *Herald Tribune* every day, if you're abroad and want to know about your net worth) is the official bank exchange rate and does not particularly apply to tourists. Even by trading your money at a bank you will not necessarily get the same rate of exchange that's announced in the papers.

▼ You will get a better rate of exchange for a travelers check than for cash because there is less paperwork involved for banks, hotels, etc.

▼ The rate of exchange you get is not usually negotiable per that establishment. Hotels do not give a more favorable exchange rate to regular patrons, etc. If you have a letter of introduction to a banker, or have zillions in a sister bank, you may get a better rate—but it's unlikely and would take some personal arranging. Although you can shop for the best rate available, you cannot haggle for a better rate from a certain source.

▼ Hotels generally give the least favorable rate of exchange, but with the current strength of the dollar, we find some flexibility here. Hilton and Sheraton hotels have been giving the bank rate lately, without a service charge, to their guests. Each Inter • Continental hotel makes its own rules, so ask at these hotels. Shops may negotiate on the rate of exchange. Say the item you buy costs the equivalent of $40 and you sign over a $50 travelers check. The shopkeeper may ask you the rate of exchange, or say something like, "Let's see, today the dollar is trading at ..." He (or you) will then pull out a calculator and figure out how much change you will get. If you have bought a lot, you may ask for a more favorable rate of exchange on your change, or bargain a bit. Exclusive shops will be insulted at this maneuver (use credit cards there, anyway). Likewise, the time involved in getting a better rate may be so preposterous that it doesn't matter how expensive your hotel is. One day we decided to go to one of the change bureaus at Piccadilly Circus that was giving a higher rate than our hotel. After one-half hour in line, we quit. It would have taken three hours to reach the head of that line. We would have saved $3.

▼ Do not expect a bank to give you any better rate than your hotel, although they may. We've generally found the best rate of exchange at the American Express office. Usually they give as close to the bank rate as is humanly possible. (We really don't work for American Express, we just use them a lot and like most of their services—chances are you will, too.)

▼ Don't change money (or a lot of it, anyway) with airport vendors because they will have the worst rates in town; yes, higher than your hotel.

▼ If you want to change money back to dollars when you leave a country, remember that you will pay a higher rate for them. You are now "buying" dollars rather than "selling" them. Therefore, never change more money than you think you will need, unless you stockpile for another trip.

▼ Have some foreign currency on hand for arrivals. After a lengthy transatlantic flight, you will not want to stand in line at some airport booth to get your cab fare. You'll pay a very high rate of exchange and be wasting your precious bathtub time. Your home bank or local currency exchange office can sell you small amounts of foreign currency. No matter how much of a premium you pay for this money, the convenience will be worth it. We ask for $50 worth of currency for each country we are visiting. This will pay for the taxi to the hotel, tips, and the immediate necessities until you decide where to change the rest of your money. (Since we also go to Europe rather frequently, we stockpile amounts under $100 for reentry money.) And do keep this money readily available on landing—you don't want to have to undress in the taxicab to reach your money belt, nor do you want the money packed in a suitcase in a very safe place.

▼ Keep track of what you pay for your currency. If you are going to several countries, or if you must make several money-changing trips to the cashier, write the sums down. When you get home and wonder what you did with all the money you used to have, it'll be easier to trace your cash. When you are budgeting, adjust to the rate you paid for the money, not the rate you read in the newspaper. *Do not* be embarrassed if you are confused by rates and various denominations. Learn as much as you can, and ask for help. Take time to count your change and understand what has been placed in your hand. The people you are dealing with already know you are an American (for the most part, they can tell just from looking at you), so feel satisfied that you understand each financial transaction. In some countries, the numbers you will be dealing with are so astronomical that it will be hard for you to adjust to the mathematical gymnastics you will have to perform to know how much you have paid for an item in U.S. terms and to count your change.

▼ Make mental comparative rates for quick price reactions. Know the conversion rate for $50 and $100 so within an instant you can make a judgment. If you're still interested in an item, then slow down and figure out the true and accurate price. Do not make the mistake of equating the pound to the dollar on a one-on-one basis, even as a quick mental fix. You'll be sorry later. And poorer.

How to Get Cash Overseas

We've run out of cash on more international trips than we like to admit (to ourselves or to our husbands, who happen to think that only women run out of cash). This happens to us not so much due to our inability to budget properly but because of our patriotic feelings in wanting to rescue a sagging economy by buying more and more goods. Besides, men run out of money, too.

If you do run out of money, know where to turn so you can do so during business hours. Holidays, saints' days, weekends, and late nights are not good times to be without funds. If you think you can sail into your deluxe hotel and present your credit card to the cashier for an instant injection of cash or the redemption of a personal check from your U.S. bank, think again. Despite misleading ads to the contrary, American Express gold cards do not bring the respect you want when you are in this ticklish situation. The people who are most anxious to see your American Express card (be it gold, platinum, or plain old adorable green) are the people at American Express. Go there for quick cash. Green-card members may draw up to $1,000; gold cards can get $2,000; platinum cards, $5,000. You may also cash a check there. (*Never travel without your checkbook.*)

It's all a relatively simple transaction: You write a personal check at a special desk and show your card; it is approved; you go to another desk and get the money in the currency you request. Allow about a half hour for the whole process, unless there are long lines. Usually you get the credit advance on your card at the same desk.

Bank cash machines are just beginning to be used in Europe; don't count on finding them everywhere you go, but don't be surprised to find them in major cities. There are even more of them in major airports. Bank cards usually allow you to withdraw the rest of your credit line through their participating banks. (If you are able, pay off your balance on your bank cards before you leave home, giving you maximum purchase and rescue power on the trip.)

Personal Checks

It's unlikely that your hotel will take your personal check, unless they know you very, very, very well and you are (a) famous or (b) rich, rich, rich, or (c) *both*. Be prepared to cry, whine, or go to extraordinary lengths to get your hotel to provide this service. But carry your checkbook anyway, because all sorts of places will take your old-fashioned American check.

You will also most likely want to write a check to U.S. Customs to welcome yourself home. We always do.

E.T. Send Money

You can have money sent to you from home, a process that usually takes about two days. Money can be wired through Western Union (someone brings them the cash or a certified check and Western Union does the rest—this may take up to a week) or through an international money order, which is cleared by telex through the bank where you cash it. Money can be wired from bank to bank, but this really only works simply with big-city major banks that have European branches or sister banks. Banks usually charge a nice, fat fee for doing you this favor. If you have a letter of credit, however, and a corresponding bank that is expecting you, you will have little difficulty getting your hands on some extra green . . . or pink or blue or orange.

In an emergency, the American Consulate may lend you money. You must repay this money. (There's no such thing as a free lunch.)

Banking Abroad

A s ridiculous as it sounds at first, it just may be very convenient for you to have a foreign bank account. We are not talking about a secret Swiss account for stashing cash so you don't have to pay taxes on it or comingle it with your husband's money. If you travel to a specific city (or even a country) often, it may make life easier to have a checking account there. Ask your own bank about making these arrangements. There are also British banks that do business in the United States and allow you to open accounts in both countries—it's a new twist on being bicoastal.

Foreign bank accounts must be reported to the IRS.

The Big Payoff

W hen traveling, we've found that three things make some of the difficulties of the world a little bit better:

▼ a fabulous smile

▼ a pleasant tone of voice

▼ CASH

What we're really talking about is what Mother would call the "schmeer"—part tip, part bribe, the payoff that can make your life a lot easier. A generous or even *overgenerous* tip in the right hands can work magic, particularly if you are a woman traveling (or shopping) alone, who may need some help—schlepping packages, shipping, getting taxis, getting extra luggage through the airline desk, etc. Concierges, taxi drivers, and even escort and shopping service representatives will be ever so helpful if you cross their palm with some of the local currency. (We've even tipped in dollars when it seemed appropriate, or was all we had.)

While each person has different needs, here are some of the rough spots a little schmeer can help you out of:

▼ There is an internationally famous designer giving a fashion show you'd love to attend. The concierge of your hotel can make this arrangement for you; the more you want to go, or the harder it is to get the seat, the more cash should cross his hand. Point of order: It's almost impossible to get a press seat to a big show if you are not a legitimate member of the press and on an approved list of international journalists.

▼ This is similar to the previous situation, but let's say you hear of a party you'd like to attend. The concierge of a properly deluxe hotel can make you the right social connections—especially if you are attractive, rich, famous, or all three.

▼ You want to know where locals go to buy a specific item.

▼ You have extra baggage and hope not to be charged for it by your airline.

▼ You do not like your assigned hotel room and would like something nicer but without much of a price increase.

▼ You want a taxi driver to function as personal chauffeur for an afternoon or a day.

▼ You want to keep your room past check-out time and not be charged for extra time since your flight isn't until later in the day.

▼ You want your shipping office to pick up your packages for you, or you want someone from the hotel to pick up your packages for you.

No matter how much you smile or tip or beg, the concierge cannot get you a lunch date with Fergie.

Getting Refunds

The problem with returns, repairs, and rip-offs is that they take more time than cash to fix, and your time is valuable. Never buy merchandise abroad that you think may have to be returned. However, should you have a problem, see to it at once. Send a telex rather than a letter (too slow) or a phone call (there will be no record of your call). A telex costs only 35 cents per word and can be dictated over the phone to Western Union. It will be charged to your phone bill or credit card. You probably have a friend who has a telex at his or her office and can send the message for you free, if you want to trouble that person. Notify your credit-card company of the problem as well.

Don't just return something to the place of origin without a confirming telex that your package is expected. If you are desperate, you may want to contact the designer directly, just to rat on the retail account. Don't send an item back with a friend whom you expect to do battle for you unless it's a very good friend who doesn't mind getting involved. Don't be surprised if European merchandise doesn't match—or coordinate with—its American counterparts, even when sold in that vendor's American boutique. While the merchandise sent to the United States is not different from that available in Europe, dye lots may vary, seasons may have changed, shopkeepers may be pulling the wool over your eyes, etc.

Sometimes you can exchange designer merchandise in an American shop, of the same designer or owner. Many of the shops are franchises, so if the actual shopowner likes what you have, he or she just may make a deal. This is an unusual transaction, however. The bigger the firm, the better your chances. Expect a store credit, not cash. This only happens to work with British-American goods, by the way.

American outlets should repair European-bought merchandise, provided it's genuine. There may or may not be a fee for this; this matter may be negotiable.

If your credit-card bill shows a purchase that you have no recollection of making, or if the signatures on the credit-card slips don't match yours or your husband's, notify the credit-card company or bank immediately. Do not pay that portion of the bill until you get further clarification. Bank cards usually just list your charges rather than provide a copy of the sales slip. You may not even recognize the names of some of the shops you have been in. We know one woman who had a $200 charge on her bank card from Orly in Paris. Since she did not fly in or out of Orly International Airport, she was certain it was a mistake and so notified the credit-card company. She did not pay that part of her bill. The bank provided her with a copy of the sales slip, she verified her own signature, and she had to admit that Orly must be the name of a shop she could not even remember visiting. (It happens to be a great discount scarf shop on the Rue Rivoli in Paris.) Sometimes these dealings with the credit-card company can go on for months.

It will always be difficult to handle foreign financial matters through the mails. Use credit cards whenever possible, since they will expedite matters somewhat; have your sales slips and charge records and a copy of your side of the correspondence with the vendor and the bank or credit-card company; persevere but have patience. The better the reputation of the shop or designer you buy from, the better your chances of not being ripped off in the first place and of making returns for refund.

So remember the words of that famous seer Oscar Hammerstein II as we paraphrase his "Some Enchanted Evening":

Who can exchange it? Who can tell you why?
Fools give you answers; wise men never try.

One Last Calculating Thought

Unless you have a Ph.D. in mathematics from MIT, we suggest you keep a calculator in your purse at all times. Furthermore, it should be the kind that uses batteries. Solar-run calculators are very cute, but your purse is dark inside, and many shops are, too. There's nothing worse than trying to do a hard bit of negotiating when your calculator won't calculate. If you use your calculator frequently, or if your children like to play with it as a toy, buy new batteries before you leave on the trip.

LONDON

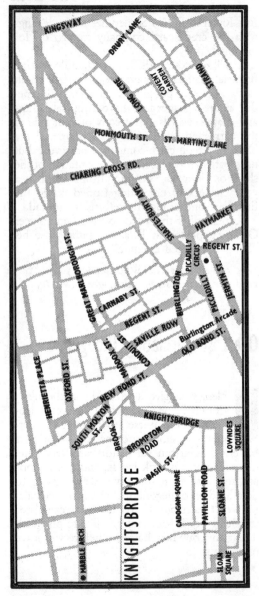

6 ▼ LONDON IN LISTS

The Big Names

AQUASCUTUM: Who would believe that a raincoat could make such a difference? Obviously, Humphrey Bogart, Detective Columbo, and Aquascutum agree that the man can't make the raincoat but the raincoat can make the man. Established in 1851, Aquascutum has grown from a tiny cottage industry to a major international name. Most people who go to London for the first time want to come home with an Aquascutum or Burberry raincoat. The Aquascutum line of goods manufactured now includes skirts, sweaters, and any accessory you could imagine. The classic men's trench coat will cost $350 lined in wool; the women's will be $295.

AQUASCUTUM, 100 Regent Street, W1

▼

ASPREY: Asprey isn't a designer name but is nonetheless one of the big names of London. They have a store in New York, with prices to match—so if you're looking for a status type of gift, Asprey is the place to go while in London. Even if you buy zip, go just to gawk.

Asprey is kind of a department store of status. It's very cluttered and posh and crystal chandeliers and whispered prices and curving staircases and "May I help you, madame?" but is still tremendous fun in its own London way. Since any gift you give from Asprey has a high status message, you may do very well here for the kind of business gifts that have to look like money but you hope to get a good buy on. We've found pens that are similar to the S.T. Dupont pen for about $50 that could cost $500 elsewhere. The picture frames and small leathergoods also make reasonable gifts.

Asprey does hold a royal warrant—and has for over a hundred years. They are jewelers—Princess Margaret has her pearls restrung here—but have become more famous for their gift items and luggage items for the person who has everything. The mail-order catalogue (a must for your coffee table) is free if you get it while in the shop; the catalogue costs $5 if you order it through the mail.

If Asprey is too stuffy for you, run out the door really fast, gulp in some fresh air, and then clear your head across the street at Zandra Rhodes.

ASPREY, 165–69 New Bond Street, W1

▼

GIORGIO ARMANI: Armani has left the comforts of Brown's and opened a franchise shop that looks like most other Armani shops—gorgeous. All the many lines are represented, including the children's, which is in the back. Have you seen the underwear? We only wish we could afford it. If we're ever in a car accident and get taken to the hospital and everyone sees our underwear, this is what we want them to see. You'll pay a little over $1,000 for a woman's fall suit *sans* blouse.

GIORGIO ARMANI, 123 New Bond Street, W1

▼

LAURA ASHLEY: Americans who love the Laura Ashley look, unite and spend your money here. There are no seconds shops, there are no discounts—but there are scads of shops, and the savings are large. We like the stores in the suburbs best—such as the one in Hampstead or even the one in Bath. But London has some new shops, including a biggie that has gone in on Regent Street. The Laura Ashley look of Victorian prints is produced at the headquarters in Wales. The line encompasses everything that has to do with the home and also a complete line of dresses, kids' wear, and sleepwear. Prices in London are very good, with wallpaper selling for $4.00 to $6.00 per double roll, chintz fabric $7.25 per meter, and bed linens $16.00 and up for double-bed size. Each store has its own closeout policy—you may see baskets filled with discontinued wallpapers (these are sold in double rolls, for added bargains) that sell for $3.00. Usually there is enough of one or two patterns to paper a small room. This is one of the world's best deals.

LAURA ASHLEY

 183 Sloane Street, SW1 (furnishings)
 7–9 Harriet Street, SW1 (garments and fragrances)
 35–36 Bow Street, Covent Garden, WC2
 71–73 Lower Sloane Street, SW1 (decorator showroom)
 256–58 Regent Street, W1 (Oxford Circus)
 208–10 Regent Street, W1
 MacMillan House, Kensington High Street, W8

▼

BASILE: Basile is designed by Luciano Sopriani and Gigi Monti. Everything about these wonderful designs is dramatic! He cuts so that no matter what you have on, or how many layers, you look sexy. Prices are hefty but the look is sheer Italian chic.

BASILE, 21 New Bond Street, W1

▼

BELLEVILLE-SASSOON: With a royal warrant, and the Princess of Wales as a loyal customer, the Belleville-Sassoon design team has little to worry about. David Sassoon also designs clothing to buy off the rack. Their shop on Pavilion Road has limited-edition day and evening dresses with rather high prices. A simple black cocktail dress starts at $250. A ball gown will cost $800 and up, and if you want your wedding dress designed, expect to pay at least $2,000. However, if these prices scare you away, take heart. The Belleville-Sassoon patterns are available in the *Vogue* designer catalogue; ask Jacob Gordon to get you their fabrics. (See page 176.)

BELLEVILLE-SASSOON, 93 Pavilion Road, SW1

▼

BENETTON/STEFANEL: Benetton and Stefanel are as popular in London as they are in Italy. With their easy style and prices, the Benetton and Stefanel lines appeal to the young set. We like the shops, three of them, on Kings Road, for the best selection. A pair of tweedy wool pants sells for $35, and a sweater to go with it can be purchased for about the same price. Sweatshirts cost in the range of $15, and nice, cozy, wool scarves are $10. In the 0–12 Benetton, boys' corduroy pants cost $18, and a girl's basic crew-neck sweater is $20. All three shops are within walking distance of each other.

BENETTON/STEFANEL, 88 Kings Road, SW3

BURBERRY: The design element that distinguishes a Burberry product from any other is the distinctive camel, red, and black check tartan plaid. We have never been fond of everything matching, but clearly the Burberry's customer is. The shop is multilevel, and if you love the tartan plaid, you will be in heaven. The raincoat itself, we must admit, is superb; it will cost in the area of $350 for a man's and $300 and up for a woman's. You can also purchase sweaters, hats, shawls, umbrellas, scarves, and luggage to match your trench coat. There is even a special minitrench being made for the five-and-up set. Check out Westaway & Westaway for a small but slightly discounted selection. You can get traditional English fashions here as well as bespoke suits. Some items in the store, such as the umbrella, seem to be outrageously expensive ($50), while others seem quite reasonable.

BURBERRY
165 Regent Street, W1
18–22 Haymarket, SW1

CHANEL: Chanel has renovated the London boutique. The sales help will insist on showing you everything and don't seem to mind if you are only looking. We found that the prices in the U.S. Chanel boutiques were exactly the same as those in London—except for the

VAT. This is where you will save and save. If you can keep your purchases low and don't have to pay duty, buying in London is well worth the time. Jewelry, makeup, and handbags are upstairs, and clothing is downstairs. A classic suit costs $1,600; traditional leather handbag, $500; and necklaces are priced from $155 to $400. Earrings are by far the best buy, starting at $50. The fresh lilies will make your day.

CHANEL, 26 Old Bond Street, W1

▼

COLLINGWOOD: All right, so you've never heard of Collingwood and don't know why we call it a big name. Well, it's a very big name to the British, especially to the British royal family. If you are a Di-watcher, you know about the necklace of cultured pearls and diamonds that Charles gave her after the birth of Prince Wills. This is where you can get one just like it.

Queen Victoria granted the firm's royal warrant; both the Queen Mother and Queen Elizabeth II have granted the most recent royal warrants. Don't forget to ask for the catalogue while you're there. You can always dream, you know.

COLLINGWOOD, 46 Conduit Street, W1

▼

ADOLFO DOMINGUEZ: If the only Adolfo in your life is the man who makes the knit suits à la Chanel, meet up with Spanish designer Dominguez and his Japanese-European look. If the boutique looks sparse and frightening, don't be put off. Go on, go downstairs and see the men's and women's things. Even if you can't afford the clothes, you can afford to be inspired. Miami Vice clothiers shop here.

ADOLFO DOMINGUEZ, South Molton Street, W1

▼

ALFRED DUNHILL LTD.: This is the largest and most extensive collection of Dunhill products we have ever seen, or could ever hope to see. The shop actually looks a little more like a Dunhill museum than a retail store. Nevertheless, the merchandise is absolutely top-of-the-line as far as quality goes. Those wonderful Dunhill lighters that everyone who smokes uses come in a variety of styles and prices. The Rolls-Royce of the lighters (*solid gold*) will cost you just under $5,000. However, you can have the same lighter (jacketed in gold only) for approximately $1,800. Now, do we know how to spot a bargain? A sterling silver lighter can cost from $500 to $750, while a silver-plated one will be only $150. Our favorite lighter to buy is the enamel one. Its price in London will be $190 to $250 depending on the model. There's also a complete line of ready-to-wear goods and leathergoods and, of course, cigars. Dunhill is probably most famous as a tobacconist. Once again, its quality is aimed at the top of the market. The cigars are stored in a climate-controlled room to ensure their freshness. The pipe tobaccos are available for sampling. Dunhill also has a beautiful line of humidors, or will convert your prized antique box into one for you. REMEMBER: It is illegal to bring Cuban cigars into the United States.

ALFRED DUNHILL LTD., 30 Duke Street, SW1

▼

ESCADA: Escada, a German line, is less expensive in London than in the United States—which is a good thing since sweaters are $200 in the London shop. Escada fans don't care. This rather new shop feels all modern and good and rich and just the way you'll feel if you can buy an outfit or two.

ESCADA, 67 New Bond Street, W1

▼

GUCCI: A superb example of the Gucci experience awaits you in this boutique. On the main floor you will find the leathergoods, accessories, and shoes; upstairs, the men's and ladies' clothing. Downstairs, the gift section is extensive, with a leather key case costing $30, a memo pad $38, and a fabric wallet $60. The store is always jammed with people. Closed for lunch.

GUCCI, 27 Old Bond Street, W1

▼

HERMÈS: The selection is fabulous even though the space is limited. See scarves, handbags, and ladies' clothing. The famous scarf is $113 (it's $130 in the United States). A savings here. Most interestingly, we watched a man pay with a travelers check and get change in sterling—Hermès gave him the best rate in town.

HERMÈS, 155 New Bond Street, W1

▼

HILDITCH & KEY: One of several very proper men's shirtmakers on Jermyn Street, Hilditch & Key now has two different men's shops, and a women's shop that sells the women's version of the famous men's shirt as well as women's ready-to-wear—in keeping with the look. All the shops have been redone (it was about time) and now look like Old World gems. Please note that there is a full inch of shirt fabric under the cuff, so should the shirt need to be lengthened, the fabric is readily available. Shirts can be fixed in a day or two if the standard size does not fit you. There's made-to-measure (six minimum) or a special stock shirt, which is not quite as expensive and means the sleeves are made to measure but the body is not. Sold at Saks in the United States. Mail order is available. If you want a private visit to your hotel room, call 030-4126 to make an appointment.

HILDITCH & KEY, 73 Jermyn Street, SW1

▼

JAEGER: Jaeger is a basic British resource sold in their own shops and in many department stores. They have a way with wools in particular and stride the fine line between boring English clothes and high fashion. For quality, you can always trust Jaeger. The shop on Regent Street is almost a department store. Not only is this shop easy to find, but also it has everything. Wherever you buy Jaeger, the value is good. Clothing is automatically coordinated, saving the working woman lots of time. You can buy a good suit for $225, a great silk blouse for $125, and a high-fashion jacket-coat for $150.

For men, a wool trench coat will cost $300 and a classic gray flannel suit $225. Sweaters are about $50. The department store D. H.

Evans has one of the best Jaegar boutiques in a store—men's on the ground floor and women's upstairs.

JAEGER, 204 Regent Street, W1

ROLAND KLEIN: If you can't choose between Calvin Klein or Anne Klein, why not go for Roland Klein? He's pricey, a little too inventive if Calvin is your cup of Darjeeling, and very hot. His clothes are at most of the department stores, or in his tiny, tony boutique—don't miss the downstairs. We find the silk dresses very Joan Collins.

ROLAND KLEIN, 26 Brook Street, W1

KARL LAGERFELD: Finally it is possible to see Karl Lagerfeld designing under his own name. The shop is small, but the clothes are wonderful. The knit sweater-jackets are $500 but have enough classic good sense to them that you would always look stunning—we think they're worth the price. Of course, we didn't buy any. This line is carried at Barney's in N.Y. but costs less in London.

KARL LAGERFELD, 173 New Bond Street, W1

KEN LANE: This is a designer we have always loved. His *faux* jewelry is a delight to look at and wear. The shop is filled with designs of every style. We like to wear the antique look-alike jewelry—bracelets cost about $50 each. In the Bulgari *faux* line, a necklace with pearls, diamonds, and rubies is only $35! If you want pearls, try a three-strand choker with black onyx, and diamond drop clasp: $65. He has a shop in Paris, too, but the South Molton Street shop has more pizzazz. The merchandise in each shop varies.

KEN LANE
66 South Molton Street, W1
Burlington Arcade, W1

▼

LOEWE: Leather at its finest is what you will find in Loewe. (Do get into the swing of things by pronouncing this one correctly—it's Louvay. We've been *so* embarrassed by saying Loew's. The store now is large and elegant and smells divine. You can't knock the location, between Gucci and Ungaro—pricey. However, if you are searching for a fine leather handbag, the quality of the Loewe leather certainly equals that of Gucci or Hermès. Prices in London are very close to the Spanish prices (handbags are $200; suede coats begin at $350) or just a touch higher.

LOEWE
25 Old Bond Street, W1
47–49 Brompton Road, SW3

▼

ISSEY MIYAKE: This Japanese designer, who once worked for Givenchy and Guy Laroche, beautifully combines Oriental style and Western tailoring. His shop on Sloane

Street has the Oriental simplicity that is the perfect backdrop to highlight his designs. Prices are high; buy on sale or in Tokyo.

ISSEY MIYAKE, 21 Sloane Street, SW1

▼

BRUCE OLDFIELD LIMITED: The Princess of Wales brought Bruce Oldfield into the spotlight, but he has been a British social secret for many years. He is most admired for his fabulous ball gowns and luxurious evening wear, which are anything but plain or simple. Most of his designs flow and rustle, and if they are black, there is always something glistening attached. He operates from his Beauchamp Place boutique—both a retail and a bespoke operation.

BRUCE OLDFIELD LIMITED, 41 Beauchamp Place, SW3

▼

POLO/RALPH LAUREN: Expanding like crazy, Polo is the British look done once through American eyes and brought back. The shop is homey and cozy and is not a carbon copy of Paris or Madison Avenue but still feels rich and elegant. Ralphie, you should be proud of yourself. Buy it on sale at home or fly to the factory outlet in Puerto Rico. But do stop in to stare at and to enjoy this shop and all its luxe sets.

POLO/RALPH LAUREN, 143 New Bond Street, W1

▼

ZANDRA RHODES: Fantasy is what Zandra Rhodes is all about. She began designing for affluent hippies in the sixties and was discovered by Diana Vreeland. Her tattered hemlines, flowing chiffons, and handpainted taffeta designs are now sought by museums. She is also famous for her incredible wedding dresses. Some of the stars who buy from her include Barbra Streisand, Lauren Bacall, and Bianca Jagger. We love to whisk through her boutique and watch all the beautifully painted chiffons ruffle; you must walk in here even if it's just to stare at the seashells that are incorporated into the handmade chandelier. Zandra has maintained her business as a cottage industry, so the quality of each piece is superb. Prices are high, but less than in the U.S. You can get a sweatshirt for $150.

ZANDRA RHODES, 14A Grafton Street, W1

▼

YVES SAINT LAURENT: There is not just one but four Rive Gauche boutiques in London. The two shops on Brompton Road are actually side by side and just look like one big shop. The shops on New Bond Street are slightly more snooty, but the selection usually is better.

We have found Yves Saint Laurent so changed in recent years that we aren't knocked out.

YVES SAINT LAURENT
  113 New Bond Street, W1
  135 New Bond Street, W1
  35–37 Brompton Road, SW3

▼

SOULEIADO: This tiny shop is off the beaten track, on Fulham Road. You will find the accessories upstairs and fabrics downstairs. The sales help is very friendly, and prices range from $12 to $15 per meter for the classic Souleiado prints. Tablecloths cost in the range of $70 and placemats $8 each. Handbags are $40 to $50 depending upon the size.

SOULEIADO, 171 Fulham Road, SW3

▼

SULKA: We love going into Sulka and touching all the fabrics. The shop caters to men, and the sales help isn't quite sure what to do with women. We have always made friends there by exclaiming in hushed tones about the quality of their merchandise. It is indeed fine, although for shirts we still prefer Turnbull & Asser. However, Sulka carries a line of hand-brocaded silk paisley robes that really should be in a museum. They cost in the range of $2,000 (and up) and would look good on any duke or baron you might know. This is the only shop in town that told us that VAT was 13% and that charges a £3 service charge for the paperwork. We'd love to own one of those bathrobes, but really!

SULKA, 19 Old Bond Street, W1

▼

TURNBULL & ASSER: Prince Charles buys his p.j.'s here. He also buys his shirts, as do many other famous and not-so-famous men who just love the finest cotton and tailoring money can buy! Shopping at Turnbull & Asser is quite an experience. The main store is on two levels, with the ready-to-wear shirts, bathrobes, and underwear downstairs, and ties, sweaters, and accessories upstairs. One door down Jermyn Street is the Churchill Room, which houses the bespoke department for shirts and the ready-to-wear suits. Entering the shop is like going back in time to the days (1885) when Reginald Turnbull and Ernest Asser first began making hunting gear for the nobility. The walls are wood-paneled and the atmosphere is hushed. However, the sales help is quite helpful and will tell you that if you have time to be fitted, a bespoke shirt will not cost you much more than a ready-to-wear one— approximately $10 more, to be exact. The Turnbull & Asser staff travels to New York and Los Angeles twice a year to see their clients. They take up residence in a hotel suite and make appointments with their longtime customers. When you are in the London shop, ask to be put on their list. We have tried this and are not always contacted. Ask to meet the manager and let him know that you are seriously interested. It's worth a try for the money you will save. Turnbull & Asser is carried in the United States through Bergdorf Goodman in New York and Neiman-Marcus in other cities. The popularity of the Turnbull & Asser shirts is so great that when Bergdorf's has its once-a-year sale before Christmas, the lines begin to form at 7:00 A.M. We have heard rumors of tea and crumpets being served. Turnbull & Asser makes their ready-made shirts with only one sleeve length; if you are tall, have long arms, or are a chimpanzee, you are out of luck. If your arm is shorter than their shirts, you will be fitted accordingly at the store that sells the shirts. But if you're going to this much trouble to begin with, why not get a custom-made shirt? It is actually cheaper to buy a custom-made shirt in a hotel in the United States from the Turnbull & Asser representative than it is to walk into Bergdorf's or Neiman's and buy a shirt that will have to be altered. Another tip for saving money: When in London, check out the shop across the street from Turnbull & Asser (Hilditch & Key) —it's supposed to be a secret, but everyone knows about it: Unsold Turnbull shirts are sold here with different collars and cuffs.

TURNBULL & ASSER, 71–72 Jermyn Street, SW1

▼

JOSEPH TRICOT: Not to think that this man only makes goods out of that fiber but Tricot is not really his last name. But Bis is, so if you happen upon a Joseph Bis, it's just another of his many shops. There are shops in London, Paris, and New York. Joseph has graduated from being hot to one of London's leading forces in retailing. Prices are in what's called the moderate range: $135 for a big cowlneck sweater; $90 for a more simple sweater; $125 for a sweater dress. The clothes are young (but not too young), spontaneous, and vibrant. Some 20 shops, worldwide.

JOSEPH TRICOT
    18 Sloane Street, SW1
    16 South Molton Street, W1

▼

TRUSSARDI: The shop looks tiny as you enter, but don't let appearances be deceiving. Downstairs is a larger room filled with luggage and the like. Upstairs you will find the clothing line, with a silk blouse selling for $140, a man's jacket for $300, and a woman's skirt for $85. Trussardi is expanding and getting more and more attention for the ready-to-wear designs.

TRUSSARDI, 51 South Molton Street, W1

▼

EMANUEL UNGARO: Ungaro makes a lot of his clothing in Italy now, so it probably is better to shop there or in Paris. However, this is a good boutique with a wide selection of merchandise, including skiwear and cruisewear. Silk blouses range from $425 to $550. Sweaters cost around $225, and a silk dress will run about $700. The best things are the sales; recently we spied the famous Ungaro coat jacket marked down from $1,000 to $350. It was worth every penny—and that's without the VAT discount.

EMANUEL UNGARO, 153A New Bond Street, W1

▼

VALENTINO: Our favorite thing about this boutique is that they hand out free postcards—what other sights would you tell your friends you were visiting? Big Ben? Yawn. The prices are high ($700 for a sweater); there's more downstairs. Men's, women's, accessories. Usually you can find a pin for about $100.

VALENTINO, 160 New Bond Street, W1

▼

GIANNI VERSACE: Located between South Molton Street and New Bond Street, this Versace boutique seems to float between two worlds. In fact, it very much has a Bond Street feeling. The stock of merchandise is extensive and very well priced. We have seen the same merchandise in Beverly Hills for at least double the price found here. Also a second location on New Bond Street, for men.

GIANNI VERSACE
  34 Brook Street, W1
  18 New Bond Street, W1

Finds

London, more than any other city—yes, even Paris—offers its unique fashion selection through a variety of boutiques. You could probably spend a lifetime going from cute shop to cute shop, trying to keep up with it all. But since that's a dream, we've whittled the list down to a precious few shops that we consider old standards. Some of them carry designer labels, some of them offer their own designs or their own selection of their favorite designers—whom we have never heard of. (That's fashion in London—it's hard even to keep track of who the movers and shakers are. . . .) These boutiques are from our personal list; if you are shopping for less expensive clothes, for children, or for teens, you may want to bypass this group. Otherwise, have a ball.

THE BEAUCHAMP PLACE SHOP: Two tiny little shops on the quaint street of the same name, they represent many of the up-and-coming designers. Jasper Conran started here but now has his own shop—almost across the street. During sale times, one shop is taken over as a sale boutique.

THE BEAUCHAMP PLACE SHOP, 37 and 55 Beauchamp Place, SW3

BERTIE: We shop Bertie at Covent Garden and now in Beverly Hills, where we get a big kick out of the hearty savings in London. Fun shoes in the midprice range in London—under $100 for a real fashion statement, without going in the Maud Frizon direction. This is just the kind of thing you came to London to buy. Flats are as low as $45; boots start at $95. Fabulous colors. If you like low heels but have trouble finding ones with flair, race over here as soon as your plane lands.

BERTIE

48 South Molton Street, W1
8A Sloane Street, SW1
409 Oxford Street, W1
118 Kings Road, SW3
Brent Cross Shopping Centre V-16, NW4
15 Covent Garden, WC2

▼

BIP: Maybe the initials mean something to someone, but to us, BIP stands for New Man. There're men's, women's, and children's fashions in the shop—children's are toward the back and are a bit hard to find. We don't find the New Man much cheaper here than in the United States. Wait for Paris if you can. A down jacket is about $100, which isn't bad, but it's just no bargain. But the shop is fun and well laid out and you'll pass it anyway, so stop in.

BIP, 69 Duke Street, W1

▼

BLADES: One of our favorite shops for Mr. Right—although we've seen the same sweaters at Key Largo for 20% less. Located right in the Savile Row cadre of tailors, Blades is a very with-it shop in an old-fashioned setting.

Go in to get out of the chill (if it's cold) or to rest your feet—the sales staff is very nice. The clientele is rich, hip, and has a good sense of humor about dressing in an elegant but snazzy way. Prices are a bit *cher*. Key Largo has some of the same jumpers, for less money.

BLADES, 8 Burlington Gardens, W1

▼

JOHN BOYD: If you have been caught up in the Princess Di hat craze, then this is the place to come. Mr. Boyd has been making hats for the royal family for many, many, many years. What is wonderful about John Boyd is that he doesn't just produce one look. Princess Anne and Margaret Thatcher are obviously different looks. Can you imagine them in each other's hats? There are over a gross (that's 144) of hats on display in the showroom, ranging in price from $50 and up. Mr. Boyd will add or subtract bows, veils, and feathers depending on your taste and needs. And, yes, you can wear your Boyd backward and he'll never tell.

JOHN BOYD, 91 Walton Street, SW3

▼

BRADLEYS LIMITED: If you want to feel like Alice in Wonderland, check out Bradleys, known as "the largest specialist lingerie store in England." If it is not, we would love to know one that is better. This successful operation is run by a dynamic mother-daughter duo who know their briefs. They also have a trained staff that can fit you professionally in a bra or corset, which they've been doing for the royals for several years. (And we thought royals had good posture because they walked around with books on their heads.)

One of Bradleys specialties is specialty fitting; if you need a nursing bra or a mastectomy bra, they have just the thing. House calls or hospital calls are part of their business. If you live in a small town and feel you have not gotten a proper postsurgical fit and have never been to a specialist in a big U.S. city, it's worth taking some of your vacation time in London to stop by at Bradleys.

If your taste runs more toward the seductive than the practical, Bradleys still can help you. We would be afraid to sleep in a $1,500 nightgown, but obviously not everyone is. You can also get a little something to sleep in for about $25. Princess Anne and the Princess of Wales, along with many of the European royal families, make this a stop when in need of a lift.

BRADLEYS LIMITED, 83 Knightsbridge, SW1

▼

BROWN'S: If you can visit only one shop in London, this is our choice. It's filled with a ready-to-wear selection from the top designers in Europe. Sonia Rykiel, Chloé, Kamali, Jean Muir, Ralph Lauren, and Geoffrey Beene are all represented. The store is a string of connecting town houses; see the upstairs and downstairs levels in each. This can be confusing but is worth the trouble. This very chic and with-it shop is patronized by a very prestigious clientele, and that includes celebs and movie stars. Prices are high because these are expensive clothes—but you'll find the velour and cotton groups in the Sonia collection, the cheap line by Jean Muir with her expensive line, and many well-priced unisex items in the men's shop. We bought a Jean Paul Gaultier coat on sale here for $200 and thought it the bargain of the century; a Sonia skirt on sale for $120 was not the best price we've ever seen, but it was reasonable enough to be competitive. Sale merchandise is put in specially made shopping bags that say "Brown's Sale," which labels you to the whole world as a piker with good taste. VAT after £100, even on sale items.

BROWN'S, 23 South Molton Street, W1

BUTLER & WILSON: If you are a fan of authentic or reproduction Art Deco or Art Nouveau jewelry, or just love the chunky costume "glitz," this tiny shop is a must. Their collection of antique jewelry is the best. Many of the identical pieces of costume jewelry that we've seen in the United States were here for less than half. Making a choice can be difficult, but the sales staff always is helpful and patient. Expect to pay between $40 and $70 for their costume necklaces, and about $30 for their costume earrings.

BUTLER & WILSON, 189 Fulham Road, SW3

CAROLINE CHARLES: If you are a fan of this very talented British designer, stop by this shop, decorated in pink and beige, to find her complete collection. We saw quite a selection of both daytime and evening wear. Her clothes are chic and elegant, and it is no wonder that Princess Diana favors them. The prices are moderate for the quality and styling. You can expect to pay between $100 and $350.

CAROLINE CHARLES, 9 Beauchamp Place, SW3

COURTNEY: We don't understand these two shops that are next door to each other and obviously related—the lingerie shop is so rich and elegant and the ready-to-wear shop offers exactly the clothes you imagine Lady Annabella to wear to a shoot or a weekend at Balmoral— tweed skirts ($150) and hand-knit sweaters ($150). Does Lady Annabella perhaps wear a pale pink corset under her tweeds? We've seen these same sweaters for less money at other places, but the shop is so nice in its Anglophile way that we almost don't mind overspending. Ralph Lauren meets Laura Ashley.

COURTNEY, 22 and 24 Brook Street, W1

▼

DANA: These are the kinds of clothes that say you are chic, and rich enough just to look beautifully tailored. These are the outfits you put on when you want to get the job, or when you have no idea what to wear and want to look terrific. The prices are not bargain basement by any means; in fact they equal those at Ted Lapidus. However, the Dana jackets, skirts, and silk blouses that we have collected over the years seem to be seasonless and yearless. We are still combining jackets from five years ago with new blouses and skirts from this year. In other words, buying here is a good investment. The shop is on a funny little street that runs just above Oxford Street and intersects Duke Street right behind Selfridges. The clothing is French and manufactured in Nice. They have an outlet in New York and private-label for some other companies we know.

DANA, 138 Wigmore Street, W1

▼

ADELE DAVIS: This New Bond Street shop carries a wide selection of conservative designer clothes. You can find the clothes of designers such as Louis Feraud and Albert Nippon priced very well here. We think this is the Lily Rubin of London.

ADELE DAVIS, 10 New Bond Street, W1

▼

EDINA & LENA: One of our very favorite boutiques featuring an array of gorgeous hand-knit sweaters, Edina & Lena is in the Antiquarius antiques supermarket. Their styles range from conservative to chic, and the prices here are high, but about half of what you'd pay in U.S. outlets. For these fabulous handknits you can expect to pay $240 for a silk and wool cardigan, $160 for cashmere, $230 for a rhinestone-studded evening sweater, and $200 for a silk and wool basic cable knit. U.S. prices are 25% more.

EDINA & LENA, 141 Kings Road, SW3

▼

FIL À FIL: A newish chain that many locals are raving about, Fil à Fil is a French firm that sells men's shirts to men and women. There probably are a half dozen or more of these shops in London now. We think it's boring; if you want boring you might just as well buy it from a famous London house when it's on sale. But this is considered trendy. Prices are about $50 a shirt.

FIL À FIL, Brompton Arcade

GALLERY OF LONDON: Of course you came to London to buy blazer buttons, or better yet, those embroidered patches from a royal regiment that you sew on a sweater or blazer for just the best fashion look ever. So you want to go to Gallery of London, off Jermyn Street, for a wide selection at good prices. We paid $20 for our Merchant Navy patch (we saw it elsewhere for $25). This is one of our favorite gift items, by the way.

GALLERY OF LONDON, 1 Duke of York Street, SW1

▼

HABITAT: Habitat made British home furnishings history, although not in the same way as Mr. Chippendale. After the spare Scandinavian look came the modern British look—an update of Scandinavian chic with a touch of high tech. It was all begun by Terence Conran, who was later knighted for his contribution to the world. Habitat, which Conran has since sold, is still a glorious place to shop even if the look isn't the newest look and you can see a lot of this stuff at home. But its clean lines and low prices make everything seem possible. This is where we love to buy kitchenware—since the chairs and tables won't fit into our suitcases. If you shop Pottery Barn in the United States, you'll love Habitat in London. (They are not related, but the look is similar.) One of the best things about shopping at Habitat is the wealth of ideas you will come away with and the realization that you can furnish anything with total charm and style without spending a lot of money. If you're just into your first house or apartment, stop by with a notepad. The Conran's store is a little more pricey. Don't forget that there is a Conran's in the United States and they mail-order; we haven't found that it pays to ship from here.

HABITAT
  206 Kings Road, SW3
  Conran's, 77–79 Fulham Road, SW3

▼

HALCYON DAYS: For all you collectors of fine English enamels (Battersea boxes), it's time to go hog-wild crazy. The Halcyon Days shop in London is small but loaded with bargains. You can find both antique English enamels and contemporary designs that include clocks, picture frames, musical boxes, sewing accessories, pens, etc. The prices are seemingly dirt cheap. Expect to pay $50 to $60 for a box that retails for $110 in the United States. Mail order is a cinch.

    Best of all, once you buy an item, for years afterward you'll be on the mailing list, and gorgeous brochures will come to you a few times a year—all with the London prices.

HALCYON DAYS, 14 Brook Street, W1

▼

JIGSAW: If you love the Adrienne Vittadini slouchy look, or the crushed silk look, or the body suit with the pull-on knit skirt look, you'll appreciate any of the Jigsaw stores. It's a small chain with wovens and knits and inexpensive to moderate clothes and great sales.

JIGSAW, 14 James Street, W1

▼

KEY LARGO: There are a couple of shops in London that carry these specially handknit sweaters (actually made by little old ladies in Leicester), but Key Largo is the least expensive and the actual supplier to Princess Di—so they get our business. Unisex in design, the sweaters come with car logos, Superman or cartoon logos, major brand labels, and all sorts of sayings on them (for example, TYCOON spelled out in big silver lurex letters). You can get a custom order; you can even have your signature made for you. The regular sweater, as made up in the shop, costs $75.00. Special orders are $85.00 and take five weeks. Add $8.25 for postage to the United States. Yes, they'll make up a child's sweater—but they are the same price. VAT arranged on mail order as well as in-shop purchases. Do not miss this chance—an especially good gift item for the man who has everything; for women we sew in shoulder pads.

KEY LARGO, 2 Bow Street, Covent Garden, WC2

▼

ALAIN MANOUCHIAN: A young hot, inexpensive designer from France who is famous for his sweaters, Manouchian isn't sold much in the United States. We make up for all that once we hit this store. It's a bit like a Benetton but with a more designer touch. A dressy sweater with pearls and satin embroidery is $100; the traditional cowl in great colors is $35.

ALAIN MANOUCHIAN, 49 South Molton Street, W1

▼

MONSOON: Brewing up a storm, all right—there's a Monsoon everywhere you look. This place is almost another Benetton. The clothes are rather ethnic in style and modest of price. We've seen a few things we like, but mostly we think it's kind of cheap-looking. The South Molton Street shop has the top-of-the-line look; other branches are not so upscale.

MONSOON
  68 South Molton Street, W1
  26–28 Kensington Church Street, W8
  Head office: 74 Winslow Road, W6

▼

NEXT: Obviously some genius walked around the world and saw all the Benetton shops and the Ann Taylor shops and the Conran shops and said to himself, "What's Next?" Next has emerged as a full-blown phenomenon all over England, with many shops in London and an interior-design branch called Next Too (which gets our shopping bag award). In some stores the men's things are to one side and the women's to another; in other locations there are separate men's and women's stores. While you won't see anything extraordinary here, soak up the ambience and think how American the whole thing is.

NEXT
9 South Molton Street, W1
72 Kings Road, SW3
160 Regent Street, W1

▼

TOMMY NUTTER: Rock stars and scions know exactly who Tommy Nutter is, and so should you if you—or your man—need a with-it tailor. Clothes here are not stiff like Savile Row duds, yet the workmanship is comparable. It must be the address. Besides being pricey, the clothes have a sort of California British feel, if you get our gist . . . with maybe a touch of the Italian design community thrown in. We love the clothes, and we love to stop by the store to watch the men come and go—we once fell in love with a tall, thin Italian count who was all of twenty-three years old and oozed charm and slubbed silk. Very Nutters. This isn't for everyone in either price or style, but the tailoring can't be matched.

TOMMY NUTTER, 19 Savile Row, W1

▼

LUCIENNE PHILLIPS: If you've figured out that Jasper Conran is indeed related to Terence (Terence is his father) and you can't return home without showing your friends how trendy you are by having discovered the Conran who isn't as well known in America, then you'll be happy to shop at Lucienne Phillips, where Conran and several other up-and-coming—but not downright crazy—deigners are sold. Prices are not giveaway, but they're reasonable. Good

Jean Muir selection here, also. This is a good example of the best kind of London boutique—lots of fun stuff that you won't see at home.

LUCIENNE PHILLIPS, 89 Knightsbridge, SW1

▼

RICHARDS: Look, Mom, it's Ann Taylor in London. The young working woman can find it all here—high style, low to moderate prices, pantyhose to business suits to belts to hats. The store has a lot of bleached wood and actually feels like a rip-off of an Ann Taylor shop. We didn't mind when we bought a great dress for $50—the kind of dress that looks like it cost $200. This is a small chain. You can pool receipts for VAT.

RICHARDS, 374 Oxford Street, W1

▼

SAVOY TAYLORS GUILD: This newly decorated, very fancy men's store often has big sales. Perhaps this is the fanciest men's discounter in town, we don't know—but for big-name-designer men's ready-to-wear, you should look at the wide selection and very good prices here.

SAVOY TAYLORS GUILD, 164 New Bond Street, W1

▼

THE SCOTCH HOUSE: A must stop for the lover of those classic Scottish tartans and kilts. They carry all the major brands, and have matching sweaters and jackets for many styles. This is also a wonderful place to purchase scarves in the traditional tartans or in more subtle colors to take home as gifts for your family. Remember when you were six and Mommy brought you back a kilt of your own? (you always lost the pin, too, didn't you?)—this is where you can return the favor for someone on your gift list.

THE SCOTCH HOUSE
   84 Regent Street, W1
   191 Regent Street, W1
   2 Brompton Road, SW1
   7 Marble Arch, W1
   187 Oxford Street, W1

▼

PAUL SMITH: In this austere, tiny little shop with wonderful wood-planked flooring are all the wonderful men's clothes from this very talented English designer. What makes these conservative clothes work so well is the marvelous array of colors they are made in. Piled in stacks are their famous sweaters and shirts. You can also find a great selection of tweed suits, sport coats, corduroy pants, and shoes. Prices are moderate. Expect to pay between $44 and $75 for sweaters, $44 for shirts (their most expensive is $100 for a silk print), $70 for shoes, $100 for corduroy slacks, and $240 for a sport coat. The location is a bit **tric**ky; walk into the alley next to Gianni Versace and then look to your right.

PAUL SMITH, 44 Floral Street, WC1

▼

WAREHOUSE: This is a small chain featuring London look clothes at moderate prices. This isn't totally punk, unwearable stuff and is suitable for American working women. Their prices are moderate, in keeping with the neighborhood in which it's located (Miss Selfridge's is across the street). There are other locations scattered throughout London, but this location is our favorite. It is a great shopping place for teens, for inexpensive summer clothes, or even if you want your friends or neighbors back home to see that you've acquired the "London Look" (even though you wouldn't ordinarily be seen in it). Don't forget to pick up their catalogue!

WAREHOUSE, 27 Duke Street, W1

▼

WARM & WONDERFUL: Warm & Wonderful knits those fabulous handknit sweaters that have really caught on since you-know-who began wearing them. You remember the sweater with all the white lambs and the one black sheep? Enter Warm & Wonderful. The sweaters are sold all over the world and are pretty cheap if you've come to the place in your life where more and more handknits cost $300. The sheep sweater costs $75. We bought one for our friend José Eber—who we think of as our favorite frog—that was solid red with hand-clasping frogs running around it in stripes. Saks carries the line in the United States; there is an outlet across the river that is so wonderful we're willing to swim the Thames to get there.

St. John's Hill is also a fun neighborhood for making new discoveries; plan to spend a few hours investigating the whole area.

WARM & WONDERFUL
    191 St. John's Hill, SW11
    233 Camberwell New Road, SE5

▼

WHISTLES: You know how to whistle, don't you? You just put your lips together and pull out your charge card. Whistles is fun, funny, and fabulous. No matter what your age, you'll love the young looks and hot new fashions. Princess you-know-who has been known to indulge.

WHISTLES
12–14 St. Christopher Place, W1
1 Thayer Street, W1
14 Beauchamp Place, SW3
20 Covent Garden, WC2
89 Marylebone High Street, W1

Department Stores

American department stores are mostly patterned on British ones, so you will feel right at home at just about any department store in London. All are in big, old fashioned buildings and offer the kind of security that enables you to know you could live in them. Most of them have several restaurants or tearooms. If you are seriously interested in eating in any of these, sneak a peek at your Egon Ronay guide, which critiques all the department-store eateries! If you need the facilities, don't forget to ask for the "ladies" or the "W.C."

If you happen to be in London for Christmas with your children, we offer one of our famous motherhood tricks: Hire a baby-sitter and send her and the kids off to see "Father Christmas," who has a seat of honor in each department store, just like at home. The lines for this visitation are enormous, and your children will be occupied for at least half the day. You are free to go shopping. If you need more time, expand the trick to a daily ritual or one big trip with stops at several department stores—a lot of them are close together. Some of the stores give the kids little free gifts after they have seen Father Christmas.

During the Christmas shopping days, department stores are open later than usual, which may mean until 7:00 P.M. They are never open until 9:00 P.M. Other than at Christmastime, department stores have one night a week—either Wednesday or Thursday—during which they stay open until 7:00 P.M. Otherwise, stores open at 9:00 or 9:30 A.M. and close at 5:00 or 5:30 P.M. They have never gotten into the American habit of offering longer hours.

Many of the stores are members of a chain, as are American department stores, but the British stores allow you to use a group charge plan. Thus a Sears (not the same as our Sears, Roebuck) charge or a House of Fraser charge card may come in handy for a bevy of stores. Yes, Americans can have charge cards in Britain. Most interestingly, aside from Harrods, few London department stores cater to tourists. Real people go to shop here, and you'll see them all turned out—especially on a Saturday. But all department stores have export desks that will help you with the VAT forms; all department stores allow you to collect your receipts over a period of time to qualify for the VAT. Some may charge $3 for administrative work on a multiticket VAT form.

▼

HARRODS: We were once having one of those chic little publishing lunches at a hot new restaurant on Twenty-third Street in Manhattan and happened to overhear these two very British editors having a wonderful chat. In their very British accent and manner, they were heard to say:

"Can you imagine, she went to Harrods to buy it?"

"That just proves how American she still is, my dear. Only the Americans and the Arabs shop at Harrods."

Well, the Princess of Wales used to shop there, and while it may not be our single most favorite shop in all of London, we like the store (especially the food halls) and think it's a great place to see a lot in a small amount of time or to escape from a rainstorm. We don't think tea there is great, but you can get a good milkshake, and the bathrooms are always clean. Besides, the place is a university of retailing.

Upon entering Harrods, it is hard to imagine that Henry Charles Harrod began his store as a little grocery business in 1849. From a small family business with a staff of two, Harrods has grown to be the most complete department store in London. The food halls, located on the ground floor, are internationally known, with seventeen departments in all. The department store itself covers four and a half acres of land and has fifteen acres of selling space. This is good to remember when your feet are telling you to stop but you don't even feel that you have made a dent in the store.

Ground floor: food halls, men's fashions, fabrics, perfume and cosmetics, fashion accessories, jewelry, stationery, and clocks; one: designer clothing: (a definite must stop); two: china, glass, books, records, housewares; three: furniture; four: sports, kids, toys.

Another of our favorite departments on the fourth floor is sporting goods. Located just behind the toys, the selection of merchandise is complete, with all major brands represented in clothing and equipment. Know your prices at home, because the merchandise might not be any cheaper—unless you hit a sale.

Don't forget that Harrods prides itself on being a full-service department store. Because of that, also on the fourth floor you will find a complete travel service agency, export department, London Tourist Board, bank, and theater ticket agency. We highly recommend the morning tour of London that Harrods conducts, if it is your first time in the city—they take you through all the different neighborhoods in a double-decker bus, and you can see everything while getting a great feeling for the city.

When you need some refreshment, Harrods has five restaurants, three of them on the fourth floor. We like the Terrace Bar on the fourth floor for that Mary Poppins feeling of looking over London, chimneys and all. You can sit and look out over the London skyline, ponder your purchases, and feel a little smug knowing that Harrods is "practically perfect in every way."

Now then, if you decide to go to Harrods for the after-Christmas sale, there are a few things you should know:

▼ Brits queue quietly and politely. They expect to stand in line for everything, and they do so almost like robots. There will be queues, and, yes, a few people do sleep on the pavement the night before. We don't suggest you do. In fact, we don't believe in standing in line and have found that once was enough for us at this sale. It's for the young and the strong.

▼ Brits have a stiff upper lip. Don't complain while standing in line. They resent Americans who come over, snap up bargains, and complain about it.

▼ Know your way around the store before the sale. If possible, get a map of the store. If not, study our list of what's where. First know what floor you are going to and what department you want. Saletime is wartime; this is no time to wander around aimlessly.

▼ Use cash to pay for your purchases, if possible. This will speed up the process. Remember that it takes time to fill in the VAT forms.

Harrods does the refund right on your credit card for big purchases. Ask.

▼ Wear appropriate clothes—if you plan on buying clothes, wear something you can get into and out of easily. Since it's winter, you will be carrying the weight of your winter coat with you. We wear our coats to keep our arms free; you can check them, but the line to claim them is enormous. We wear boots with low heels (consider combat boots with reinforced toes for kicking aside anyone who is the same size as you); high heels slow you down when you are running down the aisles.

▼ We rarely waste time on merchandise in bins. We have heard that this merchandise is bought especially for the sale. This may be a blatant lie, so we pass it on to you as such. The merchandise in bins is the cheapest.

▼ Limit the amount of time you will be in the war zone. If you don't, you may snap. This sale is murder on the nerves. The weak and the pregnant should shop at Brown's.

HARRODS, Knightsbridge, SW1

▼

SELFRIDGES: The other example of one-stop shopping, besides Harrods, is Selfridges. Harrods, we feel, offers a touch more quality merchandise. However, when we want to find a really good value for our pound, we come here. Their specialty is fashion at a moderate price; clothes for working women.

Harry Gordon Selfridge was an American who believed that the European market could benefit from a full-service department store. He was unable to convince his employers at Marshall Field in Chicago of that fact, so in

1909 he opened his own version of the American department store. Now Selfridges covers an entire city block.

Basement: housewares; ground floor: souvenirs, food halls (not as interesting as Harrods), cosmetics, cameras; one: export bureau, men's clothing; two: women's clothing (designers); three: kid's clothing; four: sportswear; five: personnel.

Selfridges has three restaurants, four coffee shops, and a juice bar. The service department includes a bank, an optician, theater tickets, fur storage, ear piercing, export services, and gift wrapping. We've bought our theater tickets from their broker and found the markup was less than at our hotel; you just may save a few dollars. Don't forget the Miss Selfridge part of the store—great fashions for the working woman, and a great resource for teens and college students. Miss Selfridge is now sold in the U.S., by the way.

SELFRIDGES, Oxford Street, W1

▼

LIBERTY: Originally opened in 1875 by Arthur Lazenby Liberty as an artists' source for fine materials from the Orient, Liberty has grown but retained its original flavor. Liberty is known worldwide for their fine Liberty prints. The fabric department takes up an entire floor and distributes fabrics for most of the famous designers.

Within the store are many little boutiques. One of these is composed of Oriental goods. On the top floor is a collection of antique pewter, originally called "Tudric," which is considered desirable by collectors. The gift department on the ground floor is filled with wonderful little nothings costing much more than they should but also hard to resist.

Our two other favorite pur[chases]
are the silk scarves and tie[s.] [The]
London prints are recognized [by]
even the toughest of relatives. If you[']re looking for a bit more to take home, the patchwork duvet covers and Liberty linens are well
worth the money.

Don't leave Liberty without their catalogue—
we use it frequently. Liberty's location makes
them a convenient stop for any shopping spree;
we do find their prices a tad high, however.

LIBERTYS, 210–20 Regent Street, W1

▼

HARVEY NICHOLS: Although Knightsbridge's other department store is much smaller
than Harrods, it makes up for size with quality. Harvey Nichols does not try to be everything to every person. They concentrate their
energy on the latest of high fashion for men,
women, and children. They are, frankly, *our*
kind of store. Styles are always the latest,
and most of the major design houses are
represented—even American designers such as
Liz Claiborne and Carole Little.

There is a tiny Oriental rug department,
although the selection in dhurries is good. The
glass department specializes in Lalique. Leathergoods and luggage are well represented, with a
fine selection of small items such as notebooks,
wallets, and keychains.

For the weary, there are two restaurants,
top floor and bottom floor.

HARVEY NICHOLS, Knightsbridge (corner of
Sloane), SW1

▼

FORTNUM & MASON: As with many of the old department stores, Fortnum & Mason began in 1707 as a grocery store. However, unlike the others, its founder, William Fortnum, was a footman in the household of Queen Anne. He collected and traded the used candle ends from the palace, saving his funds until he could open his own shop. He persuaded Hugh Mason, who owned a small shop in St. James Market, to become his partner, and thus began Fortnum & Mason.

The firm's great success during the empire's reign had to do with supplying goods not only in London, but also to the British families overseas. In the Victorian era, Fortnum & Mason also became famous for their fine-quality preserved fruits, jellies, and hams.

After World War I, Fortnum & Mason greatly expanded to its present size and became a department store. The ground floor is still dominated by the food halls. Here you can purchase the finest in caviar, foie gras, teas, chocolates, jellies, coffee, and wines. Upstairs is a collection of the best in British and international collections of leathergoods, fashions, gifts, and luggage. We find the fashion selection quite fitting for the Queen Mother, but not our cup of tea. No offense, mum.

Don't miss the famous Fountain Restaurant on Jermyn Street. It is open for breakfast at 9:30 A.M. and remains open all day until 11:00 P.M. Look, too, at the wonderful Fortnum & Mason clock. Added only in 1964, the clock features Mr. Fortnum and Mr. Mason bowing to each other while the clock chimes play a selection of eighteenth-century tunes. This is almost as much fun as watching the blackamoors in the clock in Venice at St. Mark's Square. We also adore the formal dining room on the fourth floor, where you can get roast beef from the trolley. The W.C. is on the fourth floor as well.

FORTNUM & MASON, 181 Piccadilly, W1

BARKERS: This is Grandma Mary's favorite department store in London, but we remain lukewarm. It's nice, it's serviceable, it's not a zoo like Harrods. We prefer Harvey Nichols—it's more "with it"—but Grandma Mary takes after the Queen Mother, so there you are. The location makes it convenient to your Kensington High Street tour of Hyper-Hyper and your stroll to Portobello Road.

Lowest floor: china, luggage; ground floor: cosmetics, accessories; one: ladies' fashion; two: hairdressing.

BARKERS, 63 Kensington High Street, W8

▼

LILYWHITE: Lilywhite is a department store of sporting goods. Kids' clothes are mixed with adults' clothes in many categories; there isn't anything they don't sell here. (Well, come to think of it, they had no boxing gloves for a small boy. But then we weren't sure we really wanted them, anyway.) All brand names are sold, including America's and Europe's finest. The Fila prices, when the items are on sale, are very low; we bought a boy's Nike nylon windbreaker lined with fleece for $15 on sale. The sport shoe selection is flabbergasting. Our favorite sweatsuit: "Marc O'Polo" for $45.

Ground floor: track suits; one: shoes; two: gym; three: books, video, ski; four: racket sports; five: darts, snooker, water sports, shooting, riding.

LILYWHITE, Piccadilly Circus, SW1

▼

AUSTIN REED: Technically this is a specialty store. But after you've been in some of the big department stores, you come to appreciate a little department store. Austin Reed has no food halls, but they do sell just about everything else you need, and it's all of style, grace, and high quality. Made-to-measure is available, but the ready-to-wear selection for men and women is very British and very much in keeping with old wood, Irish setters, and rare books. This is what you came to London to buy. They bill themselves as the home of British style.

Lowest floor: toiletries, gift items, shoes; ground floor: gifts, luggage, sweaters; one: country shop: two, coats.

AUSTIN REED, 103–13 Regent Street, W1

▼

DEBENHAMS: This is very much a real-people store, sitting high and mighty on Oxford Street and attracting working-class locals. It's a little nicer than Marks & Sparks and sells copies of many hot tickets—such as the Microfile, which is the $50 copy of the $100 Filofax. There's an in-store Benetton and other name-brand fashion items. The Christian Dior pantyhose costs about $1.25 a pair—this is worth the trip. Brightly colored umbrellas in a rainbow of shades cost $8—should it happen to rain while you're in town.

Lowest level: restaurants; ground floor: cosmetics, accessories; one: kids', ladies', Jaeger; two: home furnishings; three: furniture.

DEBENHAMS, Oxford Street, W1

▼

D. H. EVANS: Just like the old Macy's, or the large department store of your coming of age, Evans has a good selection of their own private-label items and many designer names. You'll see things here that you just won't find in other shops; you'll also find that they billboard midrange designers who can get buried in glitzier stores. We found Planet here, and Jill Barnes, and many names we didn't know well but later discovered were moving up in the world of fashion. This is a House of Fraser store; it's not the fanciest store you'll find in London, but if you like bread-and-butter clothes, you may want to give it a try. Jaeger boutiques on two floors. Kids' items are boring.

Ground floor: cosmetics, accessories, men's; one: women's fashion; two: kids', designers; three: fabrics, linens, bath shop; four: silver, kitchen; five: furniture.

D. H. EVANS, 318 Oxford Street, W1

▼

DICKINS & JONES: A more high-end House of Fraser store, Dickins & Jones sells fabric and knitting yarns, but also big-name designers and snazzy clothes. Here you'll find Yves Saint Laurent Variations and all that sort of thing. Recently they have emphasized lower-priced designer goods and clothes fitting for smartly dressed executive or working women.

Ground floor: accessories, fabrics, wools; one: designer; two: executive woman; three: coats, British collections.

DICKINS & JONES, 224 Regent Street, W1

Sweaters and Knitgoods

N. PEAL: For the quality- and convenience-conscious, N. Peal offers quite a variety of wools and cashmeres in a multitude of colors and styles. They are top of the line in the business, but frankly, we don't spend $300 for a sweater very often! N. Peal is in the Burlington Arcade, where you'll be anyway—the women's shop is at 37 and the men's shop is at 54 Burlington Arcade. Both shops look small, but they have underground levels. Peal's is the kind of shop you swear you won't patronize because of the high prices but then you go back after you've been to every discount resource in London. While you can get traditional sweaters in any number of places and at a variety of prices, Peal's is one of the few outlets that sells fashion merchandise made out of cashmere. Notice that their sweaters are entirely different from the look-alikes you'll see everywhere else. And look at that cashmere bathrobe.

N. PEAL, 37 and 54 Burlington Arcade

THE SCOTCH HOUSE: A must stop for the lover of those classic Scottish tartans and kilts, for sweater-lovers, for lovers of grand wooden staircases and stores that look like stores should look. Our favorite Scotch House is the Brompton Road one in Knightsbridge (because of the staircase, not the selection), but the Regent Street one is large and wonderful also. They carry all the major brands and have matching sweaters and jackets for many styles. This also is a wonderful place to purchase scarves in the traditional tartans or in more subtle colors to take home as gifts for your family. Remember when you were six and Mommy brought you back a kilt of your own? (you always lost the pin, too, didn't you?); this is where you can return the favor for someone on your gift list. The kids' department is excellent; don't miss their chart of tartans and clans.

THE SCOTCH HOUSE
   84 Regent Street, W1
   191 Regent Street, W1
   2 Brompton Road, SW1
   7 Marble Arch
   187 Oxford Street, W1

▼

S. FISHER: Another good find if you want to buy the classic cashmere, lamb's-wool, or shetland wool sweater is S. Fisher. At a certain point, all the merchandise begins to look alike in each of the shops like this one, but this is a well-thought-of and famous shop. They also carry the tartan plaids that everyone seems to like.

S. FISHER, 22 Burlington Arcade, W1

▼

BRAININ CASHMERES: If you are shopping Old Bond Street, this is a good resource for Ballantyne cashmere sweaters. The shocking thing about Brainin is that after you think you've seen every sweater style ever made and there are no twists, Brainin comes up with a few different looks. The shop isn't as fashionable as N. Peal, but does have some fashion-style cashmere (expect to pay $200 to $300 for it, though). The shop is painfully small, with only one counter and barely room to stand. However, the merchandise is extensive and the sales staff is lovely even if you are just browsing. They carry both men's and women's styles in both single- and double-knit weights.

BRAININ CASHMERES, 11 Old Bond Street, W1

▼

WESTAWAY & WESTAWAY: If you can't stand wondering who has the cheapest sweaters and the best selection, take our word for it and head to Westaway & Westaway, or to Portobello Road—the two are tied in price but offer something slightly different. Westaway & Westaway has more shops, is neater, and has more selection. It's located across the street from the British Museum, and you are guaranteed to find any sweater in any color and style that might be desired. The shop carries a large selection of handknitted garments from Scotland and Ireland as well as the classic cashmere and lamb's-wool favorites. There are several shops, so make sure to see all of them. They have slightly discounted Burberry and Aquascutum items, kilts, shawls, and yardgoods in one shop and then sweaters, sweaters, sweaters in the other shop. In the sweaters shop, notice there are two rooms upstairs and two downstairs as well as a back, back room that you might have trouble finding if you don't know it's there. We buy men's cashmere sweaters for all our lady friends and sew in some shoulder pads. You'll pay $80 for a cashmere sweater here and then get VAT on your credit card. Don't forget to look at the sale merchandise in the lower shelves in the downstairs rooms. There also is a more fashion-oriented shop one block away. The merchandise in each of the shops is somewhat different. All the more fun.

WESTAWAY & WESTAWAY, 62–65 Great Russell Street, WC1

▼

W. BILL LTD.: If Westaway & Westaway did not have the colors you wanted (sometimes they just stock traditional colors) and you must have a turquoise or a shocking pink sweater, stop by at W. Bill Ltd. The prices are reasonable, although not nearly as inexpensive as at Westaway & Westaway. W. Bill is a famous tourist shop, but the downstairs selection of men's sweaters is excellent in a way we've seldom seen in any of our other sweater resources. The shop is conveniently located in the Royal Arcade, which just happens to lead to our favorite spot for tea (Brown's Hotel). The last time we stopped at W. Bill, we were able to pick up mohair open-weave scarves that cost us all of $8 each. (These same scarves are $5 at Westaway & Westaway.) The larger cashmere scarves are $25; cashmere capes cost only $250. (But don't buy here until you've seen if Westaway & Westaway has your colors; they have the same cape for $200.)

W. BILL LTD., 28 Old Bond Street (Royal Arcade)

▼

CROCHETTA: If you are looking for an incredibly unusual sweater instead of the traditional British sweater to take home, this is the company that makes them. Sweaters are designed with beading, leather, fur—you name it, they design it. Prices are about half of what you would pay in the United States if you could even find them. Our friend Donna was going to sell them in the United States, but she couldn't find enough people to plunk down $500 for the sweaters, which is what they would have to cost once Stateside. Every now and then, Saks gets a few of these in. You'll also see them in the pages of all the European fashion mags. Especially check out the ones

that have pieces of mink or fox tails knitted in.
Prices are high.

CROCHETTA
   68 South Molton Street, W1
   61 Beauchamp Place, SW3
   140 Fortis Green, N10

▼

THE SCOTTISH MERCHANT: Prices are
high, but the street is so cute that we almost
forgive them. And, amazingly, we saw styles
here that were noplace else. If you can't leave
London without an Irish fisherman sweater,
get it at Marks & Spencer (see page 178) or try
The Scottish Merchant. Here, too, you will
find the Fair Isle and Channel Island sweaters.
Really, the prices at Marks & Sparks are the
best around—unless you are going to Hong
Kong. You can also knit your own Irish fisherman sweater. But alas, this is a good resource for the basics and isn't nearly as touristy as most of the big shops. Walk this street
as you connect from Leicester Square to Covent
Garden.

THE SCOTTISH MERCHANT, 16 New Row, WC2

▼

BENETTON/STEFANEL: Benetton and Stefanel are as popular in London as they are in
Italy. With their easy style and prices, the
Benetton and Stefanel lines appeal to the young
set. There's a shop or two or three everywhere
you look. Since shops are individually owned,
prices—especially sale prices—can vary. There're
too many shops to list them individually, but
there's always a Benetton at crowded shopping
areas. Oxford Circus has several shops.

▼

NO. I COPENHAGEN STREET: Those of us who love a good sweater know that London weather demands that each well-dressed woman have her own resources for fashionable sweaters. If you want them at discount, we've got just the place for you. This is one of the few shops in London that sells designer samples and seconds and has many original handknits for less than you could knit them for. Since the name of the shop is the address, you'll have no trouble finding it. This is a little off the beaten track, but get off at the tube stop Angel.

NO. I COPENHAGEN STREET, 1 Copenhagen Street, N1

▼

PORTOBELLO PORCELAIN & WOOL MARKET: If you love crazy fun, this one's for you. This is a bargain basement in the traditional sense of the words and it is sweater city. There are no labels and the proud cry that this merchandise is the finest. Sweaters that elsewhere cost $100 are $70 here. There are seconds, much of the merchandise is big-name without labels, but the help will tell you what it is. It is worse than mobbed on Saturdays, and you have to be the kind who likes this kind of stuff to endure it. But any friend of ours wants to be on Portobello Road on a Saturday, anyway. So what the hell? Prices here, along with those at Westaway & Westaway, are the best in London—probably in all England. We have heard of prices at sweater mills that are higher.

They have a catalogue and clear instructions on how to order from home. You get VAT at £50. They also have a porcelain market next door, which may or may not offer bargains. The porcelains offered in the catalogue are top drawer, but the prices are the same as at regular china shops. Wedgwood's dark blue Runnymeade, $76 (that's no bargain or a few dollars high).

PORTOBELLO PORCELAIN & WOOL MARKET, 101–3 Portobello Road, W2

Shoes and Leathergoods

KURT GEIGER: This contemporary shop, with expansive window displays, carries the complete selection of the wonderful Bruno Magli line. You'll find, upon entering, that they have combined the Jaeger—each occupying one side of the shop. Geiger also is sold in some department stores; the name is synonymous with good style to locals.

KURT GEIGER, 10 Old Bond Street, W1

MAUD FRIZON: We're really not the kind to go on about this sort of thing, but the salesman who helped us at Maud Frizon on our last trip was the most beautiful young man we ever saw. We almost asked if he was Elizabeth Taylor's son, but we didn't have the nerve. This tiny shop stocks men's, women's, and handbags; prices on sale can be as low as $50 for a pair of flats. Standard prices for nonsale pumps are $125 to $150. Boots can go up to $400. Prices are a little higher than in Italy but a little lower than in the United States.

MAUD FRIZON, 31 Old Bond Street, W1

▼

RAYNE: The elegance of this shop is in direct contrast to the blandness of the sturdy-looking styles of the Rayne line, which happens to supply the Queen and the Queen Mother with shoes. The more stylish Andrea Pfister shoes also are carried here, as well as the St. John knits (the only shop in London to carry this line). Don't dump on Rayne as dumpy—they are a good bread-and-butter choice, and some of the zippy shoes will surprise you.

RAYNE, 31 Old Bond Street, W1

▼

BALLY: There are eight branches of Bally in London, but this New Bond Street branch is our favorite. In this very spacious shop you can find a wonderful selection for both men and women of the famous Bally of Switzerland styles. We find the prices to be about half of what they are in the United States. Men can expect to pay $100 for loafers, $125 for wing tips, and $110 for short-topped leather boots. Ladies will pay $95 for their traditional pumps.

BALLY, 116 New Bond Street, W1

▼

CHURCH'S: What did you come to London for, if not to buy Church's shoes for him? Don't forget there is a factory outlet in Darien, Connecticut, if you happen to live nearby; otherwise enjoy this tiny, tiny shop with your typical "well worn" English interior. Prices are great! Expect to pay half of what you would in the United States.

CHURCH'S, 163 New Bond Street, W1

RUSSEL AND BROMELY: If you are looking for your favorite European designer shoe such as Bruno Magli, Walter Steiger, or Charles Jourdan, stop by this very fashionable shop. There are several locations throughout London, but this elegant store is our favorite. There are styles here for both men and women. This is bread-and-butter traditional stuff with the understanding that Britannia rules the waves. There are shops everywhere.

RUSSEL AND BROMELY, 24–25 New Bond Street, W1

▼

CHARLES JOURDAN: Located conveniently near Harrods, the Jourdan shop sports a good selection of both clothing and shoes. The best news is that the prices are the same as in Paris! You can do quite well for $100 to $150.

CHARLES JOURDAN, 47 Brompton Road, SW3

▼

BERTIE: A famous London shoe resource at the moderate price level, Bertie has shops in the United States and some distribution in the United States. We saw boots in an ad for Saks retailing for $119, so we tried to find them in

London for, say, $75. Nowhere to be seen, and no one at any of several Bertie shops knew what we were talking about. On the other hand, Bertie does offer a lot of style for the money (leather briefcase for $40; boots for $100; half boots for $60), and there are scads of shops all around town.

BERTIE, Covent Garden

Children

HAMLEY'S: Pussycat, pussycat, where have you been? To Hamley's, of course, then later, the Queen. Whether you have children or not, Hamley's deserves attention. They ship, they give VAT at £50, they make returns easily, they are in the business of satisfying you and your kids.

Basement: gobots, transformers, etc; one: stuffed animals, cutesy-pie knickknacks, souvenirs; two: knights and soldiers; three: sporting goods; four: books, cafeteria.

If you are beginning to find yourself feeling dizzy, you will be relieved to find a snack bar on the fourth floor. We find the prices great on many items—American toys are more expensive here, but Corgi toys are a bargain. If you're looking for that unusual toy not readily available in the United States, Hamley's is a must. The gift shop on the street level is the best (and easiest) place we know of to buy gifts for all your friends and neighbors. Our favorites are the Snoopy T-shirts complete with British slogans, key chains, and the famous metal Hamley's buses and taxis in all sizes. If you or your child collects dolls, you will have a tough time making a final decision. We are especially fond of the Catherine Nesbitt dolls that have reproduced all the royalty famous in

British history, as well as the small metal British Regiment Guard for all the collectors in your family. We also like the sports shop on the third floor, for every possible sporting accessory your child might need. If you are wondering how you will get your packages home, Hamley's will ship them to your door. The paperwork takes about twenty minutes but is well worth the time. Our packages, always sent surface, always have arrived home before we did! Don't forget to pick up their fabulous mail-order catalogue.

HAMLEY'S, 200 Regent Street, W1

▼

GALT TOYS: For mothers of invention, this shop on the corner of Great Marlborough and Carnaby streets is for you. These are the educational-type toys that are in no way related to television shows or cartoons. You'll find only the wonderful, sturdy, wooden toys that Galt is famous for. Prices are much better than in the United States. Ask for the excellent color brochure.

GALT TOYS, 30 Great Marlborough Street, W1

▼

LA CIGOGNA: The London branch of La Cigogna, on Sloane Street (behind Harrods), still is our favorite place to buy children's clothing for infants through age thirteen. This shop is loaded with all those wonderful Italian designer clothes and shoes that we love to dress our children in but can't always afford. If you have a daughter, the gorgeous array of party dresses next to the entrance seems endless. Also available for your princess are lovely skirts, pants, and sweaters (some handknits). There is a small area for infants and toddlers, and the back of the shop is devoted just to boys. Don't miss the basement for dazzling Italian shoes. We find shopping in the London shop to be much easier than in Rome because in the former they seem to carry the best of the La Cigogna collection. The prices are slightly higher, though (10 to 15%).

LA CIGOGNA, 6A Sloane Street, SW1

▼

BENETTON 0–12: This tiny little shop on South Molton Street is crammed with stacks of their famous cotton and woolen separates. If you have the time to dig through the stacks, you can uncover a multitude of styles (jumpers, pants, sweaters, shirts, scarfs, and gloves) in bright colors. These Italian-made classics are always stylish and fun, but they are not inexpensive. If you traditionally shop at Sears or Penney's for your kids, you will not like the prices here or in any other 0–12 shop. We wish this stuff were cheaper because it is adorable. Good sales in July and January.

BENETTON 0–12, 22 South Molton Street, W1

▼

ZERO FOUR PLUS: Across from Benetton 0–12 and a million miles away in style, Zero Four Plus is the expensive and chic look you think royal children wear on a daily basis. We love the selection of French and Italian designer clothes in this simple and small rectangular shop. The Cacharel line is well represented here. They carry clothing for children under the age of thirteen, but you'll find the largest variety for the smaller child. Expect to pay dearly for the European chic sold here—rich mums may want to splurge, but a lot of others will be heartsick at the high price of style.

ZERO FOUR PLUS, 53 South Molton Street, W1

Horse and Rider

I f you're sick to death of everyone drooling over Princess Diana and the Duchess of York and you find that Princess Anne has been underrated by the public, you're probably into the horsey set and won't find your trip to London complete without the sniff of saddle soap. Whether you're buying or browsing, you'll find the horse trail of retailing to be marvelously old-fashioned England, steeped in dark grain wood and tradition and fox tails.

▼

J. A. ALLEN: If you have a horse-crazy daughter, perhaps she'd like a book from J. A. Allen's, the foremost equestrian bookstore and publisher. You name it, and they've got it here. If you just want to soak up horse vibes, this is the place to do it. The sales help is most helpful, and they never say "neigh."

J. A. ALLEN, 1 Lower Grosvenor Place

HENRY MAXWELL: Once you've got a leg up on horse lore, you'll need boots. So trot on over to Maxwell (in the basement), where you will be glad you're close to ground zero when you see the prices. We're talking heavy-duty royalty and polo player playboys for customers and over $1,000 for a pair of polo boots. A Maxwell boot is *le dernier cri* to those in the know, so if you've got it—flaunt it. If you're planning on crashing Virginia fox-hunting society, Maxwell will start you on the right foot.

HENRY MAXWELL, 11 Savile Row

▼

TRICKER'S: If you find Maxwell a tad pricey but don't mind spending up to $500 for a pair of riding boots, try Tricker's.

TRICKER'S, 67 Jermyn Street

▼

JAMES LOCK & CO.: If you need the right hat for the fox hunt, you'll pay about $75 for a very proper bowler at a firm that has been in business since the mid-1700s and knows a lot about crowning glory; silks here, too. Lock sells all sorts of hats, by the way, and they hold a royal warrant.

JAMES LOCK & CO., 6 St. James Street

▼

J. DEGE & SONS: For traditional riding garb, try J. Dege & Sons, which specializes in garments for showmen and hunters and will fit you in London and then send your clothes overseas for you. This is dressage heaven.

J. DEGE & SONS, 16 Clifford Street

▼

Don't forget that Turnbull & Asser, besides making Chuck's pajamas, also makes his hunting shirts; they'll make them for you, too, for about $100. Harrods has an entire department devoted to horses, so if you don't need the Savile Row look for your Mr. Ed, prices at Harrods are also much less than in these shops.

China, Crystal, and Silver

We know people who fly to London just to buy their china and crystal. The savings are so great, we don't blame them. There are innumerable places to shop for these items, so we have checked them all out (until our feet felt like they were made of china and soon would break) and have weeded the list down to what we think are the best one-stop shops—both for price and selection. Remember the big department stores when you are pricing and shipping china—Harrods especially has a good selection and will crate and ship for you. Also remember when you comparison-price (United States to United Kingdom, that is) that crating and shipping will almost double the price of your purchase. Be sure to buy items that offer more than a 50% saving if bought in the United Kingdom. One last tip: Not to spoil your fun, but if you are planning on a big haul, please check out U.S. discounters and shipping prices. Major markets (Los Angeles, New York, Chicago) always have discounters who offer you 20% off list. With the price of shipping from the United Kingdom what it is, you may come out even. Do your homework before you leave town; that way you'll never face a dilemma as you stand at the china counter in a London shop. And, yes, of course we've been to Stoke-on-Trent to check out all the china factories. Prices on seconds are good, but on best ware, here's the news: The prices in London are the same. See page 256 for the full report on the factories and their outlets, but in quick summation, if you want top-of-the-line quality and selection, London is the answer.

▼

CHINACRAFT: This is one of our favorite shops specializing in English bone china (no French or German patterns here). There are several in London, even one in Bath; you'll find them easily. They offer stock on all the biggies — Spode, Minton, Royal Crown Derby, Wedgwood, Aynsley, Coalport, and Royal Worcester. Walk down the steps to a vast array of gift items, including bone china figurines, cachepots, and paperweights. Quite a selection of crystal is also available, including patterns from Waterford and Baccarat. We continue to marvel at the amount we can save when we buy here. We have always done our business with Tony at the New Bond Street shop, but we trust their personnel everywhere. Oh, yes, and here's a little secret or two for you about Chinacraft: If you buy a lot (over $500), see if you can politely negotiate a discount. Tony is used to big spenders who will come in and order half a million pounds' worth (that's about $750,000 worth, as in expensive, not heavy) of delectables, but you can buy less and still get a discount—if you are nice. Discounts vary on stock—if Tony has a lot of something he wants to move out, he will discount it up front. Anyone walking in may ask about a pattern and he may tell you that they'll take 15% off on that pattern. On another pattern—perhaps one that is out of stock and has to be ordered for you—a discount would be impossible. It's all very flexible.

A catalogue with prices in dollars costs $5, but best news of all, Chinacraft comes to the United States and takes hotel space to show their goodies in major U.S. cities. You may go for tea, and order your goods at London prices. You also may phone. You are guaranteed safe delivery.

People often ask us why we would shop here rather than at Reject China (see page 169). The two offer entirely different attitudes, and we shop at both of them. Chinacraft is an elegant store; Reject China is not. Chinacraft gives you the personal attention of a specialty shop; Relect China is nice, but not in the same way. Reject China is a major discounter; Chinacraft is a major specialty store. If you want selection, perhaps a special order, and service, Chinacraft will handle all that for you without being quite as fancy as a place such as Lawley's.

CHINACRAFT, 130 New Bond Street, W1

▼

THOMAS GOODE: If you're looking for the ultimate shopping experience for your selection of china, glassware, silver, or exquisite accessory pieces, this elegant shop with the two Minton elephants in the window is a must. They carry all the top European brands of china and crystal and have monogram services available on the premises.

No bargains here, so we suggest you browse

only. If they have an item you can't get elsewhere, expect it to be 30% cheaper than the U.S. price. But remember, Goode is more expensive than Chinacraft—generally speaking.

THOMAS GOODE, 19 South Audley Street, W1

▼

GERED: There are several Gered shops, and they sell Wedgwood and Wedgwood-owned factory-made items only. Because of their connection to Wedgwood, we'd go here if you want Wedgwood and if Reject China didn't have what you wanted. Gered is well equipped to send you a price quotation in U.S. dollars and to ship—you may pay with personal check on mail order. Although all china prices are fixed, we find Gered up to $5 a place setting cheaper than Chinacraft. To whet your appetite or help you begin your homework on price comparisons, here's a few of the 1986 prices for a five-piece place setting: Runnymeade Dark Blue (W4472), $72.51; Raspberry Cane oven to tableware, $19.52; Coalport April (59104), $38.77.

GERED, 173–74 Piccadilly, W1

▼

CHRISTOPHER STRANGEWAYS: This shop is the home of creative, funny, witty ceramicsware. You can find anything from camel cups to Memphis Milano–inspired triangular plates. What you won't find is "boring." Many of the designs are one-of-a-kind, hand-painted items. We love to visit here even when we have nothing we need to buy. For everyone who raves about fine English china, this is a good lesson in what else you can make with a hunk of clay.

CHRISTOPHER STRANGEWAYS, Covent Garden

▼

PORTOBELLO ANTIQUE COMPANY: Although this sounds like a furniture company, in actuality it is a wonderful source for everyday china and silver. Terry Goldsmith runs the company, mostly for the trade. He supplies other shops in the area, and ships goods to hotels and private customers all over the world. Don't expect to find Grandmother's 1823 Georgian candlesticks. But you might find a nice silver-plate pair. He is open Monday to Thursday to the trade only. Friday and Saturday he is open to the public. If you are planning to ship your goods home, be aware that he will not ship under two hundred pounds of merchandise, so be prepared to buy in quantity.

PORTOBELLO ANTIQUE COMPANY, 133 Portobello Road, W11

▼

LAWLEY'S: If we were local brides, we probably would register at Lawley's, with its blue carpets and velvet cases and department-store elegance. The selection is vast, the prices are fixed—as are everyone else's. We like the more intimate relationship we have with Tony at Chinacraft, but Lawley's is a fine choice.

LAWLEY'S, 154 Regent Street, W1

▼

LEATHER & SNOOK: Another traditional shop with a large selection, Leather & Snook has the Doulton collectors' club in its lower level. They seem to specialize more in figurines and gift china, but they certainly have the patterns and choices that other shops have.

LEATHER & SNOOK, 167 Piccadilly, W1

▼

REJECT CHINA SHOP: We have a very complex relationship with the Reject China Shop. We love the shop on Regent Street, we love that this is one of the few businesses in Britain that seems to understand retailing at its finest, that knows how to move merchandise. But we hate that they don't always have everything we want. (That's why we need a backup such as Chinacraft and why we sometimes go to Stoke-on-Trent.) The Regent Street store is our favorite because its lower level is almost like a warehouse of the world's most beautiful china (crystal is upstairs). We have fallen in love with more patterns than we care to admit— and have had the feeling that we had to get out of there before we thought we were Nancy Reagan and ordered service for the White House. The Beauchamp Place shops in Knightsbridge are divided up and therefore are harder to shop, but each one is fun. They are used to tourists and will ship for you with ease. Catalogues/mail order/telephone orders with credit cards. Our Baccarat glasses are $45 in New York, $20 in Cannes, and $25 from Reject China; prices are exactly 20% less than the fixed prices posted in the fancy shops.

Note: Reject China also has added sweater goods to some of its shops.

REJECT CHINA SHOP
    134 Regent Street, W1
    33–35 Beauchamp Place, SW3
    56–57 Beauchamp Place, SW3

Fun Jewelry

BUTLER & WILSON: If you are a fan of authentic or reproduction Art Deco or Art Nouveau jewelry, or just love the chunky costume "glitz," this tiny shop is a must. Their collection of antique jewelry is the best. Many of the identical pieces of costume jewelry we've seen in the United States were here for less than half. Making a choice can be difficult, but the sales staff always is helpful and patient. Expect to pay between $40 and $70 for their costume necklaces and about $30 for their costume earrings.

BUTLER & WILSON, 189 Fulham Road, SW3

▼

ELIZABETH GAGE: A new, hotshot, society jeweler with a salon filled with banquettes and ruffled pillows and necklaces that are a cross between the elegant hippie look and Bulgari. Each piece is made of the finest metals and gemstones but is unique in a way that jewelry should be; this is expensive and important stuff, not silly glitz.

ELIZABETH GAGE, 20 Albemarle Street, W1

▼

KEN LANE: If you love fake, then fake it is, and it has to be Kenny Lane—for big-time glitz, anyway. His *faux* jewelry is a delight to look at and wear. The shop is filled with designs of every style. We like to wear the antique look-alike jewelry; bracelets cost about $50 each.

KEN LANE
66 South Molton Street, W1
Burlington Arcade

▼

ROCKS: More glitzy jewelry in a shop that is similar to Butler & Wilson but has fewer retro pieces and more splashy ones. You'll pay $50 for a bracelet that we bought wholesale in Paris for $15. There are a few Rocks shops around town at elegant addresses.

ROCKS, 2 South Molton Street, W1

▼

TIFFANY: If you hate English breakfast and want to consider Tiffany, they have indeed just opened in London. Actually, they have re-opened after hiatus. While there have been some Tiffany in-store jobs in various foreign markets (Tokyo), this is their first free-standing foreign store.

TIFFANY, 25 Old Bond Street, W1

Papergoods

PAPERCHASE: The "in" paper place for the look we rather call American in papergoods, but it's charming nonetheless and right on Tottenham Court Road. Paperchase offers a wide range of paper products—everything from greeting cards, stationery, wrapping papers, and party items to a variety of materials for the serious artist. If you like a well-decorated Christmas tree, check out the marvelous selection of decorations and glass ornaments. It's chic here, without being too terribly old-fashioned.

PAPERCHASE, 213 Tottenham Court Road, W1

▼

SMYTHSON: If you're looking for stationery fit for a queen, stop by this very elegant shop, which has been producing top-quality paper since the turn of the century. If you buy your writing papers at Cartier in New York, or any of America's finest paper shops, you'll see some old friends here in London. Aside from the selection of writing papers, there's a wide variety of leatherbound goods, including address books and notebooks, diaries, and lovely desktop accessories. This is an old-fashioned, blue-blood, blue-haired, very regal kind of place, a bit expensive, but cheaper than in the United States for the same goods. Be sure to go downstairs to the stationery department to see the Christmas cards (about $1 each) and our faves— the change-of-address cards that are engraved, fill-in-the-blanks jobs that are the last word in drop-dead chic.

SMYTHSON, 54 New Bond Street, W1

▼

ITALIAN PAPER SHOP: If you love that swirly, marbleized antique Italian paper look as much as we do, you may want to poke into the Italian Paper Shop, which is in an arcade right between Harrods and Harvey Nichols.

PERFUME/MOLTON PHARMACY ▼ 173

Prices are higher than in Italy and lower than in the United States. The store lacks the charm of similar shops in Venice or Florence, but the goods are the same. The pencils, at about $1 each, make smashing gift items.

ITALIAN PAPER SHOP, Brompton Arcade

Perfume

France has the discounts, not London, but if you insist—please use a discounter.

▼

MOLTON PHARMACY: This is convenient and fun and claims to be as cheap as Paris. (We don't think so.) You'll get the VAT if you buy enough, and discounts on smaller purchases are negotiable. The owners are very friendly and let you try everything—no snobs here. If you've heard of a new European fragrance that hasn't yet come to the United States and you want to try it out, this is the place. We've found that Boots has almost identical prices, but they're mobbed and not as easy to work with. They, too, will let you test, but you have to keep asking for help, since everything is behind counters out of reach. We think the prices on Orlane beauty treatment products are the lowest we've seen anywhere.

MOLTON PHARMACY, 64 South Molton Street, W1

▼

C. W. ANDREW CHEMIST: Here they say they'll match any discount price on perfumes in town. The selection here is huge; the staff is as nice as at Molton Pharmacy. There's a David Hicks designer carpet here—a novelty for a pharmacy—and complete beauty treatment and makeup lines as well as all the fragrances. Prices match those at our other two resources. We got a present for buying just a few items when we didn't qualify for the VAT. All the Mary Quant cosmetics are here.

C. W. ANDREW CHEMIST, 78 New Bond Street, W1

▼

J. FLORIS LIMITED: London has two leading local perfumiers; Floris is one of them. If you are as crazy for the "English Look" as many travelers who come to London are, then you don't want to miss the "English Scent," which you can buy at J. Floris. Special floral perfumes include Roses, Lilies, Lavender, and on and on. Nice for gift items.

J. FLORIS LIMITED, 89 Jermyn Street, SW1

▼

PENHALIGONS: Especially well known for their toilet water and soap that men adore, Penhaligons holds a royal warrant. Their products are produced according to the original formulas of William Penhaligon, who began his business as a barber shop in 1841. It's very olde England in here and we love to sniff around. Kids seem to like it here, too.

PENHALIGONS, 41 Wellington Street, WC2

Beauty Parlor Buys

I t's no secret that just about every hairdresser in the world sells a few items from the front counter to bring in a little extra cash. It's also no secret that we are devout shoppers and will find something to buy anywhere. Well, when in London we have a few beauty parlor tricks that we can't pass up.

▼

MOLTON-BROWN: One of the chicest salons in London is Molton-Brown, right on South Molton Street. We've never tried out their beauty services, so we can't comment on them, but we do go there to buy hair combs, headbands, and hair accessories, to say nothing of it being the best resource for Molton-Browners. While Harrods also carries Molton-Browners, the shop selection is superior at Molton-Brown. What is a Molton-Browner? Well, it's a hair curler that is rather like a big pipe cleaner. You twist them around wet hair, let dry, and voilà—Annie with a twist. Rollers come in two different sizes and covered in a variety of fashion fabrics. About $20 for a set of ten; a fabulous gift item. Don't forget to try the seaweed setting lotion as well.

MOLTON-BROWN, 64 South Molton Street, W1

▼

MICHAELJOHN: Another chic salon is Michaeljohn, which does a lot of royal heads and won't talk about it. Their products are for sale in London at the shop and in the United

States in major department stores although the packaging is different. Prices are no lower in London, but the salon is fun to visit and is conveniently located near Brown's Hotel.

MICHAELJOHN, 23A Albemarle Street, W1

▼

NEVILLE DANIEL LTD.: This salon holds the royal warrant for HRM the Queen. It's a full-line beauty salon where products are also available for sale.

NEVILLE DANIEL LTD., 175 Sloane Street, SW1

Fabrics and Notions

JACOB GORDON LTD.: We discovered Jacob Gordon Ltd. the same day that costumers from *Dynasty* were shopping there, so it was quite glamorous. Known for their couture silks and woolens, Gordon's will gladly tell you the names of all the celebs and royals who shop there. They have twice-a-year sales during which silks are marked down to $12.50 a meter.

JACOB GORDON LTD., 75 Duke Street, Oxford Street (there are two Duke streets), W1

▼

ALLANS OF DUKE STREET: Here you'll find that all the designer pictures are on the wall with swatches taped to them. It's very elegant and impressive here; prices are not low but they are lower than in the United States.

ALLANS OF DUKE STREET, 56–58 Duke
  Street, W1

▼

PATRICIA ROBERTS: If you knit, your
life will not be complete unless you visit Patricia Roberts. She has her own books and patterns, the yarn is well priced, and the designs
are explosive. Expect to pay $8 per 25 grams
of cashmere, $4 for 50 grams of cotton bouclé,
and $2 for 28 grams of real Shetland. Mail
order is okay; they will make the sweater for
you if you can't knit, but when you hear the
finished price, you'll learn how to knit. Many
of Ms. Roberts's sweaters are displayed at the
Victoria & Albert Museum.

PATRICIA ROBERTS, 31 James Street (and
  other locations)

▼

LIBERTY: Liberty sells a raft of designer
fabrics, their own and others, with names such
as Armani, Valentino, Yves Saint Laurent, etc.
Most of these fabrics are made at a factory in
Italy (see page 144). Liberty prints run about
$15 a meter in wool challis to $22 a meter in
silk; designer silks are closer to $40 a meter.

LIBERTY, 210-20 Regent Street, W1

Bargain Basements

I n an informal survey of every taxi driver any of us has ever had in London over a period of three years, we have a unanimous decision to announce: Every single one of them cited Marks & Spencer as the best discount source in London. Going even further, most of them were surprised that we were looking for other discount outlets, since they couldn't understand anyone wanting to go anywhere else. Known as Marks & Sparks to the locals, this quasi-department store is more like a fancy dime store than anything else. We always go here first thing in the morning, when we are well rested and the crowds are their least lethal. At Christmastime this place is a madhouse. Never mind. Bargains are bargains: Traditional lamb's-wool and angora cardigans are $25; fashion acrylic sweaters are $12; evening sweaters with sequins are $25; traditional fisherman sweaters are $20; cashmere sweaters are $52. There's clothing for every member of your family; there're books, video tapes, beauty products, active sportswear, etc. There's even a food market, à la Prisunic in France. There are 255 Marks & Spencer stores in the United Kingdom; our regular store is the one across from Selfridges, known as the Marble Arch store.

MARKS & SPENCER, 458 Oxford Street, W1

▼

CONSTANT SALE SHOP: A far cry from the inexpensive merchandise sold at many bargain basements, the Constant Sale Shop is just that—it's always on sale here. The store is owned by a man who owns other shops that sell designer merchandise at regular prices. Rather than suffer serious markdowns in his shops, he takes his no-goes to this outlet. We're so glad, too. On a clear day you can see forever—Armani, Krizia, Basile, Soprani, etc. Armani blouses may be priced as low as $100.

CONSTANT SALE SHOP, 54 Fulham Road, SW3

▼

LOST PROPERTY SALES: If you have endless intellectual curiosity, a good sense of humor, some money to burn, and time on your side, you may get a kick out of one of our favorite places in London: Lost Property Sales. Anything not claimed at Waterloo Station meets its Waterloo here. If you're used to post office auctions, this is your kind of place.

LOST PROPERTY SALES, 113 Oxford Street, W1

▼

REJECT SHOP HOUSEWARES: If you're already shipping a container or such, you might want to look in at Reject Shop Housewares. This is neither The Reject Shop nor the Reject China Shop but another resource, with kitchen equipment, dishes, and pine furniture. Some things are seconds or samples. They also have small gift items, but if you're not furnishing your house, or in the block already, don't make a special trip.

REJECT SHOP HOUSEWARES, 209 Tottenham Court Road, W1

▼

THE REJECT SHOP: We cannot be in London without spending at least an hour at The Reject Shop, which is not the Reject China Shop. The Reject Shop is large, clean, bright, and conveniently located right on Brompton Road. There's enough children's merchandise here that it's an easy place to shop if you have kids with you. What kind of bargains you'll find varies; not all will be portable. We once got fabulous handpainted wooden Christmas tree ornaments for $1 each there—and during the Christmas season! There were also enough Winnie-the-Pooh items to plan an entire birthday party for a four-year-old. Then there were the bargains we didn't know what to do with—crystal wine decanters, clay cookpots, etc. Don't buy anything electrical because of the difference in United States and United Kingdom current.

THE REJECT SHOP, 245 Brompton Road, SW3

▼

THE SALE SHOP: A few British friends suggested that we visit The Sale Shop after we complained that there is no Loehmann's in London. We were disappointed when we finally got there—no big names. But for working women, students, or those who don't care if they've ever heard of the designer or not, there are some good buys here. It's nice to come here because it's very "real people" and not at all touristy or grabby or pushy. Women trade around their finds, help each other look for sizes or matches, and just have a good time while saving money. Merchandise does change quickly, but it's mostly classic and simple stuff.

THE SALE SHOP
  2 Barnabus Street, NW1
  5 Park Walk, SW10

▼

OUTGROANS: Nearby is this used-clothing resource for kids. Clothes are for those up to about age twelve and include previously worn but in-great-shape merchandise that is sold on commission, and designer samples and seconds that have yet to see the playground. We've always done well here.

OUTGROANS, 190 Albany Street, NW1

▼

WALLIS: This probably shouldn't be listed as a bargain basement, but you should know about Wallis. Wallis is owned by Sears (like Selfridges) and concentrates on reasonable fashion for the working woman. The secret is that all their clothes are line-for-line copies of the best of the international designers—many of them the French names you wish you could afford. We'll never get over the line-for-line copies of the Ungaro jackets for a mere $125. If you want something nice in the $100 range (often less), you can find it at Wallis. The dressy clothes are not nearly as nice as the sportswear and work clothes.

WALLIS
    490 Oxford Street, W1
    215 Oxford Street, W1
    9 Brompton Road, SW3
    96 Kings Road, SW3

▼

PANDORA: For the real thing in designer clothes but cheaper in price than the first time out, try Pandora, which sells used designer wear. Things are not necessarily laughable-cheap, but they are at least half price from the original price. There is one section of the store devoted to the items that are under £30 (about $45, depending on the rate of exchange). It's fun to browse, since you'll surely be in the neighborhood anyway.

PANDORA, 54 Sloane Square, SW1

Fur Bargain Basements

Perhaps you find it chilly in London and don't need a raincoat, but maybe you need a fur coat. We've got two used- (and new-) fur shops that have spectacular buys: NOBLE FURS, 183 Regent Street, W1, and KONRAD FURS, 90 New Bond Street, W1. Konrad has incredible pre-Christmas sales in which the saving can be 70%. Then there's JINDO, 10 Old Bond Street, W1, which sells new furs as if it were a supermarket of furriers. The furs are made in the Orient to keep labor costs low. The selection is vast and prices are quite reasonable—we've had trouble finding the kind of quality we find at Mr. Kahn's showroom in New York, so know what you want before you plunk down your money. Prices are quoted in U.S. dollars or sterling, and a full-length, traditionally styled mink coat is not much more than $1,600. There are many nice coats for under $1,000.

Books, Maps, and Autographs

The West End

MAGGS BROTHERS LTD.: Don't believe those ghost stories you hear about Maggs.

While it has been rumored for years that the

Maggs mansion built in 1740 was haunted, no ghosts were spotted during World War II, when fire-watch rules required at least one Maggs employee to sleep on the premises each night. Of course, the house next door was completely destroyed ... and the one across Berkeley Square suffered heavy damage ... but there are no ghosts.

The only remaining mystery at Maggs's is just how many books they have on hand. They've been accumulating since Uriah Maggs founded the firm in 1857, and not even their insurance company has been able to come up with a correct figure. (When Maggs's broke down and bought a computer to catalogue the collection, it stood unboxed for eight months until John Maggs hired a consultant, whose first move was to plug it in.)

Such eccentricities are allowed any bookseller with an enormous collection of travel books, militaria, maps, illuminated manuscripts, autographs, and Orientalia. Maggs's travel section alone would fill the average bookstore with first-edition on-the-spot reminiscences by the likes of Stanley, Livingstone, Robert Falcon Scott, and Admiral Byrd. Whenever the stock gets dangerously low, it is replenished by ten specialists who attend auctions around the world to keep current.

Maggs's also boasts of a sizable autograph collection. Recent offerings have included:

▼ a letter from Catherine the Great ordering the treasury to pay her lover Field Marshal Potemkin 15,000 rubles

▼ an order from Queen Elizabeth I signed April 24, 1572, naming five men to the Order of the Garter

▼ a memo from Lord Nelson updating his plan four days before the Battle of Trafalgar, and a letter from his mistress Lady Emma Hamilton begging the Duke of Hamilton to get her a government pension

Whether you're a bibliophile or not, you should visit Maggs's to see just what a civilized delight bookbuying can be.

MAGGS BROTHERS LTD., 50 Berkeley Square, W1

▼

G. HEYWOOD HILL, LTD.: If Maggs's is a showplace for books and autographs of the illustrious, nearby G. Heywood Hill on Curzon Street represents the cramped, Dickensian bookshop most visitors associate with literary London. For fifty years Heywood's has been a beacon to authors, librarians, and collectors around the world.

Although space is limited, the shop is packed to the rafters with books that meet the standards of its knowledgeable staff. You won't find the newest Judith Krantz novel here, but employees know the stock and can lay hands on thousands of volumes of which they approve quickly. Moreover, while antiquarian books pay the light bills, Heywood's stocks contemporary books on a variety of subjects merely to satisfy its clients' needs. (It is also probably the only bookseller that will refuse to sell its clients books that don't meet its Olympian standards.)

The shop specializes in books on design, architecture, gardening, and the allied decorative arts. There's also an extensive collection of biographies and a subspecialty in literary criticism; Heywood's bookishness has attracted many writers as steady customers, including Evelyn Waugh, Anthony Powell, Nancy Mitford (who worked there during World War II), and other Waughs, Mitfords, and Sitwells for several generations.

This family feeling and the respect for the shop's high standards often give Heywood's first crack at extensive private libraries. Recent additions included Stendhal's *The Red and the Black* in the original paper covers *en français,* and a rare complete set of *Buck's Antiquities* in three volumes with all the botanical illustrations, a steal at $37,000.

G. HEYWOOD HILL LTD., 10 Curzon Street, W1

Piccadilly

BERNARD QUARITCH, LTD.: In October 1847, Bernard Quaritch came to London, determined to become a bookseller. He succeeded, attracting clients along the way, such as Prime Ministers William Gladstone and Benjamin Disraeli, publishing Edward FitzGerald's *The Rubáiyát of Omar Khayyám,* and being eulogized by *The Times* as "the greatest bookseller who ever lived."

By this time, Quaritch's has attained an international reputation. That reputation was heightened when, representing the Carl and Lily Pforzheimer Foundation, Quaritch's recently sold *The Gospels of Henry the Lion,* the German bible, to H. Ross Perot, for $8.25 million, the highest price ever received for an item at auction.

The firm recently offered a totally unrestored copy of the first edition—in the first state—of *Don Quixote* and has bought and sold no less than eight copies of the Gutenberg Bible. Recent offerings included a perfect set of *David Copperfield* in the original blue printed wrappers, a first edition of *Paradise Lost* in four volumes (one of only four copies known to exist), and *The Vegetable System,* the most extensive eighteenth-century botanical publication, in twenty-six volumes with 1,547 plates.

Boasting perhaps the largest stock of antiquarian books in London and thirty-two experts in fields as diverse as Arabic, bibliography, and psychiatry, Quaritch's atmosphere is quiet but not formal. The firm attends auctions on the Continent (sometimes bidding for the British Museum) and assembles collections that can run the gamut from Tibet to Henry James to rigging and shipbuilding.

Because of its size, Quaritch's is able to air-freight its own crate of books to New York once a week; the contents are then sent separately to clients via UPS, bypassing the post office and possibly careless (and financially damaging) handling.

BERNARD QUARITCH LTD., 5–8 Lower John Street, Golden Square, W1

▼

SOTHERAN'S OF SACKVILLE STREET: Sotheran's has been selling books since 1761 in York and has been established in London since 1815. Charles Dickens was a regular customer, and when he died, Sotheran's sold his library. The firm also purchased a number of volumes from Winston Churchill's library and was the agent for the sale of Sir Isaac Newton's library to Cambridge.

The firm specializes in ornithology and natural science, although Sotheran's recently offered Gibbon's *History of the Decline and Fall of the Roman Empire,* edited by Dr. Thomas Bowdler. (In Gibbon's case, the man whose prudish censorship has given us the word "bowdlerized" omitted Chapters 15 and 16 entirely.)

Books line the extensive perimeter of the ground floor, and the atmosphere is neat, formal, and as silent as a library. A lower floor is given over exclusively to antiquarian prints and maps, drawings by book illustrators such as Kate Greenaway and Arthur Rackham, sporting prints, and military and naval subjects.

There's also an attractive private office in an adjoining building for private negotiations.

Sotheran's offers search service, handbinds serial publications such as the Bills and Acts of Parliament, restores books, and also maintains subscriptions to overseas periodicals for its customers.

SOTHERAN'S OF SACKVILLE STREET, 2–5 Sackville Street, Piccadilly, W1

▼

PHILLIPS: Even though books are not on Phillips's weekly calendar like rugs, ceramics, furniture, and silver, the firm auctions books, maps, and autographs thirteen times a year and provides auction catalogues in these categories by subscription.

Phillips's books generally cover English literature, militaria, modern first editions, and incunabula. Recent lots included Darwin's *Voyages of the Beagle* in four uncut volumes; a six-page letter from George Eliot to Lord Frederic Leighton concerning his illustrations for *Romola*; and a limited edition of Charles and Mary Lamb's *Tales from Shakespeare* signed by the illustrator, Arthur Rackham.

PHILLIPS, 7 Blenheim Street, New Bond Street, W1

Charing Cross Road

Visitors searching for 84 Charing Cross Road will be disappointed to find a record store, not the bookshop that inspired Helen Hanff's bestseller; nevertheless, the long street is filled with other, equally engaging book emporiums, all of which are open Monday through Saturday from 9:00 A.M. to 6:00 P.M.

▼

FOYLE'S: Foyle's is the largest bookstore in London, with over four million volumes in stock. It's as crowded as ever, but the somewhat lackadaisical staff has been replaced by earnest and mostly helpful college students. There are large children's and fiction sections on the main floor; upper floors are devoted to technical books; a small antiquarian library; and huge sections on hobbies, art, and commerce. The business section is particularly noteworthy. Hours: Monday to Wednesday, and Friday and Saturday, 9:00 A.M. to 6:00 P.M.; Thursday, 9:00 A.M. to 7:00 P.M.

FOYLE'S, 119 Charing Cross Road, WC2

▼

ZWEMMER: Zwemmer has three stores in Charing Cross: (1) the Oxford University Press Bookshop, company store for one of the most respected publishers in the world; (2) a shop across the street devoted to the graphic arts—illustration, photography, etc. (there were three different books on Issey Miyake the last time we looked); and (3) a shop devoted to the fine arts (at 24 Litchfield Street). All three are open from 9:30 A.M. to 6:00 P.M. Monday to Friday and from 9:30 A.M. to 5:30 P.M. on Saturday.

ZWEMMER
   Oxford University Press Bookshop, 72 Charing Cross Road, WC2
   24 Litchfield Street, WC2 (fine arts)

ZWEMMER ART BOOKSHOP, 80 Charing Cross Road, WC2 (graphic arts)

ANY AMOUNT OF BOOKS, 62 Charing Cross Road, WC2

▼

FRANCIS EDWARDS: Francis Edwards is the leading antiquarian bookseller on the street and carries natural history and militaria. Open Monday to Friday from 9:00 A.M. to 5:00 P.M.

FRANCIS EDWARDS, 48A Charing Cross Road, WC2

Covent Garden

While by no means antiquarian, Long Acre, the "Main Street" of Covent Garden, is lined with bookstores on both sides of the road.

▼

ARTS COUNCIL SHOP: The ACS is open Monday to Saturday from 10:00 A.M. to 6:45 P.M. and stocks posters, postcards, and a full selection of arts books, including architecture, theater, film, photography, music, and opera.

ARTS COUNCIL SHOP, 8 Long Acre, WC2

▼

EDWARD STANFORD: Stanford's is Mecca for maps, charts, atlases, and travel books, not the reminiscences that Maggs's stocks, but rather the how-to variety. A particular specialty is guides for mountain climbers, skiers, and other outdoorsy types. Open Monday to Friday from 9:00 A.M. to 5:30 P.M. and from 10:00 A.M. to 4:00 P.M. Saturday.

EDWARD STANFORD, 12–14 Long Acre, WC2

▼

BERNARD STONE: Just off Long Acre, Stone specializes in poetry, children's books, and whodunits and has been called "addictive" for its seamless blend of rare and secondhand books as well as a large selection of new stock. They're open from 10:00 A.M. to 7:00 P.M. Monday to Saturday.

BERNARD STONE, 43 Floral Street, WC2

Cecil Court

Cecil Court, a block-long street between Charing Cross Road and St. Martin's Lane, has some charming secondhand bookshops. Most are open from 9:30 A.M. to 6:00 P.M. Monday to Saturday. By number, they are:

▼4—Bell, Book & Radmall: English and American first editions

▼ 11—Pleasures of Past Times: theater, music halls, juvenilia

▼ 17—Travis & Emery: music, ballet, opera

▼ 18—Frognal: law, economics, history, caricatures

▼ 24—Alan Brett: *Vanity Fair* cartoons, topography, acts of Parliament

▼ 25—Quevedo: Spanish books

▼ 27—H. M. Fletcher: early English literature

Yet More

Other bookstores that demand a visit include:

▼

DILLON'S: The bookstore for London University; open from 9:10 A.M. to 5:30 P.M. Monday to Saturday.

DILLON'S, 82 Gower Street, WC1

▼

HATCHARD'S: Far and away the most complete of the modern booksellers. The main Hatchard's is in a town house near Fortnum & Mason and is filled with treasures. The children's book section is a good one—this is where we discovered James the Red Engine. Hatchard's also has a branch in Harvey Nichols's and in Fulham. All are open from 9:00 A.M. to 5:30 P.M. Monday to Friday and from 9:00 A.M. to 5:00 P.M. Saturday.

HATCHARD'S,
    187 Piccadilly, W1
    Harvey Nichols, 75 Knightsbridge, SW1
    150–52 Kings Road, Fulham, SW3

▼

WATERSTONE'S: A chain, not so different from B. Dalton, but with a large selection of everything and many locations near the shopping areas you automatically gravitate to. A good shop for extra guidebooks (no one can survive in London without an "A to Zed"), airplane reading books, art books, etc.

WATERSTONE'S
    88 Regent Street, W1
    99–101 Old Brompton Road, SW3
    193 Kensington High Street, W8

Collectors' note: Collectors of antiquarian books should also consult two new magazines devoted to the topic—*Driff's* and *Slightly Soiled*—which are available at Sotheran's and the Cecil Court stores. Both carry news of auctions, sales, and book fairs, not to mention gossip about booksellers.

Addictions

CHARBONNET ET WALKER: If you can't get through the day without a fix of chocolate, stop by Charbonnet et Walker, which happens to hold a royal warrant. Either the Queen has a sweet tooth, or mice, but she is rumored to do a big business in chocolate-covered creams. Sources outside of Buckingham Palace say that Charbonnet et Walker is the best chocolatier in the world. Prince Philip likes the Mocha Crisp. Prices, by the way, are fit for a king's ransom.

CHARBONNET ET WALKER, 28 Old Bond Street, W1

▼

CLARE'S: For those who adore the liquor-filled chocolates you can't buy in the United States and are illegal to import, stop by Clare's if you're in the neighborhood. They're even open on Sundays.

CLARE'S, 3 Park Road, NW1

▼

THORNTONS: If you're more the type who needs a candy fix and not a royal pedigree for your bonbons, there's a large British chain called Thorntons, which is popular all over the United Kingdom. It's not much of a tourist place, since chocolate doesn't travel, but if you need an on-the-spot sugar high, try the shop in Covent Garden.

THORNTONS, Covent Garden, Unit 2, WC2

▼

PRESTAT: Should the West End prices be all too much for you and you're looking for a shop where you can find something luxurious and grand that you can easily afford, try Prestat, right on swank South Molton Street. We stop here when we have the kids with us because the chocolate Paddington the Bear is a big fave of ours. Prestat does a mostly in-town business with chocolate telegrams and specialty sculptures, much like Kron in the United States, but Prestat is an old-fashioned fun place to get a bite, and they hold a royal warrant.

PRESTAT, 40 South Molton Street, W1

▼

H. R. HIGGINS: One of the great gifts to take back home is a tin of tea—which is okay with Customs. Coffee also can be brought back. H. R. Higgins is the "in" coffee provider, and since it's conveniently located to all our West End shopping, we always stop in for a sniff and a bag of beans. This really impresses your friends when they rave about your brew and you tell them it's from London. Ho-hum. (They do mail order.) We buy the Chagga, which comes from Tanzania and reminds us of our days staring at Mount Kilimanjaro. There are twenty-five other equally exotic brands. Travel with beans rather than grounds, and ask for your package to be wrapped in plastic in case of a leak in your suitcase. We buy the four-flavor gift pack as a house present and great $10 gift item.

H. R. HIGGINS, 42 South Molton Street, W1

▼

SAVOY HOTEL COFFEE DEPARTMENT: You'll wonder what the Boston Tea Party was all about if you happen into the coffee department of the Savoy Hotel. This department has been in biz since right before World War II and was set up specifically to sell the hotel's coffee blend to their guests who were begging for the recipe. Mick Jagger swears by it; the Queen has granted a royal warrant.

SAVOY HOTEL COFFEE DEPARTMENT, SAVOY HOTEL, 1 Savoy Hill, WC2

▼

R. TWINING & CO., LTD.: We buy all our tea at Fortnum & Mason or at R. Twining & Co., Ltd., which holds the royal warrant and is famous world over. We've been drinking their black-currant tea for a dozen years now—although the shop's best-selling tea is Earl Grey.

R. TWINING & CO., LTD., 216 The Strand, WC2

▼

DAVIDOFF: We're a bit reluctant to admit this, since we are very happily married women, but well—here goes. Whenever we are in London, we spend a few minutes at Davidoff. We do not smoke cigars and only occasionally bring back a smoke or two for our hubbies—only because the best cigars still are made with Cuban tobacky, which is illegal to import into the United States. But Davidoff is a great place to meet men. We fall in love every time we go there. Since a box of cigars costs about $200, the demographics are excellent here. This is where rich men hang out. It's a small shop, every one is very friendly, and you can play dumb and ask a handsome man to help you choose a gift for a friend. Who needs singles clubs when there's Davidoff? They also sell lighters, pipes, and smoking accessories. The perfect location makes them easy to include on your shopping itinerary.

DAVIDOFF, 35 St. James Street, SW1

▼

ALFRED DUNHILL LTD.: If Davidoff is too small for your taste, or not quite swank enough, you may want to run upstairs to Dunhill, where the humidors and cigar mavens hang out. It's much like a very fancy bank, and we buy three cigars (about $15 for the three), which are placed in a gorgeous blue box that tucks nicely in the purse. While you're at Dunhill, don't forget all their other items and the ready-to-wear line. Pipes begin at $50 and are quite a status item. British prices are exactly half the U.S. prices on the same merchandise. Dunhill holds several royal warrants.

ALFRED DUNHILL LTD., 30 Duke Street, SW1

7 ▾ HOME FURNISHINGS, ANTIQUES, AND COLLECTIBLES

English Style

While a large number of the tourists who go to London are seeking raincoats with zip-out linings and matching kilts for the kids, more and more of our friends are interested in home furnishings and antiques. The "Country English" look is as popular as "Country French," and with the recent revitalization of flowered chintz, everyone is mad for a home that looks like Balmoral.

Country English is a life-style that incorporates a compilation of colors, patterns, fabrics, and furniture styles that are both comfortable and rich. The English look in decorating represents the highest form of eclecticism, which has come to be associated with the "good life" that was, in the British Empire's heyday—the way of life for the nobility. The English look is casually elegant. The manor homes look like generations of children and golden retrievers have played in the rooms and sat on the chairs. The window curtains are never crisp and starched. The tables are always cluttered. The smell in the air is of rose gardens and rose water.

This look has taken generations to develop. However, fear not. Thanks to the foresight of a group of designers, antiques dealers, and fabric manufacturers, the English look has been packaged and is for sale in London . . . and is much cheaper than in the United States.

Many designers give Laura Ashley credit for popularizing the use of English patterns and actually sprucing up the colors to appeal to a more worldwide audience. It is true that her firm has had the largest impact on an international market. However, the popularization of the look actually goes back to the beginnings of Colefax & Fowler over fifty years ago. And the roots of the look really go back to Martha Washington.

In the 1930s in New York, "Sister" Parish (Mrs. Henry Parish II) gained fame for her style of decorating in a comfortable lived-in yet elegant style. As it so happened her good friend Nancy Lancaster was simultaneously working in London and took an interest in the firm of Colefax & Fowler, well known at the time for providing the same look, in the English tradition. When Sybil Colefax retired, Nancy Lancaster became partners with John Fowler and continued not only to promote but also to market the "English style." On either side of the Atlantic, these two powerful women influenced a design trend that has only continued to gain momentum in the 1980s.

As for the furniture, British antiques have been leaving home since the *Mayflower* crossing. In recent years, more and more big pieces of furniture have crossed over the ocean, making one wonder if there will ever be a shortage of antiques in London.

The current antiques and collectibles markets are many and varied. There is no question that you can make a find and save yourself pounds of money. There is also no question that you can get gypped. At most of the markets, you will not find fine pieces of furniture, and for this reason we have dealt with markets under a different section (see page 218). However, they are our favorite way to shop for small silver items and odd collectibles.

The best news about shopping for fabrics and furniture in London is that there are no barriers between the buyer and the seller. You don't need a resale card or a designer at your side. You don't have to pretend that you are buying for a mansion or buying a quantity of anything. You are welcome in most of the showrooms just because you want to buy. (These people are our kind of sellers!)

There are a few rules to be aware of when buying in London:

▼ British decorating and design houses are not in the business of reducing prices unless you are an established client with an open account. Be prepared to show that you are in business, have a credit rating, have at least three references from big U.S. firms where you hold open accounts, and make a minimum purchase of at least $1,000, although this varies (upward only) with some firms.

▼ Very often English design firms will not take personal orders from out-of-towners. This is especially true if the firm has an agency in the country where you wish the goods to be shipped. They will not compete with their own overseas agents. However, they will sell goods to anyone directly from their London showrooms.

▼ Be prepared to handle your own shipping.

▼ When shopping in a market such as Bermondsey, or on Portobello Road, expect to bargain. If you pay the price as marked, you will be overpaying. In this kind of circumstance, having a knowledgeable local at your side can be beneficial. The English accent may give you the bargaining power that a tourist does not have.

▼ Always deal with cash. Very often a store will offer a discount for cash transactions because they do not have to deal with credit-card fees. In the markets, only cash is accepted. Many stalls will not even take travelers checks. If the store does not offer a discount for cash, ask to see the owner and make your point.

▼ Remember that European fabrics are sold by the meter, not the yard, and that wallpaper rolls are very often double rolls, not single rolls. Always verify the width of the fabrics (most American fabrics are fifty-four inches wide), as that can affect the amount you need to purchase. If you are buying for a particular piece of furniture, take the measurements of the piece, and a photo with you. Most fabric houses have trained staff who will help you determine how much fabric is necessary for your job. If there is any question, buy extra. Yes, you might be able to find the same fabric at home, but the dye lot will be completely different and your two pieces will never match. You are safer having the extra for pillows if you don't need it for your job.

▼ When you are in the fabric house, ask if there are any close-out bins. Quite often fabrics are discontinued or half rolls are sold and the showroom cannot sell the pieces left. There just might be some wonderful leftovers that are perfect for your home or a piece of furniture you hadn't thought of re-covering. Laura Ashley is famous for its close-out bins. We have purchased wonderful fabrics for $1 a meter in this manner.

▼ When buying European wallpaper, ask about the life expectancy of the paper. Once again, printing processes sometimes are different, and the wallpaper you are dying for could in fact be printed on a paper that is not as sturdy as your needs. Many of the Laura Ashley papers are wonderful but have a life expectancy of only four to five years. They are not coated, and they absorb dirt at a rapid rate. These are considerations that every designer worries about when doing a design job. Since you will be doing it yourself, you, too, must be aware! There are Laura Ashley vinyl wallpapers, but they are made for the U.S. market and are sold through designers here.

▼ If you are buying fabrics that need trimmings to match, buy them at the same time and with the fabrics in hand. The English trimmings (fringes, ropes, tassles, etc.) are designed and colored to match the fabrics. Most of them are not available to the regular consumer in the United States. As a matter of fact, most of the wonderful English trimmings are not even imported for the designers. The French fringes seem to be more popular in the United States than are the English ones. However, the colors are vastly different. The fabric showroom will give you their best resource for these items, and be sure to see our following listings.

▼ If you are planning to buy a lot of furniture, make arrangements with a shipper before you start your spree. (See our section on shipping.) Very often the fabric houses will ship for you, but the furniture dealers prefer that you make your own arrangements. If you are buying antiques valued over £2,000 (about $3,000), you will need to have an export license from the British Customs offices. A good shipper will also help arrange this for you. It is easier to have all your goods arrive in one container than in dispersed shipments. Ask your shipper if they will pick up from a variety of sources and if there is any charge for this extra service. Be sure to get the best insurance possible on your goods. Don't save money on shipping. Shop the options, but buy the best! In areas such as this it saves to pay. And you know how we love a bargain!

▼ When buying at auction be aware that you will be bidding against dealers who know their goods and what they are worth. Do a very careful inspection of the auction items the day before and check carefully for repairs and/or replacement of parts. The technology of furniture repair has made it possible to repair and/or replace damaged parts of a piece of furniture without the untrained eye being able to see the work. If you are not buying to collect but only to enjoy, this won't matter. However, if you are collecting Georgian antiques, every repair changes the value of the piece. If the dealers are not bidding, take their clue that something is wrong. If you want a piece badly enough, however, you can very often outbid the dealers. They need to resell the piece to make a profit and therefore need to stop well under the street value for that piece. This is where you will have the advantage. You can save money and get a valuable piece of furniture/ art/carpet or collectible while having the fun of beating the dealer. There is nothing more satisfying than a good bargain!

▼ When buying period pieces, whether at auction, through a dealer, or at a stall, remember to get papers of authenticity. Any item a hundred years old or older is free of Customs duties. However, you will be asked for proof of age by the Customs officials. They are on to tricks in this area, so don't try to pass off a new tea service as antique. However, this is also a gray area in English law. If you buy a chair that is Georgian but has had some parts replaced, this would be considered a reasonable restoration and would be fine. However, if more than half of the chair has been restored so that most of the parts are new, the law is not clear, and your chair may not be considered duty-free.

▼ Don't expect to be able to buy a national treasure. Important pieces must be approved for export by the curator of the National Museum before they are granted an export license. If you are bidding against a museum in an auction it is quite possible that the work will be awarded to the museum even though you can outbid them. All countries are unwilling to let go of their finest works of art and furniture.

▼ If the work of art or piece of furniture is not wanted by the museum, be sure that the price you are paying is not more expensive (taking shipping, insurance, etc., into account) than it would be to buy a similar piece through a dealer in the United States. If it is a special, one-of-a-kind find, of course the value is there regardless of the price. But the average antiques shopper is not a pure collector and possibly could do better by buying at home. Doing your research at home before you go always is the key to a good buy.

Dealers: Fabrics/Furniture/Collectibles

I t is hard to separate the fabrics, furniture, and collectibles sources from each other. Most often a fabric showroom also will carry a line of furniture, and a furniture dealer will have an exclusive line of fabrics. Some shops specialize in home collectibles, and most showrooms carry their own selection. Therefore, we list each source for their specialty, and we will mention the other goods they carry in the showroom.

Often while shopping you will note a sign on a particular item that says, "Selected for the Design Centre of London." This tag marks that particular product as having been recognized by the British government for superior design, and in essence it grants that product a government warrant. Each year approximately two thousand products are selected for this honor. Of those two thousand, thirty receive an additional design award, the most prestigious of which is the Duke of Edinburgh's Designer's Prize. This prize has been won by many of the fabric collections that you will see in the showrooms. The award, however, is not limited to the interior-design trade. The Design Centre of London is at 28 Haymarket, very near the Piccadilly Circus tube station. It is well worth a visit to see what is happening in the world of British design and is open from 10:00 A.M. to 8:00 P.M. every day. Some products are available for sale there, and there is a very complete directory telling you where other products are being sold. We think this is a great place to pick up a gift for a "difficult" friend.

Since any reasonable person does her shopping by neighborhood (especially this kind of shopping), we have divided up the dealers by neighborhoods. Needless to say, there are thousands of dealers in London, and we didn't list all of them. But here are some must-sees:

Kings Road

The best area in which to begin shopping for fabrics and furniture is the wonderful, eclectic Kings Road. Among the teenagers with orange and purple hair, the rock music, and the eighteenth-century pubs can be found some of London's most popular design studios. Some are more famous than others, and these we have described in more detail. However, there are so many in this particular chic area that we urge you to walk and explore the streets of Fulham Road, Lower Sloane Street, Pimlico Road, Kings Road, and the smaller streets surrounding Sloane Square.

▼

DESIGNER'S GUILD has always been one of our faves. Tricia Guild has a unique and subtle way with color and design that makes her fabrics English but with a French flair. The fabrics also are coordinated with an accessory line that is housed next door and includes sheets, towels, padded hangers, sachets, pottery, lampshades, and other fun items. The work is presented in actual settings, which helps the less imaginative buyer realize how to mix and match all the wonderful patterns and colors. We have often thought about moving into the showroom but realize that there are not enough closets!

DESIGNER'S GUILD, 271 and 277 Kings Road, SW3

▼

OSBORNE & LITTLE is not far away and is one of the most important design houses for the English look. The firm began as antiquarian booksellers, with a sideline of handprinted wallpapers. However, when Sir Peter Osborne and his brother-in-law Anthony Little won the Council of Industrial Design Award for their first wallpaper collection in 1968, they began a revolution in the interior design and manufacturing business. Shortly after, the firm gave up the interior-design aspect of the business to concentrate on the design and production of fine English wallpapers and fabrics. Osborne & Little designs are wonderful because they are always based in history but not limited by it. A charming English botanical print might be reinterpreted in bolder colors. A whole line of wallpapers reflects the paint effects of marbleizing and stippling found in old Italian villas. Because they are now machine-produced, the fabrics and wallpapers are even affordable, running an average of $18 per roll and $20 per meter. The showroom is quiet and dignified, just the kind of place where you might like to have high tea.

OSBORNE & LITTLE, 304 Kings Road, SW3

▼

JEREMY is a jewel of an antiques shop where you won't find tons of anything, but what you will find will be worth it.

JEREMY, 255 Kings Road, SW3

▼

NOTE: Our other favorite antiques shops to stop into while on Kings Road include DAVID TRON (No. 275), CARLTON HOBBS (No. 533), GALLERY 360 (No. 564), and GUINEVERE (No. 578).

▼

CHARLES HAMMOND LIMITED has been providing the best in eighteenth-century antiques, custom upholstery, exclusive fabrics, prints, accessories, *objets d'art,* and interior design services since the firm's founding in 1907. The designer room of the showroom is a wonderful resource for learning how to put together the English look complete with trimmings and accessories.

CHARLES HAMMOND LIMITED, 165 Sloane Street, SW1

▼

L. M. KINCOME DESIGN LTD. specializes in custom-made sofas. However, they also carry the Manuel Canovas line of fabrics and a selection of antique furniture and accessories. At their Walton Street showroom they exhibit their fabric lines (Boussac, Percheron, Tissunique, Fontaine Nobilis, and Pallu & Lake, among others) as an exhibition of style and design that is quite informative and beautiful. The Fulham Road shop specializes more in sofa production and design.

L. M. KINCOME DESIGN LTD.
  13 Walton Street, SW3
  304 Fulham Road, SW10

▼

ZOFFANY LTD. has a showroom specializing in wallcoverings including their own Zoffany Print collection, and Alber Van Luit. They also carry a line of antique furniture, upholstered pieces, and accessories. Especially interesting are their antique lampbases. Motcomb Street intersects Lowndes Street and is reachable by walking from Sloane Street to Cadogan Place, left on Lowndes, and right on Motcomb.

ZOFFANY LTD., 27A Motcomb Street, SW1

▼

HOTSPUR considered by many antiques lovers to be the best dealer in London, is housed in a beautiful Regency house. Their stock is small, but all of the pieces are quality.

HOTSPUR, 14 Lowndes Street, SW1

▼

GLAISHER & NASH counts as one of the upper crust of antiques dealers in London. They specialize in English eighteenth- and early-nineteenth-century pieces of elegance and quality. Their prices are high, but when you buy a piece here, you have the comfort of knowing that it is special.

GLAISHER & NASH, Lowndes Lodge, Cadogan Place, SW1

CLARE HOUSE is not the home of the Queen Mother or part of the firm Clarence House, but it's still a great find. We have often wondered over the years of being fans of Elizabeth Hanley's incredible lamps, if she decided to settle on Elizabeth Street because of her name, or if the street were named after her. She certainly is famous enough. We've never asked and probably never will because every time we visit her shop we are so struck with the wonderful craftsmanship of her lamps and shades that our minds get carried away with fantasies of buying everything. We are not the only shoppers who crave the Hanley touch, for she also holds a royal warrant. Elizabeth Hanley is actually a Michigan- (yes, U.S.A.) born and Parsons School of Design–trained designer who has made England her home. She can create a lamp out of practically any kind of vase or urn and has some of her own for sale in the shop. Wait till we turn Aunt Sadie on to her. . . . Her lampshades are custom-designed to fit the base and are made out of the finest of Chinese, French, or Belgian silks and moires. Of course, she will ship.

CLARE HOUSE, 35 Elizabeth Street, SW1

▼

JANE CHURCHILL. The fabric line designed by Jane Churchill was once described as being English in feeling (it goes with her last name). It's higher in cost than Laura Ashley's but with a younger look than Colefax & Fowler. If this doesn't suit your needs, nothing will. As the wife of the younger brother of the Duke of Marlborough, Ms. Churchill has certainly had firsthand exposure to English style. She runs an international design business along with selling and designing her own fabric and wallpaper lines.

JANE CHURCHILL, 81 Pimlico Road, SW1

West End

COLEFAX & FOWLER is located, appropriately, near South Molton Street and Old Bond Street—home to all the best designers. Entering the Colefax & Fowler showrooms is like taking a step into an English country home. The building was built in 1766 by Sir Jeffrey Wyattville and is clearly being held together with chintz. Inside, the rooms are the size of small sitting rooms, the carpet is worn, and the furnishings are old. However, this is all part of the mystique. Upstairs is housed the most magnificent collection of English chintzes ever to be desired by an Anglophile. Every year their designers bring out a new collection of fabrics and wallpapers more beautiful than the previous year's—assuming you like the look, of course. Sybil Colefax, the wonderful socialite who began the firm with the incredibly talented interior designer John Fowler, has long been absent from the business, having passed her interest on to Nancy Lancaster in the 1940s. John Fowler passed away in the late 1970s. However, their firm has become an institution and is run by the charming Tom Parr, who oversees his teams of designers while they carry out design jobs around the world. Casual shoppers are welcome to come in and browse, or to take home some of the gorgeous fabrics. The sales staff is young and pleasant, happy to help you match curtains to upholstery fabrics. Don't expect to buy those pieces you "should have bought" when you get home, however. Colefax & Fowler U.S.A. frowns on competing with their overseas agents. If you want it in London, buy it in London.

COLEFAX & FOWLER, 3A Brook Street, W1

▼

MALLETT & SON remains one of the finest antiques dealers in London after 120 years of being in business. Originally begun as an antiques shop by John Mallett and his son Walter in Bath in 1865, it was moved to its present address in 1908. The Mallett family left the business in 1930, and it is now privately owned. Just as Colefax & Fowler promotes the unmistakable rumpled elegant English look, so Mallett & Son shows the most proper Englishman how to look like the richest, in a not very rumpled way. In the eleven high-ceilinged, flower-filled display rooms are a collection of breath-taking dining-room, living-room, sitting-room, and library furniture put together in such absolute perfection that you feel a qualm about wanting to buy one piece and not the whole room—that is until you ask the price of just one piece. The furniture is undeniably some of the finest you will find assembled in one shop, and the prices are equally *cher*. Mallett & Son sells millions of dollars of furniture a year, much of it to Americans, and maintains an equally massive inventory. Managing directors Peter Maitland and David Nickerson pick and approve every piece of furniture that comes in and goes out of their shops. Every detail is attended to, down to the placement of accessories. Across the street at 2 Davies Street is the "bargain" Mallett & Son. At least the prices on the furniture and accessories in what is called the Bourdon house are a touch less expensive. Pieces of furniture and accessory items that do not sell have been known to end up on consignment on Portobello Road. Mallett & Son is not a decorating firm but will do entire homes in conjunction with a designer they recommend, or the client's own.

But of course.

MALLETT & SON, 40 New Bond Street, W1

▼

PALLU & LAKE. Founded in 1927 by Pierre Maisonneuve, Pallu & Lake has become known for its wonderful collection of handprinted damasks, brocades, and chintzes. They represent French, English, and American fabric lines of exceptional quality, including Casals, Zumsteg, and Brunswig & Fils. If you've got it, this is the place to spend it.

PALLU & LAKE, 18 Newman Street, W1

▼

CVP DESIGNS LTD. Zandra Rhodes is one of our favorite designers because of her ability to combine fantasy with color and pattern. In this case, CVP Designs carries her at-home collection of fabrics and matching wallpapers. Fabrics include cottons, voiles, satins, linen, moires, and silks, all of which are printed with lilies, swirls, and abstract images from her wonderful imagination. CVP also carries a line of their own fabrics coordinated with wallpaper.

CVP DESIGNS LTD., 5 Weighthouse Street, W1

▼

LAURA ASHLEY recently completed the largest shop to date in London on Regent Street. Two floors of the complete clothing, wallcovering, fabric, and accessories lines are shown off in sample room settings that will make you want to move in. Note the new line that is totally different: The Bloomsbury Collection. Very 1930's; '50's and New Wave.

LAURA ASHLEY
   256–58 Regent Street, W1
   183 Sloane Street, SW1
   157 Fulham Road, SW3
   35 Bow Street, WC2
   71–75 Lower Sloane Street, SW1

▼

TISSUNIQUE LTD. is on a side street that intersects Regent Street before you reach Oxford Street. It is an unusual location for a fabric firm, but when you have a royal warrant and a fabric line as unique as Tissunique's, who cares where you are located? Since its founding in 1967, the firm has grown and expanded from a French importing firm to one that also prints its own line of English antiques fabrics. We suggest you call first to see if the showroom is open to the public, and if not, where to find their collection. Sometimes you can get in; sometimes not. It depends on how convincing your story is and how much you are buying.

TISSUNIQUE LTD., 10 Princes Street, W1

▼

WARNER & SONS LTD. also has a royal warrant and contains, in its extensive archives of textile samples, as much a history of the silk industry in England as any museum. Benjamin Warner began the firm in 1870 as a silk-weaving company. As a matter of fact, Warner & Sons still uses the original silk-weaving jacquard hand looms for some of its work. The archives document over thirty thousand fabrics by name of designer, year designed, and a sample of the fabric where possible. Warner will reproduce any of the designs in their archives for a minimum order of 120 meters per colorway. They will also custom-design a fabric for your job if a reproduction is not to your liking. Getting into the showroom is difficult if you are not in the design business. However, if you have an important commission for them, you should have no problem.

WARNER & SONS LTD., 7–11 Noel Street, W1

▼

G. P. & J. BAKER LIMITED is a large distributor of fabrics to the trade and Her Majesty the Queen. The showroom is open to the public, however, and you can pick out what you would like to order. The fabrics are carried by many of the department stores and through select interior designers. Baker has a long history of trading, dating back to before 1884, when the company was officially formed. The Persian prints, on which the original collections were based, still are in the Baker archives. The designs have a distinct influence from the Far East, with an emphasis on floral patterns.

G. P. & J. BAKER LIMITED, 17–18 Berners Street, W1

▼

ARTHUR SANDERSON & SONS LIMITED had its 125th anniversary in 1985; they celebrated with an exhibit of its past designs. Back in 1860, Arthur Sanderson decided that what the English needed was a little of what the French already had—and we are not talking pâté! He began his firm to import French wallhangings to the Brits. As this did not satisfy the demand, he opened his own handblock printing factory in 1897. Shortly after his death, his sons decided to expand again and took over the printing presses of Jeffrey & Co., which was also printing the work of William Morris. In 1940 they bought the original designs of William Morris and to this day are still reprinting these handblock prints. Sanderson is now owned by a much larger company (Reed International) but still retains the original quality that made them famous and for which they received a royal warrant.

ARTHUR SANDERSON & SONS LIMITED, 52 Berners Street, W1

▼

COLE & SON LIMITED still handprints many of their wallcoverings from an extensive (over three thousand) collection of wood blocks dating back as far as the eighteenth century. If you have or are building your own palace, Cole has the original blocks used to print the wallpaper for Kensington Palace, the Brighton Pavilion, Hampton Court, and the Houses of Parliament. They even welcome mail order if you can't make it to London during your construction.

COLE & SON LIMITED, 18 Mortimer Street, W1

▼

HENRY NEWBERY & COMPANY LIMITED supplies all the trimmings—and we don't mean turkey. No English fabric looks complete without its tassles, fringe, or braid attached. Although Newbery sells to the trade only, they are happy to allow you to browse through their catalogues and will help you find the right source for purchasing its goods. They carry mostly British trimmings in stock but will happily reproduce your existing worn braid if they don't carry it.

HENRY NEWBERY & COMPANY LIMITED, 51–55 Mortimer Street, W1

▼

DISTINCTIVE TRIMMINGS COMPANY is not in the same neighborhood but is a fabulous resource for discount trimmings! The shop has been there for twenty years and is run by a charming husband-and-wife team. They buy end lots of trimmings and fabrics from some of the famous resources we have listed, and discount them. The goods are incredible and the prices even better. You can save at least half the cost of the trimmings by buying them here. One caution: You must pay in cash, and goods are not returnable. However, they will ship to the United States and other countries.

DISTINCTIVE TRIMMINGS COMPANY, 17 Kensington Church Street, W8

▼

Mount Street is not only where you will find The Connaught, but also where you can find a group of excellent antiques shops including the prestigious Stair & Company. Our favorites on this street include JOHN KEIL (No. 25), BARLING OF MOUNT STREET (No. 112), BLAIRMAN AND SONS (No. 119), STAIR & COMPANY (No. 120), and JOHN SPARKS LIMITED (No. 128).

▼

CHRISTOPHER GIBBS attracts the jet set of antiques buyers who have yachts to furnish and country homes to fill. This large and well-stocked shop is a wonderful antithesis to Mallett & Son as far as its clientele.

CHRISTOPHER GIBBS, 118 New Bond Street, W1

▼

S. J. PHILLIPS LIMITED is a holder of a royal warrant. Founded in 1869, S. J. Phillips has gained its reputation for a superb collection of antique jewelry, silver, porcelain, perfume bottles, and other collectibles.

S. J. PHILLIPS LIMITED, 139 New Bond Street, W1

Knightsbridge/Chelsea

NORMAN ADAMS has a wonderful location, being directly adjacent to Harrods. The merchandise, unlike Harrods, is not trendy. Nor is it very new. In fact, the stock is not even very large; however, whatever it lacks in size and zip it makes up for in elegance and quality. Very British down to the last eighteenth-century Chippendale chair!

NORMAN ADAMS, 8–10 Hans Road, SW3

▼

C. FREDERICKS carries seventeenth- and eighteenth-century antiques but with price tags that are affordable.

C. FREDERICKS, 92 Fulham Road, SW3

▼

RICHARD COURTNEY has a very large shop compared to some of the other antiques shops in London and has an equally good collection of eighteenth-century English furniture.

RICHARD COURTNEY, 112–14 Fulham Road, SW3

▼

MARY FOX LINTON does not have antiques, seventeenth-century or otherwise! However, she does have a wonderful contemporary design

concept and showroom that are refreshing.
When you can no longer look an ormolu in
the gilding, come here to refresh your eyes.

MARY FOX LINTON, 249 Fulham Road, SW3

Sloane Square (Knightsbridge/Chelsea/ Belgravia)

Pimlico Road is just south of Sloane Square
and is not noted for being an exceptional
long street. Considering that, it is amazing to
us how many antiques and design shops are on
this street. Some of our favorites not to miss
include CHRISTOPHER HODSOLL (No. 69),
WESTENHOLZ KIME (No. 70), ROSS HAM-
ILTON (No. 73), LOOT (Nos. 76–78), JANE
CHURCHILL (No. 81), BENNISON (No.
91), BOX HOUSE ANTIQUES (No. 105),
and LENNOX MONEY ANTIQUES (No.
105).

▼

NICHOLAS HASLAM is on a small street
that intersects Pimlico Road and Sloane Square.
His showroom is a wonderful collection of
every period and style, with preference to none.
The truth is that Nicky Haslam is one of London's more sought-after designers, with a very
versatile design ability. He will do both small
and large jobs, but you must have an appointment to meet with him. We especially like his
style because he has lived and trained in both
America and England, and his understanding
of the two life-styles makes him particularly
gifted in adapting each for the other.

NICHOLAS HASLAM, 12 Holbein Place, SW1

Collectibles

> *St. George he was for England,*
> *And before he killed the dragon*
> *He drank a pint of English ale,*
> *Out of an English flagon.*

We were offered that very flagon several times on our first visit to London, and several times again each time we ventured off to check out the collectibles market. But after the first few oh-so-convincing pitches, we began to catch on. Shopping for the real thing in London is a tricky business.

As time went on, we came to learn that:

▼ England is indeed a nation of shopkeepers.

▼ Many of the shops they keep are crammed with collectibles.

▼ Some of these collectibles are as real as England's St. George's flagon or that grand old American collectible, the Brooklyn Bridge.

The collectibles shops we list in this section, on the other hand, have stood the test of time—they are the real thing. Some are famous, others are our personal finds. When we checked them last, they were fresh out of flagons (thankfully). Instead, they offered books as sensuous to the touch as they are titillating to the mind, dolls so beautiful that they brought a tear even to our cynical eye, and toy soldiers as spiffy as anything you'll see strutting around West Point ... but these little metal guys are just a tad older than the West Point version.

While furniture, fountain pens, and fine art also are available here (see page 233), and while we know full well that people are capable of collecting *anything*, we wanted to give you at least a small taste of the tempting collectibles London has to offer to those who know that London is the first city of the world for collectors.

Collectors of antiquarian books, maps, and autographs, please see page 182.

Coins and Medals

SPINK & SON LTD.: If you've yearned for those giltzy costume jewelry medals, you'll all-out faint and go stark raving mad with delight when you see the original medals that the current fad was based on. Why was a man always so dashing in his uniform? Because of his medals, of course. And chances are, they came from Spink's. Spink's has tremendous stock in Orientalia, paperweights, and Greek and Roman coins as well as an ample supply of early English hammered coins in gold and silver and milled pieces dating back to the late 1600s; however, as Hamley's is to toys, so Spink's is to medals. Along with sheer size, Spink offers an expertise born of creating decorations for Great Britain and sixty-five other countries.

Most recently Spink's offered, among other treasures, a boxed group of four medals, including the Victoria Cross, twelve medals from various European countries awarded to Queen Victoria's footman, and a group of nineteen medals awarded in connection with the Sepoy Mutiny of 1857–58. The firm also has an extensive collection of miniature medals, correct in every detail.

In addition to fashioning the medals, Spink also has world-class experience in mounting and displaying them and even publishes a guide to wearing them. (Medals on your evening gown? Wear on sash, please. Medals on your safari jacket? Hmmmm.) The company also issues the monthly *Spink Numismatic Circular,* which includes large sections on medals, orders, and decorations. Hours: 9:30 A.M. to 5:30 P.M.

SPINK & SON LTD., 5–7 King Street, St. James's, SW1

▼

B. A. SEABY LTD.: While Seaby's recently moved from their digs on Margaret Street to nearby Cavendish Square, their service remains impeccable. Early coins bearing the likenesses of royalty from Corinth, Phoenicia, and Rome rub shoulders with tradesmen's tokens issued by coppers in Dover and fishmongers in Margate, yet each is presented with care, panache, and the necessary historical background.

The firm is deep in antiquarian coins, and that interest has led to sidelines such as collections of jewelry and copperplate from ancient Greece, Rome, and Jerusalem. Seaby's publishes a magazine, the bimonthly *Coin & Medal Bulletin,* which is likely to contain scholarly pieces related to archaeological finds, as well as price lists of coins. Hours: Monday to Friday, 9:30 A.M. to 5:00 P.M.

B. A. SEABY LTD., 8 Cavendish Square, W1

▼

FORMAN PICCADILLY LTD.: A small shop on the edge of Mayfair, Forman's specializes in medals but also sells carved ivories made by soldiers and sailors, and other specialized antiquities. But it's the gorgeous colored ribbons and enamel medals that drew us into the shop, to peer hungrily into the large wooden case. If you brush up on your Russian, you can read the inscriptions on medals awarded by the Czar. We're fond of Napoleonic medals, complete with ribbons or sashes, and wouldn't mind owning the Bulgarian Order of Civil Merit—awarded before World War I, still perfect on its willow green, rose, and white ribbon—about $400.

FORMAN PICCADILLY LTD., 92 Piccadilly, W1

ARMADA ANTIQUES: One of two important stalls in Gray's Antiques Market, Armada Antiques is crammed with militaria of all kinds. Armada Antiques (Stand 122) carries mostly edged weapons such as stilettos and sabers but also has some medals. For the total effect, shop also at Seidler (Stand 120)—together these two fabulous dealers give you a nice overview.

ARMADA ANTIQUES, Gray's Antiques Market, Stand 122, 58 Davies Street, W1

C. F. SEIDLER: Seidler (Stand 120) places greater emphasis on medals, badges, and orders. The owner will search for particular pieces and also is helpful on shipping oddly shaped pieces, such as swords. Since Gray's guarantees the authenticity of any item paid for by check (up to £1,000), these shops transcend the usual stall entrepreneurs. Hours: Monday to Friday, 10:00 A.M. to 6:00 P.M.

C. F. SEIDLER, Gray's Antiques Market, Stand 120, 58 Davies Street, W1

THE ARCHES: Soaring rents have forced small-time dealers out of Cutler Street, long a Sunday-morning fixture at the Petticoat Lane market; however, inexpensive coins still are available by the bagful at The Arches on Villiers Street, beneath the Charing Cross Road tube stop. This is where we got the coin collection for Aaron (age seven)—twenty coins from around the world for about $1.50. This is decidedly low-end, and major collectors will not be interested; however, the place is a lot of fun. In addition to coins, there are comic books, cigarette cards, military insignia, and used romance novels in this covey of little dealers nestled beside the tube station. Most proprietors are open Monday to Saturday from 9:00 A.M. to 6:00 P.M.

THE ARCHES, Villiers Street, WC2

▼

Collectors' Note: In addition to the Spink and Seaby publications, there's also a periodical called *Coin Monthly*.

Scientific Instruments

TREVOR PHILIPS & SONS LTD.: Philips recently moved from Brighton to tony Jermyn Street, the fruits of serving a large and satisfied clientele for many years. A smaller version of Arthur Middleton's (see a following listing), Philips carries gyroscopes, English drafting instruments, sundials, stethoscopes, and a selection of books about scientific instruments.

Recent finds include:

▼ a vapor lamp inhaler made about 1900 in New York, complete with a bottle of fluid to cure "whooping cough, croup, asthma or cattarrh"

▼ a field surgeon's amputation kit made in Paris in the midnineteenth century, complete with saw, dissecting forceps, scalpels, and cauterizer

The shop also carries miniature instruments, such as pocket botanical microscopes, pocket globes, and exquisite orreries—small clockwork representations of the solar system. Hours: Monday to Friday, 10:00 A.M. to 6:00 P.M.

TREVOR PHILIPS & SONS LTD., 75A Jermyn Street, SW1

▼

STEPHEN O'DONNELL: An interest in navigation led O'Donnell to begin collecting and restoring sextants, spyglasses, and telescopes. By this time, his collection of both is extensive, as is a fairly new sideline in antique postage scales. The scales run from $150 to $1,000, while telescopes start at $250 and sextants run anywhere from $700 to $3,000. Hours: Monday to Friday, 10:00 A.M. to 6:00 P.M.

STEPHEN O'DONNELL, Gray's Antiques Market, Stand 156, 58 Davies Street, W1

▼

ARTHUR MIDDLETON: Located between Leicester Square and Covent Garden, this shop is chockablock with antique clocks, telescopes, surgical instruments, and early dental equipment, all in splendid condition. Even if you're not a collector, you'll enjoy the spit and polish of these fascinating pieces. Hours: Monday to Friday, 10:00 A.M. to 6:00 P.M.; Saturday, 11:00 A.M. to 5:30 P.M.

ARTHUR MIDDLETON, 12 New Row, WC2

▼

HARRIET WYNTER: This dealer specializes in astronomical and navigational instruments—orreries, astrolabes, sextants, globes, etc. She shows her wares by appointment only. Call 352-6494.

HARRIET WYNTER, 50 Redcliffe Road, SW10

Stamps

Just as Nassau Street is home to dozens of stamp dealers in New York City, so the Strand (and offshoots such as King Street and Cecil Court) are magnets for philatelists in London. All the shops are in the Strand area, although we label some as in Charing Cross Road/Covent Garden—this is the same neighborhood and is an easy walk.

STRAND AREA

STANLEY GIBBONS LTD.: The shop has the largest collection of British Empire stamp material in the world as well as the most complete selection of stamp accessories—albums, tweezers, and perforation gauges, as well as its own well-researched catalogues.

Gibbons also sells extraordinary philatelic material. On our most recent visit, we saw an experimental version of the Penny Black, the first stamp ever issued. This particular test design (there were several) has the letters "V" and "R" in the upper left- and right-hand corners (for Victoria Regina—Queen Victoria), whereas the actual Penny Black carries decorative Maltese crosses.

As a counterpoint to this Stamp That Never Was, we were also shown an issued but unused full block of twelve of the Twopenny Blue with the original gum. Brilliantly colored and lettered "SG-TL" in the lower left- and right-hand corners (to prevent counterfeiting), this museum-quality piece was offered at a mere $20,000.

Such lofty material is viewed in private, secure surroundings on the second floor. On a more mundane level—the ground floor—Gibbons stocks a few topics such as birds and the Royal Family and has specialists in first-day covers, plate blocks, precancels, overprints, color variations, etc. The firm gave up the coin and medal business several years ago but now carries a full selection of postcards and pertinent literature.

Gibbons is impossibly famous and therefore impossibly crowded—you may get less service, and they may not have what you are looking for. Don't be afraid to wander around the neighborhood and try the competition. Smaller and less-known dealers may be more fun.

STANLEY GIBBONS LTD., 399 Strand, WC2

▼

CAMEO STAMP CENTRE: Cameo is the second-largest stamp shop on the Strand and keeps tabs on philatelic gems with its Computastamp service. Customers can enter "want lists" electronically, and Cameo will inform them when they find the stamp, plate block, sheet, or first-day cover in question. The firm also publishes a catalogue and offers mail-order sales.

CAMEO STAMP CENTRE, 75 Strand, WC2

▼

DAVID BRANDON: The second in a row of three shops across from Gibbons, Brandon has a large stock of classic material and is particularly up on postal history items of Great Britain and the Continent.

DAVID BRANDON, 77 Strand, WC2

▼

STRAND STAMPS: Three dealers operate as Strand and deal in Commonwealth material. Even though Gibbons has a larger stock in this area, the Strand dealers often come up with particular items from India or Australia that the big kid on the block doesn't stock. Moreover, Strand isn't pricey and is particularly patient with younger collectors. If you've gone to the trouble to seek the neighborhood, don't blow it now—you must stop in here.

STRAND STAMPS, 79 Strand, WC2

CHARING CROSS ROAD / COVENT GARDEN

LONDON INTERNATIONAL STAMP CENTRE: The LISC is actually an umbrella organization for forty different dealers, each with a different specialty—airmail, French Colonies, 1952 Coronation color variations, etc. The Centre also holds auctions every two weeks, with all items available for viewing three days in advance.

LONDON INTERNATIONAL STAMP CENTRE, 27 King Street, WC2

▼

CECIL COURT STAMP CO.: While Cecil Court is crowded with bookshops, this particular store is a haven for topical collectors—

philatelists who collect stamps in a given category, such as birds, the Vietnam War, Winston Churchill, the Olympics, etc. Most shops refuse to display their stock this way, instead going from catalogue order by country.

CECIL COURT STAMP CO., 6 Cecil Court, WC2

Collectors' and shoppers' note: All these shops are open Monday to Friday from 10:00 A.M. to 5:00 P.M. (Gibbons opens at 9:00 A.M.) and Saturday (the same hours) except for David Brandon (closed all day) and Strand and Gibbons, which close at 1:00 P.M.

There are also several periodicals related to stamps, including *Stamp News,* and collectors also should keep in mind the large auction houses. Phillips has a postage stamp auction nearly every Thursday, and Christie's recently offered a collection that included proofs and essays from Bradbury, Wilkinson & Co., which has printed British stamps and bank notes for nearly 150 years.

HARMER'S: 91 New Bond Street, W1
PHILLIPS: 7 Blenheim Street, New Bond Street, W1
SOTHEBY'S: 34–35 New Bond Street, W1
SPINK & SON LTD.: 5–7 King Street, St. James, SW1
CHRISTIE'S: 8 King Street, St. James, SW1

Dolls and Toys

POLLOCK'S TOY MUSEUM: Nearly a hundred years ago, Robert Louis Stevenson wrote, "If you love art, folly, or the bright eyes of children, speed to Pollock's." Thousands still do and find a treasure island of toys housed in two adjoining buildings overflowing with dolls, teddy bears, tin toys, puppets, and folk toys from Europe, India, Africa, China, and Japan.

Exhibits of mechanical toys and construction sets fill the lower floor of Pollock's Toy Museum, and the second story has exhibits of the paper "toy theaters" and cut-out actors and actresses that have fired the imagination of British children for generations.

In addition to the museum, there's a second Pollock's, a toy shop, set up in Covent Garden when the original was destroyed in the Blitz. The shop sells the theaters, popguns, and dolls, and there's no admission charge. The shop is open Monday to Saturday from 10:00 A.M. to 8:00 P.M.

The museum is at the corner of Scala and Whitfield streets, one block from the sunny Goodge Street tube stop on the Northern Line, and is open Monday to Saturday from 10:00 A.M. to 5:00 P.M. Admission is 50 pence for adults and 20 pence for children and students. The museum also holds parties for up to thirty children.

POLLOCK'S TOY MUSEUM, 1 Scala Street, W1

POLLOCK'S TOY THEATRES, 44 The Market, Covent Garden, WC2

▼

LONDON TOY AND MODEL MUSEUM:
In a case devoted to dolls based on the Royal Family, a German-made Princess Elizabeth doll, from 1932, sits next to a Princess Anne doll made in 1953.

This royal rite of passage from child to queen is nearly overshadowed by other dolls at the museum—poured wax dolls; bisque (china) dolls; a wax-headed Quaker lady in her original costume from 1840; and a Topsy Turvy doll, which can be either white or black, depending on the owner's fancy.

In addition to dolls, the museum has twenty-five thousand Matchbox and Corgi miniature cars, several working rocking horses, a collection of Paddington bears, an entire room of toy trains, and a display of toy soldiers from Pierce Carlson (see later listing).

The latest addition is the Baywest exhibit, a computer-controlled model of a thousand houses, fifty thousand lights, a railway system, and a helicopter, and that requires a separate admission charge. There also are two smaller coin-operated versions by the same designer—a snow scene and a small town at twilight.

Hours: Tuesday to Saturday, 10:00 A.M. to 5:30. P.M.; Sunday, 11:00 A.M. to 5:00 P.M. Admission charge.

LONDON TOY AND MODEL MUSEUM, 23 Craven Hill Road, W2

Collectors' note: *Doll & Toy World* covers these collectibles on a monthly basis, as does *Antique Toy World.*

Toy Soldiers

UNDER TWO FLAGS: By the time toy soldiers became popular in America (during World War II), English children were celebrating the fiftieth anniversary of William Britain & Co. Britain's went into the toy soldier business in 1893, creating a set of the Life Guards to honor Queen Victoria's forthcoming Diamond Jubilee in 1897.

Many Britain sets (including the first) are available at Under Two Flags on colorful St. Christopher's Place between Wigmore and Regent streets. The store also offers inexpensive lead soldiers for do-it-yourself painters; a selection of military books; magazines and prints; bronzes; porcelains; and curios, such as a chess set made of toy soldiers.

Hours: Monday to Saturday, 10:00 A.M. to 6:00 P.M.

UNDER TWO FLAGS, 4 St. Christopher's Place, W1

▼

PIERCE CARLSON: While most of the 1984–85 exhibition arranged by expert James Opie for the London Toy and Model Museum is gone, a windowful of Britain's soldiers still is on loan from Pierce Carlson. He runs a retail shop near the British Model Soldier Society and also maintains a stall on Portobello Road.

PIERCE CARLSON
9 Nichols Green, W5
Portobello Road Market, Stall 27

Collectors' note: Aside from Carlson's collection at the London Toy and Model Museum, the Bethnal Green Museum of Childhood (Cambridge Heath Road, E2) has many of the rarest Britains on permanent display. Collectors should also consult the monthly *Military Modelling Magazine,* contact the British Model Soldier Society (22 Lynwood Road, Ealing, W5), and check in with Phillips, which auctions toy soldiers every two months.

Miscellaneous note: While there are specialty publications for every collectible but scientific instruments, two British periodicals cover collectibles in general: *Collectors Mart* and *Collectors Gazette.* These are filled with ads for cigarette cards (the British equivalent of baseball cards), "advertiques" (specialty advertising paraphernalia, such as ashtrays), porcelain bottles of spirits, and pre-1960 boxed sets of Lego—with the original instructions, of course.

Antiques Centers, Fairs, and Markets

I f you have the collecting bug in your soul, then going to the chic antiques shops we have listed may not satisfy your urge to make a deal. Not to worry, London also has a number of antiques markets and seasonal fairs that are well worth visiting if you can schedule your trip to coincide with them.

The antiques fairs are run by different organizations, and the dates change from year to year. Therefore we have listed them by month only. We suggest that you write either the British Tourist Authority or the group itself early in the year for specific dates.

January

WEST LONDON ANTIQUES FAIR, Kensington Town Hall off Kensington High Street, W8, is one of two fairs run by the Penman Antiques Fairs Company, the other one being the Chelsea Antiques Fair. This fair, like the Chelsea, is held twice yearly (August is the second time) and attracts good-quality dealers. To find their specific dates, write to Penman Antiques Fairs Company, Cockhaise Mill, Lindfield, Haywards Heath, Sussex, England.

June

GROSVENOR HOUSE ANTIQUES FAIR, Grosvenor House Hotel, Park Lane, is one of the best antiques fairs held in London and is timed each year to run after the Derby and before Ascot and Wimbledon. The top antiques dealers from all over Britain are invited to exhibit their best pieces, and everything except paintings has to be over a hundred years old. A committee reviews all items for authenticity. This is also one of the top social events of the season, and watching the crowds is as much fun as examining the antiquities— some are the same vintage.

▼

INTERNATIONAL CERAMICS FAIR, Dorchester Hotel, Park Lane, is a relatively new addition to the fair scene but has become an annual event with a substantial following. The fair usually coincides with the Grosvenor House Antiques Fair because they complement each other. Some of the antique glass pieces on exhibit here are so delicate that the technique of getting them from the fair to your home would pose an interesting problem. All forms of ceramicsware are on exhibit, including those from other countries.

▼

ANTIQUARIAN BOOK FAIR, Park Lane, Piccadilly, does not have much to do with furnishings; however, no good library would be complete without a rare book or two in its collection. Collectors and dealers swap stories and collection items, including book illustrations and prints.

September

CHELSEA ANTIQUES FAIR, Chelsea Old Town Hall, Kings Road, SW3, is held twice yearly, in March and September. Our favorite time to go is September because the weather usually is wonderful and most of the tourists have left town. However, we must admit that the March fair is not as crowded, and better deals might be made then. This fair has been going on for over 60 years and probably will continue for another 260. See our earlier entry for the address of Penman Antiques Fairs to find out the exact dates of this event.

▼

THE BURLINGTON HOUSE FAIR, The
Royal Academy of Arts, Piccadilly, W1, is a
fair for antiques dealers but is open to the
public. All works of art and antiques are vet-
ted (reviewed for authenticity) and of superior
quality. The pieces are international and not
strictly limited to England. For information
ask your concierge for dates of the next one,
write to the Burlington House Fair, 10–16
Elm Street, London WC1X, or call 01-278-2345.

Antiques and Collectibles Supermarkets

A ntiques supermarkets have been set up to
give the smaller but established dealers a
permanent place to set up and display
their wares. They are covered shopping
centers for antiques, collectibles, and junk. The
fun is figuring out which is which. Very often
the dealer stalls change, so we hesitate to recommend any one dealer. However, the buildings are not going anywhere fast, and we highly
recommend the adventure on a rainy day. The
other advantage to shopping at a covered market is that very often other services are offered: There are repair shops at Grays, *bureaux
de change* at Antiquarius and Grays, and places
to eat at all of them.

▼

**GRAYS IN DAVIES MEWS, GRAYS IN
DAVIES STREET:** These two buildings,
located on the opposite ends of the same block,
house over three hundred antiques stalls con-
taining every variety of item, large and small.

Davies Street conveniently intersects South Molton Street at one end and Brook Street at the other, placing it directly in the heart of the big-name-designer section of London. When you need a break from fashion, it is easy to breeze over to Grays and rest your eyes on some breath-taking antique jewelry, bound to coordinate with any purchase you have made on Bond Street. Don't miss the river tributary that runs decoratively through the basement of the Davies Mews building. The shops are open Monday to Friday from 10:00 A.M. to 6:00 P.M. only. You can grab a bite in the cute cafe on the lowest floor.

GRAYS
1–7 Davies Mews, W1
58 Davies Street, W1

▼

ALFIE'S: is under the same ownership as Grays and houses another 150 stalls. The building in which it is located was a run-down department store and has been rehabed well. Open Monday to Saturday from 10:00 A.M. to 6:00 P.M.

ALFIE'S, 13–25 Church Street, NW8

▼

ANTIQUARIUS: Located in the popular Chelsea section of London, Antiquarius could be mistaken for a theater from the outside. In actuality it was constructed in an old snooker hall building dating way back when. With over two hundred stalls, Antiquarius has gained a reputation for being the place to go for Art

Nouveau and Art Deco pieces of every variety, from jewelry to furniture. Open Monday to Saturday from 10:00 A.M. to 6:00 P.M.

ANTIQUARIUS, 135–41 Kings Road, SW3

▼

CHENIL GALLERIES: is newer and more of a shopping arcade. They have an art gallery and are known for being a good place to look for antique medical instruments as well as seventeenth- and eighteenth-century paintings and smaller items. Open Monday to Saturday from 10:00 A.M. to 6:00 P.M.

CHENIL GALLERIES, 181–83 Kings Road, SW3

▼

BOND STREET ANTIQUES CENTRE: Like Grays, the Bond Street Antiques Centre is located amid the finest in fashion and specializes in the finest of miniatures, porcelain jewelry, silver, and paintings. Open Monday to Friday from 10:00 A.M. to 5:45 P.M.

BOND STREET ANTIQUES CENTRE, 124 New Bond Street, W1

▼

Antiquarius, Bond Street, and Chenil are all owned, along with the Bermondsey, Camden, and Cutler Street markets, by ABC Antiques Centres. For more information on these you can write their offices at 15 Flood Street, London, SW3.

Street markets are a special passion of ours—

sort of like the hunter who gets excited by pursuing the big game. We can't stand the sight of blood, but love the chase. There are many street markets, but our favorites for quality antique and collectible items are:

▼

BERMONDSEY MARKET: also known as the New Caledonia Market. Open Fridays only from 5:00 A.M. until 2:00 P.M. Go early for the best deals. Take a torch (flashlight) and elbow the dealers who are there to buy it all. Many of the deals are done out of the trunks of cars, or in the indoor cafe across the street. The dealers who are buying arrive early and leave just as early. The official market opens at 7:00 A.M., but by this time the good pieces will have left, only to appear the next day on Portobello Road, or in Camden Passage. Bermondsey is our very favorite market.

BERMONDSEY MARKET, corner of Long Lane and Bermondsey Street, SE1

▼

There is also a covered market building across the street called the Bermondsey Antiques Market and Warehouse, which is run by the London Borough of Southwark as a commercial retail group of dealers. There are around a hundred stalls. In this building you will find a *bureau de change* and a cafe (entrance from the outside of the building).

▼

PORTOBELLO ROAD: We find shopping on Portobello Road more of a street scene than a good shopping scene—maybe because we have seen a lot of the merchandise at Bermondsey already. However, Portobello Road is the source for some good finds if you dig, dig, dig. It is also good for specialty stands. Start at the south end at Pembridge Road. The road is actually many markets. Starting at Chepstow Villas are the five blocks of antiques shops that have made Portobello famous. After Lonsdale Road you will find food stalls and butcher stands. Once you reach Ladbroke Grove you have reached the junky section of the street. No one can do Portobello Road in one day without fainting somewhere toward the punk section. Remember to deal in cash only and to bargain. Prices on Portobello have gone up over the years as the road became respectable, and rents on the stalls have escalated. The road is liveliest on Saturdays, when all the stalls are in operation. The permanent stores are open during the week, but the stalls are where the best deals are made. Shops are open Monday to Friday from 9:00 A.M. to 5:00 P.M. On Saturday and Sunday the flea market is open from 9:00 A.M. to 6:00 P.M. And if you really care, you'll rent a video of *Bedknobs and Broomsticks* and join Angela Lansbury in the chorus of a song called "Portobello Road," which glorifies everything for sale there.

PORTOBELLO ROAD, Portobello Road, W11

▼

CAMDEN PASSAGE: is our idea of a yuppie or Sloane Ranger market. Basically this upmarket collection of shops is housed in two larger buildings: Georgian Village, which is a converted warehouse, and The Mall, which was a tram depot in the Victorian days. There are over two hundred antiques stores open every day, and on Wednesdays and Saturdays the area becomes crowded, with hundreds of stalls selling just about everything imaginable. The more permanent shops have a good collection of fine-quality antiques along with the junk. Open Monday, Tuesday, Thursday, and Friday from 10:00 A.M. to 5:00 P.M., Wednesday and Saturday from 8:00 A.M. to 4:00 P.M.

CAMDEN PASSAGE, Upper Street, Islington, N1

▼

CAMDEN LOCK: This is definitely the lower end of the antiques markets, but fun nevertheless. Located in the Regents Canal section of Camden, the canals provide a practical means to transport goods from the docks in the East and the main canal that carries on to Birmingham. However, the area around the Camden Lock has become more of a pleasure, shopping, and craft area in the past decade. Many of the warehouses have been taken over by craftsmen who sell their wares during market days on Saturday and Sunday. Crafts are the predominant product to be found here, with antiques of lesser quality. There are a couple of markets surrounding Camden Lock. One is in the vicinity of The Roundhouse to the north, and the other is at the intersection of Brick and Camden High streets to the south. Open Saturday and Sunday from 10:00 A.M. to 5:30 P.M.

CAMDEN LOCK, Camden High Street, NW1

8 ▾ DAY TRIPS AND TOURS OF LONDON

Britannia Rules the Rails

Hail, Britannia and all that. But better yet, rail Britannia. The British Empire begins at home, and trains are one of the best ways to see it. Even if you are staying in London for a short time, you can take one day out for a most complete adventure. There are several day trips—and overnight trips—that visitors to London can enjoy without ever having to rent a car, drive on "the wrong" side of the road, or worry which spoke of a roundabout is the correct one. London's subways made for great bomb shelters, but her train stations and web of commuter rails make for easy comings and goings. Trains run on regular schedules and are easy to catch and enjoy. Just a few words of warning:

▾ Trains in Britain are far more expensive than in Continental Europe. If you are used to how cheaply you can get from Venice to Vienna, or from Ventimigilia to Milan, think twice about Brit Rail. Before you decide on a day trip, understand the price and correlate it to the reason for the trip. You may be shocked at how expensive a day trip can be.

▾ There are "savers." Savers are cheaper fares—at nonpeak times (after 9:30 A.M., etc.) and nonpeak days (Monday through Thursday). Nonpeak days are called Blue Days. Blue Days are less expensive than White Days.

▾ Various trains leave from different stations. Know where you want to go and which train station you are leaving from. The tube connects to all the train stations; merely watch for the turkey tracks insignia, which stands for Brit Rail. Allow time to connect from the tube to the train. Depending on which line of the tube you take, you may have a fair walk.

▼ If you are a student, use your student pass (a special Brit Rail student pass) because you will save about 30% on the price of your tickets. If you could be a student, consider this aspect before you leave home and bring the proper papers (a letter from an appropriate source saying that you are a student). A Brit Rail student ID costs about $20.

▼ Most train stations are filled with retail shops, including bookstores that sell guidebooks to wherever you are going. There are tourist or information booths in most train stations. Look around, as this information will help you immensely, even if you are just shopping. You can also buy fast food at a train station, but your train probably will have a buffet (say "buffy") car for sandwiches, crisps (potato chips), toasted bacon sandwiches, etc.

▼ Paddington Station does not have a bear in it. Anywhere.

Planning Your Day Trip

While you can walk into a station, buy a ticket, and run off to anywhere—even to Continental Europe—we have found that our day trips are most successful if we plan them. Pick the day or days of travel early and work them into your itinerary so you can save money and be in the right city on its best day (e.g., Bath on Wednesday); ask your hotel concierge what time the trains leave and from what station so you don't panic on the morning of the journey. If there is more than one of you traveling, discuss the possibility of renting a car for the day. You can rent a car for approximately the price of the train ticket to Bath, or even less. While we're chicken to drive in England, you may be more confident. For two or more people, a car is far more cost-effective. Know where you are going and what you plan to do there: Bath is a great town for just wandering around in, but Stoke-on-Trent is not. Both cities offer a tremendous amount of stimulation (of different sorts), so be prepared to make choices. You cannot "do" Bath in a few hours, but you can see a lot of it, wander contentedly, or do some serious antiques shopping. Decide. Stoke-on-Trent is the main train destination for The Potteries, yet there are dozens of factories and factory outlets there. You can't shop all of them (but you can go down trying). Decide which ones you want to visit, and arrange your day accordingly. A little bit of homework will make your day trip from London all the more enjoyable.

Bath

Beginners' Bath

"Bath is a charming place," wrote Jane Austen, "there are so many good shops here." Who would have believed it? Jane Austen was born to shop! Did your English lit teacher ever tell you that? Of course not. But Jane Austen was right when she said it, and the fact still holds: Bath is an amazing amalgamation of the best of London shopping condensed into one workable area. All your favorite big-name English firms are here (Laura Ashley, Richards, Next), there are lots of charming smaller shops— some chains, some local specialists—and there

BATH

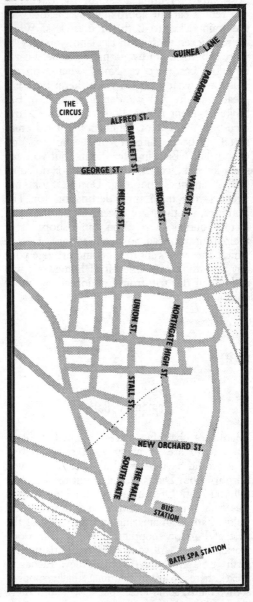

is a huge antiques business of many strata, from hoity-toity to downright tag sale. There are numerous markets, there are alleys closed to traffic, there's cute and cuter still.

But aside from shopping, Bath offers culture, culture, culture. You can easily combine a tour of antiquities and architecture with your shopping ventures—and you *must* take in the Costume Museum. There's enough to do in Bath to fill a weekend easily, or a week—so a day trip will keep you on your toes. We never stop to eat lunch when we go to Bath because the shopping is so intense and our time is limited, but there are many places to visit. There also are several hotels in the area, including the famous Royal Crescent, which is the only one we've ever tried, since we're big on expensive, grand, pretentious, outrageously wonderful Old World hotels. Indeed, if you want to do the English country weekend bit—especially nice with the husband and without the kids—use the Royal Crescent as your base and take in the heady luxury of the whole thing.

▼ Trains to Bath leave from (and return to) Paddington Station.

▼ A round-trip ticket costs about $50 on a weekday.

▼ The trip is one hour, twenty minutes and is very pleasant; while not as scenic as the trip to Stoke-on-Trent, it's nice, and the approach into Bath is beautiful. The entire landscape of small slopes filled with rows of attached homes, all beige and dancing in the light, is something inordinately special.

▼ Everything in Bath is within walking distance of the train station; you need not take a cab. There is a minibus, called Badger, that makes pickups across the street from the train station and that will deliver you to any number of in-town locations.

▼ Weather and time of year may influence how much you enjoy Bath. The first time we were there, it was October and the light was beautiful and dusty (to match the buildings) and everything looked almost as good as in the photographs in our favorite magazines. The second time we were there it was May and it was pouring rain and Bath really looked very dull and boring and provincial and not so special. The last time we were in Bath it was a sparkling bright sunny day (a rarity in England) in August—the weather made it a wonderful day for browsing, but the throng of tourists made one wonder if the entire city had been created by Walt Disney for the benefit of the paying public. Jaded travelers and those who hate crowds may find the city slightly lacking in charm if they visit it in high season.

▼ If you are going for a serious stay, you may want to consider one or both of two guidebooks: *The New Bath Guide,* published by Ashgrove, and *The Good Bath Guide,* published by Good City Guides. Each book costs about $5. The two are so totally different from each other that if you can afford to splurge the $10, we think you'll enjoy them both. On the other hand, if you're going just for a one-day shopping trip, you don't need a guidebook at all.

▼ There is a tourist information center at Abbey Green. The help is cordial, and they have free brochures for sights and tours of the surrounding area. They charge about 30 cents for a map of the city.

▼ The very best way to see Bath is to use no guidebook, have no plans, and just get lost and found. The city is a bit difficult to navigate because of all those crescents and circles, so many streets don't go through and there are all sorts of alleys and streets that look easy on maps but are nowhere to be found when you need them; but because you speak the language and because it's all so scenic, you may indeed toss books to the wind and go it alone. You may also miss a lot this way, since Bath is full of sights and you can't possibly experience them all in just hours. If you are staying the weekend, or even the night, for your first foray into the streets you may enjoy the lost-and-found technique to help you learn your way around and to let you begin to absorb some of the city delights. Then you can go to your map, guidebook, and priority list to fill in the must-do's that are most important to you.

▼ There are free walking tours, there are bus tours, there is everything you would expect in a major tourist trap. We leave all that to you, the tourist information center, et al., and we just remind you of one thing: No, you cannot take a bath in the Roman ruins. You may see the baths, but you cannot use them.

Antiques Shopping in Bath

The main reason that serious shoppers go to Bath is for the antiques. Dealers abound, and regulars with sharp eyes feel that the prices are considerably (20 to 25%) lower than in London. Naturally, London dealers are on top of the situation, and friends have friends and call friends and good stuff moves fast, but you can find some good buys and have a lot of fun in the meantime. If you have an awful lot of money to spend and are dead serious about all this, you should not pressure yourself with train schedules and perhaps should stay for a few days. We could fill a shipping container in a matter of hours, but we're not picky—we'll buy anything as long as it's gorgeous.

Day shoppers, please note: Wednesday is considered antiques day, and there is a lot of special-day traffic. Serious shoppers, please note: Most of the Wednesday markets are in collectibles and small knickknacks; if you are buying top-of-the-line fine furnishings, we don't think the day of the week will matter much. There is little in the hoity-toity arena that is available only on Wednesdays.

If you are in Bath just for antiques, you may want to begin your day with a taxi ride to the Guinea Lane Market, which is open only on Wednesdays and is the farthest point uptown that you will be visiting. This will save you the time and energy of walking through town. You'll be walking downhill toward the train station, so you'll get to see plenty of town. The Guinea Lane Market is open *on Wednesdays only.* It advertises itself as the Portobello Road of the West, but we think it makes Portobello Road look swank. The building is old and damp and musty and creaky (the bathroom is clean, however); this is the kind of place that dealers are comfortable in but that blue bloods and royals may find lacking in charm. It is not even quaint. But there are several floors of dealers. Some eighty-five stall sellers set up shop starting at 7:00 A.M. It's a very "in" crowd—most of the shoppers and the stall-holders are dealers, and they gossip about each other and about American dealers who come over to see them. There is no shipping agent for the building, but the office suggests Martin of Frome for "removals and storage." Removals are shipping arrangements.

Antiques shops and dealers and markets are dotted all over town (and the surrounding county); we suggest you walk down the hill from Guinea Lane and stop at any place that tickles your fancy. Some of our favorites:

▼ Landsdown Hill: The first roll down the hill is a crescent with a string of shops and dealers. This is Landsdown Crescent, and the hill is called—you got it—Landsdown Hill. The Antiques Warehouse is at 14 Fountain Buildings. There are several shops in Belvedere on Landsdown Road. Remember, all the architecture in Bath is similar (talk about town planning), and most buildings are blocks of units—a building can be the length of a city block, but it also may curve and have various entry halls and courtyards.

▼ Paragon Antiques Market: Across from the Royal York Hotel, this market has more stallholders and fun and some fancy junk; it is a Wednesday-only affair.

▼ Graylow & Co. Antiques: we think this is one of the best antiques shops in Bath, but since goods come and go, we have to try to stay calm. It is upper end to hoity-toity, but the people are nice and gave us the best advice we heard in England: "Buy two carefully chosen good pieces and sell them in the States and you will be able to pay for your entire trip and the container with the profit."

▼ Bartlett Street: period. If you have time only to visit one street in Bath, this is the one. There are two great antiques markets on this street (Great Western Antiques Centre and Bartlett Street Antiques Centre) as well as a few other dealers. There's more in the next block that leads to Alfred Street—and then you are next to the Costume Museum. Perfect planning. The Great Western is the single best antiques market we've ever seen—it's indoors in a nice building, and each stall is housed in bright green wooden booths with large black letters in easy-to-read Helvetica type style with the name of the shop and the stall number. On Wednesday there is a market downstairs that is more of the tag-sale type, but it is a cute addition. The Wednesday market opens at 7:30 A.M. The everyday market opens at 9:30 A.M. six days a week.

Bath is pretty much closed on Sunday, by the way, but some hoity-toity dealers will make private appointments on this day. The bigger dealers prefer appointment-only clients anyway, just as in London. A handful of the more commercial shops in the real-people area also are open on Sunday, such as Reject China Shop, National Trust, and Wellows Crafts. If you are a serious antiques shopper only, you will not have a big problem with what to do on Sunday.

▼ Walcott Street has more workshops and crafts/ artisan dealers, as well as several fun, silly junk shops. You can pass this up, but if you decide to try it, look at Quest Antiques & Pine, 27 Walcott Street, and the nearby China Doll for doll collectors and enthusiasts. There also is a cattle market on Walcott Street.

▼ The Guildhall Market does have a few dealers in it, but this is mostly a fruit and vegetables market. It's fun to visit and you should go, but don't be expecting anything nearly as fine as the Great Western. If this is your first stop (which it may be if you are working your way up the hill), it does get better. Take a good look at the building from the outside; it's far better than the inside.

▼ Wood Street also is home to several dealers— zig over one block between Milsom and New Bond. Dando and Deacon are the two biggest, most famous names on the street.

▼ A good number of dealers are open by appointment only. The tourist information center can give you brochures about antiques in the area; some of these dealers are listed with their phone numbers. Many shops are in homes (or vice versa), so dealers advertise "residency"; they will all make special appointments after hours for rich Americans. Proceed per your own interests and pocketbook.

If you are interested in shipping, any fine dealer will make arrangements for you and will organize the other dealers to put your lot together. We did our main buying through Graylow, who handled everything. All the dealers know each other—this is a very small society, they all do work together. We've heard tell that it's easier for these guys to put together a container to New York than to get some new pieces up to Manchester.

Antiques Markets

BARTLETT STREET ANTIQUES CENTRE:
Clean, well-lighted market with about fifty dealers. Across the street from Great Western. Stalls do not have names or numbers but are called "The Linen and Lace Stall" or something like that. Every type of antique is sold here. Hours: Monday, Tuesday, Thursday to Saturday, 9:30 A.M. to 5:00 P.M.; Wednesday, 8:00 A.M. to 5:00 P.M.

BARTLETT STREET ANTIQUES CENTRE, 7–10 Bartlett Street

▼

BATH ANTIQUES MARKET: For true believers and dealers. Hours: Wednesday only, 7:00 A.M. to 3:00 P.M.

BATH ANTIQUES MARKET, Guinea Lane

▼

BATH SATURDAY ANTIQUES MARKET:
What else would you do on a Saturday? Hours: Saturday only, 7:00 A.M. to 5:00 P.M.

BATH SATURDAY ANTIQUES MARKET, 7–9 Broad Street

▼

GREAT WESTERN ANTIQUES CENTRE:
Sixty stallholders during the week, over a hundred on Wednesday. It's clean, well organized, easy to shop, has a restaurant and cafe, and is very much worth the cost of the trip. If you just go here and to the nearby Costume Museum, you will be a very happy person. Hours: Monday, Tuesday, Thursday to Saturday, 9:30 A.M. to 5:00 P.M.; Wednesday, 7:30 A.M. to 4:30 P.M. in basement.

GREAT WESTERN ANTIQUES CENTRE, Bartlett Street

▼

PARAGON ANTIQUES MARKET: One block down the hill from Guinea Lane, handles the overflow from that market. Convenient to Landsdown Hill. Hours: Wednesday only, 7:00 A.M. to 4:00 P.M.

PARAGON ANTIQUES MARKET, 3 Bladud Buildings

Information on neighborhood markets and special sales is posted on a bulletin board at the Guinea Lane Market at the entrance to the main doorway. The neighboring towns in Avon have markets, fairs, and antiques dealers.

Real People

The real people of Bath (of which there are only about eighty-four thousand) must find shopping quite an adventure; the town has the benefit of the tourist traffic who make this city a vital marketplace. Yet Bath still has some very small-town, local kinds of places that remind you that Bath is a real small town. The two main shopping streets that real people and tourists alike use lead away from and back to the train station and change names at each block. Parts of these streets are mainly for pedestrians. There are sparkly special shops that are branches of well-known shops, and dull, boring local stores all nestled along these blocks. There also are a fair number of charity resale shops. Locals are not rich. There is only one big-name-designer-type shop; the London chains that have shops here are in the moderate-price range and offer the only retailing glamor that Bath has. Most of the local cutie-pie shops have been specifically created as such for the tourist market.

To hit the main shopping streets, exit the train station and turn left for one block. You'll pass the bus station and the Badger stop and get to a Boots chemist. (This is an excellent Boots, by the way.) At Boots, turn right and head up The Mall. The Mall runs parallel to Southgate, the main shopping thoroughfare. Check your map to see the giant U-tour that will take you to all the main shopping areas:

1. Turn right at The Mall and go one block, then zig left to Southgate.

2. Proceed on Southgate to Lower Borough Street, turn right, and follow the pedestrian precinct, as it is called, to Abbey Green.

3. The tourist office is at Abbey Green.

4. Pass Abbey Green to Abbey Grove and the Guildhall Market. Proceed on High Street.

5. Follow High Street up the hill to Walcott Street.

6. Cut over to Paragon Street and continue uphill to Bartlett Street.

7. Cut over on Bartlett, seeing all the antiques markets, then to Alfred, seeing the Costume Museum, and begin downhill on George Street.

8. Take George to Milsom Street, and Milsom to New Bond Street.

9. Look down side streets, such as Green Street, to see if they interest you.

10. After proceeding on both sides of New Bond Street, return to Milsom Street where it becomes Old Bond Street.

11. Continue shopping your way downhill as Milsom Street becomes Union Street.

12. Follow down; Union Street will become Stall Street.

13. Stall Street will become Southgate.

14. Follow Southgate until it dead-ends, turn left, and walk one block to the train station.

The Shops

There is little in terms of shops in Bath that isn't in London, but it's all within one neighborhood in Bath. While the shops aren't as big as the London flagship stores, you may like some of them better (we like the Bath Laura Ashley better than any of the London Laura Ashley shops), or you may enjoy the compact, easy-to-use, made-for-tourist stores. Except for antiques, there is nothing in Bath that you can't get almost anyplace else. You just might have more fun finding it in Bath than elsewhere. A warning about prices: They may be higher on ready-to-wear than in London in local stores that cater to tourists. The big-name chains all have fixed prices.

Just about any chain you can think of has a store in Bath, so this list is small and tries to veer away from chains unless they are rather special. It's easy to shop these stores, so don't hold back, and remember that everywhere you look you're bound to find a Benetton.

For some reason we do not understand, Bath is simply loaded with ethnic boutiques, places that sell Peruvian handicrafts or whatever. These shops are everywhere in the main shopping streets. The number of them is overwhelming and confusing. What are they doing here?

Don't forget to look down small streets, into alleys and arcades—they, too, are filled with shops. Here're just a few of our favorite stops, aside from antiques markets:

NEXT: A large shop with men's to the left and women's to the right, and interiors upstairs. There're other Next shops in town, but this is the main store, and going there is an easy way to see what Next is all about.

NEXT, 16–17 Union Street

COLLECTIBLE COUTURE: Lovers of antique clothes, what are you doing in London? Hop the next train. A museum-quality Victorian tea gown, with bustle, is $200. Not every piece in this shop belongs in a museum, but if you know your stuff and love old clothes, you'll want to move in. Prices are low to moderate. Prices are bargain basement on some items compared to the world market for like clothes in good condition. They close for lunch from 12:30 P.M. to 1:30 P.M.

COLLECTIBLE COUTURE, 3 Bennett Street

TRIDIAS: It will take your kids three days to be done with this excellent toy shop that has branded toys, locally crafted toys, wooden pieces, dollhouses, Galt, and three houses of cute stuff.

TRIDIAS, 6 Bennett Street

▼

JOLLY'S: This is the local department store. (There are other department stores, mostly chains, but this is the local top-of-the-line department store.) It has everything in a general-store, specialty-store approach—the makeup area is new and glitzy, with mirrors on the ceiling, while the rest of the shop is sort of Art Deco, with peacocks at the crown molding. It's a strange store with dime-store merchandise and yet a crystal and china department fit for a royal bride.

JOLLY'S, Milsom Street

▼

REJECT CHINA SHOP: One and the same.

REJECT CHINA SHOP, 34 Stall Street

▼

CHINACRAFT: Yes, Virginia. But you'll make no deals here, as you may in London if you are a big spender.

CHINACRAFT, 34 Milsom Street

▼

HAMLEY'S: A smaller and easier-to-deal-with version of the London shop.

HAMLEY'S, 4 Milsom Street

▼

JIGSAW: We loved them in London as well, a Joseph Trico-fun London look that's wearable anywhere.

JIGSAW, 8 New Bond Street

▼

LAURA ASHLEY: It's all here. Upstairs to the clothes. Wallpaper in the closeout bins is $3 a roll.

LAURA ASHLEY, 9 New Bond Street

▼

MONSOON: If you like this ethnic, cheapie look, this is a branch of the oh-so-popular chain.

MONSOON, Unit One, Upper Borough Walls, Northgate Street

▼

MOTHERCARE: One of the chain, a pleasure for those with young kids.

MOTHERCARE, 44–48 Southgate

Stoke-on-Trent

Stoke for Strangers

Stoke-on-Trent, how do we love thee? Let us count the ways.

Service for four. Service for ten. No, make that service for twelve.

Stoke is the china and crystal bargain capital of England, and if your patterns happen to be English—as ours are—be prepared to stock up on seconds, overruns and all the goodies you've wept over because you were too poor to buy the soup tureen, or the gold-rimmed salad plates.

But we digress. We foam on and drool and dribble without telling you the basics. Pardon us.

Stoke-on-Trent is the center of an area of England called The Potteries. All the big-name pottery makers have their factories—and their factory outlet shops—in this little area. Need we say more?

Yes. Before you go running off in a fit of excitement, we have several insider's tips:

▼ If you are considering the trip to Stoke as a day trip from London, note that the price of the train ticket may exceed your savings or enjoyment of the day. This is a serious buying trip. Brides should do it, without question; those on driving trips with cars at hand should do it, without question; those who have budgets to buy and don't mind the price of shipping should do it, without question. But if you're just going to browse, thinking you'll have a quaint day in the country, then you may want to think twice. Stoke is not pretty, nor are you going to have a pretty day in the country (one exception—Wedgwood) while you do this big saving adventure. You will spend three hours of your day on the train and pay about $50 to get there. After that you will undoubtedly need a taxi. So now you're down about $60. Add to this the undisputed fact that prices on best wares (that's first quality pottery) are fixed. *The price you pay in the factory shop may be the exact same price you will get in London.* This trip is tons of fun and we can't wait to do it again, but it takes time and money and effort to make a killing.

▼ Go with a friend, it's not much fun alone.

▼ Consider renting a car if there are two (or more) of you. The drive isn't that far, you'll save on the train fare and the taxis and have much more room for lugging home your purchases. Car rentals in London can be as low as $25 for one day. This trip can easily be done in a day.

▼ If you are taking the train, try to go on a Blue Day, which will save you money. It's an off-peak time of the week. Since Tuesday is the best tour day, and is a Blue Day on the train, try to organize your schedule accordingly.

▼ Yes, you can eat breakfast on the train.

▼ Stoke is the same small town in Texas that everyone couldn't wait to grow up to leave and once he left eventually wrote a movie about it all. Or a Pulitzer Prize–winning play. The economy is terrible, Stoke is not filled with renovated buildings and cutesy-pie shops or anything that resembles the Cotswolds. Think Charles Dickens. Longton is less depressing, but it's not Flemington, New Jersey.

▼ There's a good chance that it will be raining when you get to Stoke (it always rains in England), so be prepared for the extra difficulties of shopping in the rain. We had such a good time we were actually singing in the rain, but if you aren't a good sport—you might be dismayed.

▼ Stoke has a Pottery Centre attached to the train station. DO NOT MISS IT. This is the main meeting place for tourists, this is where all the tour buses leave from, this is where you get the free brochures and guides. The Pottery Centre is open seven days a week, 10 A.M. to 6 P.M.; they are closed on Sundays January to March. Tours can be arranged from here without prior booking. You can go on an all-day tour of the area, which is one of the only ways you will see it for a relatively low price. Tuesdays seem to be the best day. There are different tours on different days of the week and they go to different factories. If you want to go to a specific factory, and only that factory, you may be better off without a tour. Tours can cost as little as $5 and are worthwhile if you want to see several things in the area. Do not step off the train and decide to punt, as you will feel lost, fearful, and possibly miserable. Go directly from the train station to the adjoining Pottery Centre or get into a taxi in front of the station and go to your destination. While it's possible to walk into town, it is about a mile.

▼ If you have a car, you will not have any problems getting around the Stoke area. Be emotionally prepared for a lot of schlepping if you don't have a car—or be financially prepared to hire a taxi to drive you and wait for you, as you will never get another taxi after the first one from the train station. We hired a taxi from the front of the train station to take us to Wedgwood, to wait for us and then drive us back to the train station for less than $20. He did not charge for waiting time; we tipped $3. The total, with the tip, was $18.

▼ Most of the china outlets ship to the U.S., but some will not ship seconds. Who cares? Bring a wheelbarrow and load boxes on the train yourself, if need be. Or just buy what you can carry. If you are really planning on stocking up on seconds, rent a car just for the trunk space. It's worth it. You can arrange shipping easily from London. If you are going to one outlet only and want to make a haul of it, you may want to call from London the day before and ask about shipping (ask specifically if they ship seconds) and store hours. If the call costs $5, which it won't, it'll be worth it.

▼ There is a Tourist Information Center in downtown Stoke. Be sure to use it, although we plan to give you enough information in this section to help you make your plans prior to arriving in Stoke. The blue building with the white trim is manned by women who know the outlets and provide free brochures on all the local sights. They will also give you the local bus schedule, if you have no car and don't want to spring for a taxi.

▼ Different outlet shops have different minimum requirements for a VAT refund. Ask first. One shop quoted us the ridiculously low amount of £20 for VAT. We've never heard of anything below £50, so we doubt if this is correct. But ask. Most of the outlets give VAT at £50, one or two are at £45, and one or two are £75.

▼ Many factory outlets sell pieces from the line that you have never seen before. The best *coup* from our trip was a set of coffee cups, in the larger-than-life-grandfather size, that we never knew were made and have never seen in any other shop in the world. The savings was meaningless because we never knew the original price. But having the item is so satisfying that we feel new energy and anticipation at going back. Who knows what we'll find next time?

▼ No one in the Stoke area seems to understand merchandising and sales except for the Wedgwood people. The Potteries are not like the factory outlet villages that dot the U.S. and Canada. While this area could be extremely exciting and easy to shop, no one has plugged into that yet. If you're driving around this part of England anyway, you'll have no trouble. If you are coming up from London, be organized and know which outlets you want to visit and if they are open. This is the kind of day trip that has the potential for frustration if you are not prepared.

▼ Be sure to check the hours shops are open—they vary from day to day sometimes. Saturday is usually a half day; some shops close for lunch. Many open quite early in the morning, so don't pick a late train from London with the thought that stores don't open until 10 A.M. They often open early and close early. All factory outlet shops are closed by 5:30 P.M.

Getting There

Getting there is half the fun, or so they say. And the train ride into Stoke is a lovely one—you'll pass all the rolling pink-flowered hills, patchwork farms, and black-and-white cows you have been dreaming of. There're even a few half-timbered houses that either are props for us lucky tourists or the real McCoy.

▼ The train leaves from Euston Station in London. Make sure your return train also goes to Euston, as there are some not-so-through return trains that will get you to London but in a longer time and to another station.

▼ Since the outlet shops open rather early in the morning, you can take an early train and get in a full day. Eat breakfast in the dining car, or stop by the buffet car. By all means eat a good breakfast, since you will need the energy for the shopping ahead!

▼ The round-trip ticket will cost about $50.

▼ When you get out of the station in Stoke you will not feel any kind of welcome. In fact, you may panic. Yes, there is a statue of Josiah Wedgwood in front of the station, but unless you know what to do, there is no one who will help you out. You may: (a) go to the Pottery Centre, next door to your left as you exit the station; (b) take a taxi—this is one of the few places where you will be able to find a taxi; or (c) turn right and walk into town, about a mile away. Of course, when you get into town you won't know what to do either—so either go directly to the tourist information center or follow the huge sign on the chimney to Spode.

The Potteries

The Potteries is the local name given to the area centered around Stoke-on-Trent in Staffordshire and includes several nearby villages. Sometimes they are referred to as suburbs of Stoke, but we find that a rather generous term. If your idea of a suburb is Grosse Point, Westchester, Shaker Heights, Beverly Hills, or Buckhead, you're in for a big shock. The most lively of these villages seems to be Longton.

Public transportation connects the various villages, and you can get a schedule of the buses at the tourist office. Buses run approximately every twenty minutes, so if you miss one, you may find it worthwhile to take a taxi—if you can find one. There also is a local commuter train from Longton to Stoke that costs about $1.25 one way.

A taxi ride from Stoke to Longton costs about $3.50.

A taxi ride to and from the train station to Wedgwood, with the driver waiting for you (meter turned off for the waiting), with a tip costs about $18.

Somtimes you can book your air fare, hotel, and visit to England with a Potteries Tour included. There is such a British Heritage Tour available through BTA. For more information, contact Paul Tickner, British Heritage Tours Ltd., Richmond Place, 125 Boughton, Chester, CH3 5BJ.

The Lay of the Clay

There are two public aspects to each factory: Most factories give tours and let you see how everything is made (no children under fourteen allowed due to safety regulations); all factories have outlet shops. Sometimes the outlets are in the factory; at other times they are not. Many of the factories have museums; a few factories have several shops. We have never been to the museums or on the tours (sorry to be so heartless, but all we care about is the shopping).

The goods in the outlet shops usually are marked "best wares" and "seconds." Best wares are the same prices in London.

The outlet shops vary in style from frumpy to medium to incredibly elegant. While most of the shops are similar, Wedgwood is so wonderful and fabulous and impressive that whether you collect it or not, you cannot be in the area without visiting the stores (there are two).

Factories do close down on occasion, so be careful when you plan your trip. Outlet shops may or may not be open when factories are closed. The last week in June, the first week in July, the last week in August, and the week between Christmas and New Year's are not good times to go shopping. Even if a shop is open when a factory is closed, you will not be able to ship.

Wedgwood

Let's face it: It's a Wedgwood town. Josiah's statue greets you as you enter. Everything else for miles pales by comparison; this place is heaven. All of Stoke may make you sad; this side trip will make you happy. The factory is in the "suburb" of Barlaston in Stoke-on-Trent. It appears to be part of the original farm, with a big house, lots of private driveways, many cute cows (possibly rented; who cares?), a stream, and even a private train for the workers. No other place in the area is as pleasant, as elegant, as picturesque, or as worth visiting.

While the factory looks like a factory, it is not unattractive. Attached to it is the visitor center, which is open all year round, including bank holidays. (It's hard to find good shopping on a bank holiday.) The center is closed Sundays and for the week between Christmas and New Year's.

You do pay an admission charge to get the whole tour and see all the workshops and do the deal. But you need not enter the visitor center or pay a cent to go to the shops. The main shop sells best wares in a modern, clean, bright, one-story shop that would look good in any U.S. mall. One room, at the far left, is for the formal bone china. The rest of the shop is divided into sections—children's items, gifts, Jasperware, jewelry, crystal, etc. You may take home an order form, or order there. They will pack and ship. The second shop, behind a pale green Quonset hut, sells seconds and is not nearly as fancy as the other. They will ship for you, however, and are anxious to please— which isn't always the case at other seconds shops. Our buy of the trip was the bone china rose on a plastic stem for $3 each. Each was wrapped for us and put in its own Wedgwood gift bag. There also is a lot of Jasperware here—good gift items. It's hard to find a complete set of dinnerware, but it's easy to find great gifts at incredible prices.

For a sample of charges for packing, delivery, and insurance to the United States, check the following table provided by Wedgwood in fall 1986; calculate the rate of exchange, and understand that prices can go up in time.

NO. OF PIECES	U.S.A., CANADA, AND EUROPE
1 and 2	£6
3–6	£9
7–12	£12
13–18	£18
19–24	£24
25–30	£29
31–36	£34
37–42	£39
43–48	£44
per piece over 48	£.50

Some pieces are counted as two items for shipping purposes (such as soup tureens and other big items); please ask. Duty is the buyer's responsibility (see page 85). A deduction of 13.4% will be given to you for VAT on all items shipped, no matter what the total cost, or on £50 worth of merchandise that is taken by hand from the store. Mail order is invited; pick up a form as you leave.

Spode

The Spode factory is right in beautiful downtown Stoke. Its massive chimneys, which are marked with the company logo, are a welcome sight if you choose to walk from the train station into town, as they will guide you to just the right place. This is a factory that looks like a factory.

You may have a tour for $1.50, or you may go directly to the shop, which is inside the gate on the right-hand side. The shop sells mostly imperfect items and only a few "best wares." While the shop is far from swank, it's easy enough to shop. They have an excellent price list system tacked to the shelves that may read like this:

8″ dinner plate   4   3.75   2

The first price is the local price with VAT included. The second price is the export price— what you pay if you have the item shipped directly out of England. The last price is the cost of the shipping. Add prices two and three to get your total cost. Should you buy something in the shop and take it with you, you will pay the first price, but will qualify for VAT if you spend enough.

Portmeirion

Since we use Botanic Garden as our everyday pattern, we're always happy to find a factory outlet for Portmeirion. We're happier still to find three different ones, all close together and with somewhat different stock. The Portmeirion shops are not dressy, although the one in Stoke may be the cutest shop in town. The one in Longton is less nice. They are most heavily stocked with Botanic Garden, but they also carry all other Portmeirion patterns and some unpainted white work, should that kind of thing interest you. All items are seconds. Some have noticeable damages, some do not. Ask if you can arrange shipping—some days you cannot, other days you can. VAT at £50. The most amazing part of the whole thing is that we saw items we've never seen in the United States or in other traditional china shops in London. Prices were obscenely low. A rolling pin that retails for $32 in the United States costs $10 in Longton; cereal bowls that are $10 elsewhere are $3.75.

The Stoke Trio

If you go just to Stoke (foolish you), you can take in Spode, Portmeirion, and Minton in a matter of hours. Minton is extremely nice— they have a museum on the premises as well as a very pleasant gift shop that has carpet and

lights and amenities. We hear tell that you can
have tea at Minton if you are in a group and
make prior arrangements. Royal Doulton is a
Minton factory, so much of this merchandise
is sold in this gift shop. A five-piece setting of
Minton's "Spring Bouquet" costs $36. The
Bunnykins adult shopping bag cost $6. VAT
after £50. Minton ships best ware but not
seconds.

▼

MINTON (Royal Doulton Group): Hours:
Monday to Friday, 9:00 A.M. to 4:30 P.M.

MINTON, London Road, Stoke-on-Trent

▼

PORTMEIRION: Hours: Monday, Tuesday,
and Wednesday, 8:30 A.M. to 4:00 P.M.; Thursday, 8:30 A.M. to 3:00 P.M.; Friday, 8:30 A.M.
to 3:30 P.M.; Saturday, 9:30 A.M. to 12:30 P.M.

PORTMEIRION, 167 London Road, Stoke-on-
Trent

▼

SPODE: Hours: Monday to Thursday, 8:30
A.M. to 5:00 P.M.; Friday, 8:30 A.M. to 4:00 P.M.;
Saturday, 9:00 A.M. to 1:00 P.M.

SPODE, Church Street, Stoke-on-Trent

Pottery Factory Shops and Museums

Since it is virtually impossible to visit all the factories, and since no one is interested in any factory other than the ones from which she has china and crystal, we provide a list of essentials and suggest you have the time of your life. If you're looking for gift items, you'll never do better than Wedgwood (unless it's a gift for us; then we'll take Portmeirion). Otherwise, go to it; this list is provided by the British Ceramic Manufacturers' Federation.

CITY MUSEUM AND ART GALLERY: Bethesda Street, Hanley, Stoke-on-Trent ST1 3DE; Open: Monday to Saturday, 10:30 A.M.–5:00 P.M. Sunday, 2:00 P.M.–5:00 P.M.; Closed: Christmas holidays and Good Friday

COALPORT: CRAFT CENTRE, Park Street, Fenton, Stoke-on-Trent ST4 3JB; Open: Monday to Thursday 9:30 A.M.–4:30 P.M. Friday 9:30 A.M.–12:30 P.M.; Open most public holidays except Christmas

GLADSTONE POTTERY MUSEUM: Uttoxeter Road, Longton, Stoke-on-Trent ST3 1PQ; Open: Monday to Saturday 10:30 A.M.–5:30 P.M.; Sunday and Bank Holidays 2:00 A.M.–6:00 P.M.

MINTON MUSEUM: London Road, Stoke, Stoke-on-Trent ST4 7QD; Open: Monday to Friday 9:00 A.M.–12:30 P.M., 1:30 P.M.–4:30 P.M.; Closed: Factory holidays

THE SIR HENRY DOULTON GALLERY: Nile Street, Burslem, Stoke-on-Trent ST6 2AJ; Open: Monday to Friday 9:00 A.M.–12:30 P.M., 1:30 P.M.–4:15 P.M.; Closed: Factory holidays

WEDGWOOD VISITOR CENTRE: JOSIAH WEDGWOOD & SONS LTD, Barlaston, Stoke-on-Trent ST12 9ES; Open: Monday to Friday 9:00 A.M.–5:00 P.M. all year, including Bank and factory holidays except

Christmas; Saturday 10:00 A.M.–4:00 P.M.
April to December

Factory Visits

JOHN BESWICK (ROYAL DOULTON GROUP): Gold Street, Longton, Stoke-on-Trent ST3 2JP; Tours: Monday to Friday at 10:15 A.M. and 2:00 P.M. by arrangement with Mrs. Joan Barker

COALPORT: MINERVA WORKS, Park Street, Fenton, Stoke-on-Trent ST4 3JB; Tours: Monday to Thursday 10:30 A.M. and 1:45 P.M.. Friday 10:30 A.M.; Parties: Minimum of 10, maximum of 50. By appointment individuals may be able to join booked parties

CROWN WINSOR: SYLVAN WORKS, Normacot Road, Longton, Stoke-on-Trent ST3 1PW; Tours: By arrangement 9:30 A.M.–11:30 A.M. and 1:30 P.M.–4:00 P.M.

HEALACRAFT INTERNATIONAL LTD.: CINDERHILL TRADING ESTATE, Weston Coyney Road, Longton, Stoke-on-Trent ST3 5EX; Tours: By arrangement, Tuesday, Wednesday or Thursday at 2:00 P.M.. Minimum 20, maximum 50 people

H.& R. JOHNSON TILES LIMITED: HIGHGATE TILE WORKS, Brownhills Road, Tunstall, Stoke-on-Trent ST6 4JX; Tours; Monday to Friday 9:30 A.M.–10:00 P.M. and 2:00 P.M.–4:30 P.M.. By arrangement. Contact Mr. Billings.

JAMES KENT LIMITED (OLD FOLEY POTTERY): King Street, Longton, Stoke-on-Trent ST4 3DH; Tours: By arrangement, minimum 20, maximum 50; 10:00 A.M.–3:00 P.M.. Monday-Friday

MELBA-WAIN (ENGLAND) LIMITED: MELBA WORKS, Heathcote Road, Longton, Stoke-on-Trent ST3 2JY; Tours: Monday to Friday and some Saturdays 10:00 A.M.–12:00 noon 1:00 P.M.–3:00 P.M.. By arrangement with Mrs. Elizabeth Wain.

MINTON (ROYAL DOULTON GROUP): London Road, Stoke, Stoke-on-Trent ST4 7QD; Tours: 10:30 A.M. and 2:00 P.M.. By arrangement with Mrs. Ann Hughes

ROYAL DOULTON: Nile Street, Burslem, Stoke-on-Trent ST6 2AJ; Tours: Monday to Friday 10:15 A.M. and 2:00 P.M. by arrangement with Mrs. Sandra Baddeley; Museum Monday to Friday 9:00 A.M.–12:30 P.M. and 1:30 P.M.–4:15 P.M.

ROYAL GRAFTON CHINA: Marlborough Road, Longton, Stoke-on-Trent ST3 1ED; Tours: by arrangement with Mrs. A. Bentley, Tours Organizer

SPODE R.W.S. LIMITED: SPODE WORKS, Church Street, Stoke, Stoke-on-Trent ST4 1BX; Tours: Monday to Friday 10:00 A.M. and 2:00 P.M.; Last tour Friday 1:30 P.M. by prior arrangement

WOOD & SONS (1982) LIMITED: STANLEY POTTERY, Newport Lane, Burslem, Stoke-on-Trent ST6 3LF; Tours: By arrangement, 10:00 A.M.–11:30 A.M. and 1:30 P.M.–3:00 P.M. Monday to Thursday

Note: All tours begin at Museum. No facilities for disabled people.

NOTE: The factories are closed to the public on the following dates—

▼ EASTER
▼ MAY DAY
▼ LATE SUMMER HOLIDAY
▼ CHRISTMAS HOLIDAY

Pottery Factory Shops

ARGYLE CHINA: Waterloo Road, Burslem, Stoke-on-Trent ST6 2EL; Open: Monday to Thursday 10:00 A.M.–4:45 P.M.; Friday

10:30 A.M.–3:30 P.M.; Closed: factory holidays.

AYNSLEY CHINA: Uttoxeter Road, Longton, Stoke-on-Trent ST3 1NY; Open: Monday to Saturday 9:00 A.M.–1:30 P.M. and 2:00 P.M.–5:00 P.M.; Closed: Thursdays and factory holidays

JOHN BESWICK (ROYAL DOULTON GROUP): Barford Street, Longton, Stoke-on-Trent ST3 2JP; Open: Monday to Friday 9:00 A.M.–4:30 P.M.; Closed: factory holidays

COALPORT: King Street (A50), Fenton, Stoke-on-Trent ST4 3JB; Open: Monday to Thursday 9:30 A.M.–4:30 P.M.; Friday 9:30 A.M.–3:30 P.M., Saturday 10:00 A.M.–5:00 P.M. including Bank and factory holidays except Christmas

CROWN WINSOR: SYLVAN WORKS, Normacot Road, Longton, Stoke-on-Trent ST3 1PW; Open: Monday to Saturday 10:00 A.M.–4:00 P.M.; Closed: factory holidays

GLADSTONE POTTERY MUSEUM SHOP: Uttoxeter Road, Longton, Stoke-on-Trent ST3 1PQ; Open: Monday to Saturday 10:30 A.M.–5:30 P.M.; Sunday and Bank holidays 2:00 P.M.–6:00 P.M.

JAMES KENT LIMITED (OLD FOLEY POTTERY): King Street, Longton, Stoke-on-Trent ST4 3DH; Open: Monday to Friday 9:30 A.M.–4:30 P.M.. Closed: factory holidays

JOHNSON BROTHERS BULL IN A CHINA SHOP TABLEWARE: Lichfield Street, Hanley, Stoke-on-Trent ST1 3EB; Open: Monday to Saturday 10:00 A.M.–5:15 P.M. including factory holidays

JOHNSON CERAMICS LTD.: Victoria Road, Fenton, Stoke-on-Trent ST4 2HS; Open: Monday to Friday 9:00 A.M.–5:00 P.M. including factory holidays. Weekends and Bank holidays by appointment only with Mrs. J. E. Johnson

MASON'S IRONSTONE: Broad Street, Hanley, Stoke-on-Trent ST1 4HH; Open: Monday to

Saturday 10:00 A.M.–4:00 P.M. including Bank holidays and some factory holidays

MELBA-WAIN (ENGLAND) LIMITED: MELBA WORKS, Heathcote Road, Longton, Stoke-on-Trent ST3 2JY; Open: Monday to Saturday 9:00 A.M.–4:30 P.M. including most holidays

MINTON (ROYAL DOULTON GROUP): London Road, Stoke, Stoke-on-Trent, ST4 7QD; Open: Monday to Friday 9:00 A.M.–4:30 P.M.; Closed: factory holidays

MOORCROFT POTTERY (BOTTLE OVEN): W. MOORCROFT LTD, Sandbach Road, Cobridge, Stoke-on-Trent ST6 2DQ; Open: Monday to Friday, 10:00 A.M.–4:00 P.M.; Saturday 9:30 A.M.–12:30 P.M.

PORTMEIRION POTTERIES LTD: 523 King Street, Longton, Stoke-on-Trent ST3 1EZ; Open: Monday, Tuesday, Wednesday 8:30 A.M.–4:00 P.M.; Thursday 8:30 A.M.–3:00 P.M.; Friday 8:30 A.M.–3:30 P.M.; Saturday 9:30 A.M.–12:30 P.M.; 167 London Road, Stoke, Stoke-on-Trent ST4 7QE; 25 George Street, Newcastle, Staffs. ST4 2JS; Open: Monday, Tuesday, Wednesday, Friday 9:30 A.M.–5:00 P.M., Saturday 9:30 A.M.–4:00 P.M. 56a Gaol Street, Stafford ST16 2NR; Open: Monday, Tuesday, Thursday, Friday, Saturday 9:30 A.M.–5:00 P.M.; Closed: Wednesday

ROYAL DOULTON: Nile Street, Burslem, Stoke-on-Trent ST6 2AJ; Open: Monday to Friday 9:00 A.M.–4:30 P.M.; Closed: factory holidays

ROYAL GRAFTON CHINA: Marlborough Road, Longton, Stoke-on-Trent ST3 1ED; Open: Monday to Saturday 9:00 A.M.–4:30 P.M. including factory holidays

ROYAL STAFFORD CHINA LTD: Newcastle Street, Burslem, Stoke-on-Trent ST6 3QD; Open: Monday to Saturday 10:00 A.M.–5:00 P.M. including some factory holidays

ROYAL WINTON: THE WINTON WAREHOUSE, 10–16 Howard Place, Shelton,

Stoke-on-Trent ST3 4LR; Open: Tuesday to Friday 9:30 A.M.–5:00 P.M.; Saturday 9:30 A.M.–4:00 P.M.; Closed: factory holidays

SPODE: SPODE WORKS, Church Street, Stoke, Stone-on-Trent ST4 1BX; Open: Monday–Thursday 8:30 A.M.–5:00 P.M., Friday 8:30 A.M.–4:00 P.M., Saturday 9:00 A.M.–1:00 P.M.; including factory holidays excepting Bank Holidays

STAFFORDSHIRE FINE CERAMICS: Unit 3 Williamson Street, Tunstall, Stoke-on-Trent ST6 6EU; Open: Monday to Saturday 9:30 A.M.–5:00 P.M., including August; factory holidays

STAFFORDSHIRE POTTERIES LTD. (KILN-CRAFT): Meir Park, Stoke-on-Trent ST3 7AA; Open: Monday to Saturday 9:30 A.M.–5:30 P.M. including factory holidays

JOSIAH WEDGWOOD & SONS LTD.: WEDGWOOD VISITOR CENTRE, Barlaston, Stoke-on-Trent ST12 9ES; Open: Monday to Friday 9:00 A.M.–5:00 P.M. including Bank and factory holidays; Saturday 10:00 A.M.–4:00 P.M. April to December

Pottery Retail Shops

EDWARDS CHINA: 4 Market Lane, Hanley, Stoke-on-Trent

EDWARDS TABLEWARE: 8 Market Lane, Hanley, Stoke-on-Trent; Open: Monday to Saturday 9:00 A.M.–5:30 P.M.

LAWLEYS: 54 Ironmarket, Newcastle-under-Lyme, Staffordshire; Open: Monday, Tuesday, Wednesday, Friday, Saturday 9:00 A.M.–5:30 P.M.; Thursday 9:00 A.M.–1:00 P.M.

LEWIS'S LTD.: Hanley, Stoke-on-Trent ST1 1LT; Open: Monday to Friday 9:00 A.M.–5:30 P.M., Saturday 9:00 A.M.–6:00 P.M.

POTTERIES GIFT CENTRE: 51 Newcastle Street, Burslem, Stoke-on-Trent ST6 3QB;

Open: Monday to Saturday 10:00 A.M.–5:00
P.M.
REJECT CHINA SHOPPE: Alexander House,
88 Nile Street, Burslem, Stoke-on-Trent ST6
2BH; Open: Monday to Friday 10:00 A.M.–
4:00 P.M.

London on a Schedule

We hope you've pronounced that "shed-
ule," in proper British fashion.

Tour 1: Mayfair District/
Pound-the-Pavement Day Tour

Shopping in London always is a rewarding
experience. Not only are the best shopping
streets in the smartest and most interesting
parts of the city, but also the quality and diver-
sity of goods available are superb. If you have
only one day to spend shopping, we recommend that you concentrate your time in the
Mayfair section of the city, which includes Old
and New Bond streets, Oxford Street, South
Molton Street, Regent Street, and three arcades (Burlington, Royal, and Piccadilly). This
area is also called the West End.

1. Begin at the Marks & Spencer Department
   Store on Oxford Street, near Marble Arch.
   The British fondly refer to this store as Marks
   & Sparks, and it is a national treasure. Don't
   miss the basement, where you will want to

buy underwear once you see the quality and price! Anything you buy here will be great value for your money.

2. Next, cross Orchard Street and explore Selfridges, a great British example of one-stop shopping. Selfridges is a dumpier version of Harrods, but they do carry a ton of designer lines. Also, their brand name, Miss Selfridge, is young and kicky—perfect for the teen and twenties set.

3. Proceed away from Marble Arch (turn left) on Oxford Street and turn right onto South Molton Street. Explore the shops between Selfridges and South Molton, especially St. Christopher's Place, if you have teenagers or are looking for fun, lower-priced merchandise. Once on South Molton Street, inspect all the shops. This is tiring but fun, fun, fun. South Molton is a fabulous little street—now a pedestrian mall, closed to cars. Because of the many outdoor cafes, it is also a good place to stop for a snack or lunch. Don't miss our favorite shops on this street: Brown's (Nos. 23–27), Benetton (No. 6), Margaret Howell (No. 13), Wallis (No. 22), Hobbs (No. 47), Zero Four Plus (No. 53), Kickers (No. 66), Ken Lane (No. 66), and Trussardi (No. 51).

4. At the end of South Molton, take a left for a short block up Brook Street. Stop in Gianni Versace (No. 35) and Kenzo (Nos. 27–29). Across the street, visit Halcyon Days (14 Brook Street). This is absolutely the best place to buy enamel boxes. Be sure to buy a "Year" box, which is produced as a limited annual edition and quickly becomes a collector's piece. We like to stock up on birthday presents for our friends here.

5. Retrace your steps back to New Bond Street and do both sides of New Bond and then Old Bond streets. You will find most of the

major designer boutiques on these two streets. Don't forget that Sotheby's is at 34 New Bond Street. Two other galleries not to be missed are Wildenstein (147 New Bond Street) and Wylma Wayne (17 Old Bond Street). You might as well add a little art to your purchases! If you need a break, take a stroll through the Royal Arcade (next to 28 Old Bond Street), to Brown's Hotel, at 21–24 Dover Street. Stop in for a wonderful and classic tea, which will include tea sandwiches and scones. We vote these the best scones in London. Also use the W.C., since it's one of the most beautiful ladies' rooms we've ever frequented.

6. Fortified, walk back through the Royal Arcade. Don't miss W. Bill at 28 Old Bond. Turn right from W. Bill and finish your shopping on Old Bond. Then take a left on Piccadilly, a right through the Piccadilly Arcade, and again a right, onto Jermyn Street. Buy the man in your life a shirt at Turnbull & Asser (No. 71), or at Hilditch & Key (across the street). Turn right and walk to Dunhill, which is at the corner of Duke and Jermyn. At least look in the windows. Fortnum & Mason is one of our favorite stores, and if you look up, you will see the clock. Walk toward the clock on Duke Street and you can't miss the store, which is on the corner of Duke and Piccadilly streets. Continue on Jermyn Street until you get to the side entrance of Lilywhite, the sporting goods store. Come around and leave the store on Piccadilly, walking back toward the Burlington Arcade. You can take in Hatchard's, one of London's most famous bookstores, then cross over to the Burlington Arcade. Don't leave Hatchard's without buying at least six of the James the Red Engine books for your four-year-old.

7. The Burlington Arcade is the prettiest covered shopping street in London. This arcade was built in 1819, and its atmosphere has remained delightfully British. The arcade is the only London area that maintains Regency rules of public conduct, prohibiting whistling, singing, or hurrying. Its 585-foot passage is watched over by two guards dressed in the ceremonial garb of officers of the 10th Hussars. Most of the thirty-eight shops sell mainly British goods. We love to browse in all the stores, but our favorite still is N. Peal (Nos. 37–40), famous for their fine cashmeres.

8. Exit the arcade at the opposite end of where you entered, take a right onto Burlington Gardens, a left onto Savile Row (home of the famous Savile Row tailors), a right onto New Burlington Street, and then a left onto Regent Street. You have now entered another major shopping thoroughfare. Walk toward Oxford Street and don't miss Hamley's (No. 200), Jaeger (No. 204), Aquascutum (No. 100), Lawley's (No. 154), Burberrys (No. 165), the Reject China Shop (No. 134), and, finally, Libertys (Nos. 210–20). It's hard to even decide which side of the street to walk on; you might want to do both sides. If pressed to choose, we go for the Hamley's side and walk to Oxford Circus, shop at Top Man, and then circle back.

9. Cut back at the other side of Regent Street now. You are heading toward Piccadilly Circus. You can jump into the tube station there and go home to your hotel and order room service. And new feet.

Tour 2: Knightsbridge Day

1. Begin at Harrods (Brompton Road). Your stay here is optional—it's not un-American to admit you hate Harrods. We have friends who regularly devote a whole day every trip to Harrods. We know others who, in a hushed whisper, confide that they hate this busy and extraordinary store. If you've never seen it, at least tour the food halls and, if you are looking for children's clothing (five and under), check out the fourth floor. The values are superb!

   If you've done it and the store unnerves you, do not feel obligated to try it again for our sake. We admire their style and the fact that you really need no other store in the world, but frankly, this place can be a zoo.

2. Go out of Harrods at the Brompton Road exit and walk to the right toward Knightsbridge. Stop at Charles Jourdan (No. 47) and check out their wonderful selection of shoes and clothing (slightly cheaper in Paris). Proceed on to Harvey Nichols Department Store (corner of Knightsbridge and Sloane streets), known for its great selection of very high-style fashions. If you are hungry, stop at the basement cafeteria, where you can sample their wonderful quiches, coffees, and desserts. Harvey Nichols is a little easier to handle than Harrods; we know people who totally bypass Harrods in favor of this specialty-department store.

3. Now you are ready to take the Sloane Street exit and walk toward Sloane Square. Sloane Street is a long, straight shopping avenue filled with fun, chic boutiques. Look out for Sloane Rangers, those trendy fashion yuppies. Make sure to stop in at our favorites: Joseph's (No. 6), La Cigogna (No. 6A), Brown's

(No. 6C), Issey Miyake (No. 21), Laura Ashley (No. 183), and Descamps (No. 197).

4. Now take Pont Street (off of Sloane Street) a few yards to Pavilion Street and look for No. 73, which is the workshop of Belleville-Sassoon, the royal warrant designer patronized by Princess Diana. Go back to Pont Street and walk away from Sloane Street until you come to Beauchamp Place. Here you will find a bevy of wonderful boutiques. Our faves are: Caroline Charles (No. 9), the Beauchamp Place Shop (Nos. 37 and 55), and, of course, the fabulous Reject China Shop (Nos. 33–35).

5. At this point we suggest that you grab a cab and head to Fulham Road, where you will find Souleiado at No. 171 and Butler & Wilson at No. 189. With your last breath of energy, cross over to Kings Road and buy a pillow for your head and a pillow for your feet at Designers Guild (No. 237). Now take your tired but well-clad body back to the hotel and start repacking that suitcase.

Tour 3: Cute and Merrie Olde Hampstead

Cute England? You say you want cute England? And in a matter of hours? No big deals, no serious train trips? Here it is—just fifteen or twenty minutes from Mayfair and a world away in terms of calm. You can do it all in an hour or two.

One of our favorite escapes from the crowded excitement of central London is to the "burb" (that's suburb to us) of Hampstead, which is undeniably charming. Take the Edgeware branch of the Northern line and there you are—in the midst of Hampstead Village. You're to the north of Hampstead Heath (Heathcliff),

which is a large, rambling, untamed park.
For you literary types, Keats's house is walking distance from here, and both George Eliot
and Karl Marx (what a combination!) are
buried in the Highgate Cemetery across the
Heath.

Hampstead is inhabited by literary types
(who care about George Eliot's gravesite), actors and actresses, and, of course, British
yuppies. It's all quaint and rather perfect with
little shops, restaurants, delis, specialty food
shops, and pubs woven into one perfect urban
escape.

1. Begin your tour at the intersection of Hampstead High Street and Heath Street, where
   you are when you come out of the tube
   station.

2. Most of the good shops lie in a row on the
   left side as you descend Hampstead High
   Street. Just up the station to the right is a
   shopping center with a Whistles and other
   goodies. But we usually wander left, downward in the direction of central London.

3. As you wander, some of the fun shops you'll
   pass are branches of stores you could have
   seen in London. One of the reasons this trip
   is so much fun is that you have a capsule
   version of the best of London in one handy
   spot. Look for Fil à Fil for shirts and ties;
   Benetton, Bertie, and Next. The Laura
   Ashley at 37 Hampstead High Street never
   is crowded and is a very complete store with
   clothes and home furnishing lines—paints,
   papers, everything you need. Asparagus has a
   good local rep as a hot spot, although we
   have found it rather average (are we too
   jaded?); Nicole Farhi is a London favorite
   with very sophisticated, rather expensive designer duds that are perfect for the working
   woman who can afford them. There're
   Hobbs, Carolyn Brun, and yet another
   Monsoon. Are these people after the Benetton

world record for number of shops in a small space?

4. Crown your downhill run with a stop at Designs, 61 Rosslyn Hill (same street, different name), which is a secondhand consignment shop featuring the likes of Kenzo, Missoni, Jean Muir, Krizia, and Nipon at great prices. Downstairs is somewhat less elegant, but the clothes are in good condition. No returns; they accept Visa for purchases over $50.

5. Before you turn around, hit Moonshine for fun young fashions and the French Connections line.

6. Now you can choose to turn left on Downshire Hill to tromp on the Heath or visit with Keats. Or you can head back up the hill until you see Perrins Court, across the street. This little road cuts through to Heath Street, the other commercial lane in Hampstead.

7. Naturally, you've chosen Perrins Court—for its name, no doubt. So we're off for more shopping. On Heath Street, there's John Barry (No. 39), which sells Escada and other upscale lines; Jeeves of Belgravia for men's shirts; and the Hampstead Bazaar (No. 30), where you'll find Williwear, Betty Jackson, French Connection, etc. Don't forget the Hampstead Antiques Emporium (No. 12), a collection of small dealers that adds the whipped cream to the perfection of the day. The Emporium has about twenty dealers who have everything from silver to bric-a-brac to porcelain to important eighteenth-century furniture and is open Tuesday to Saturday, 10:00 A.M. to 6:00 P.M.

8. Finish up the adventure at Louis's, where the tea and pastries are sublime—a just reward after a hard afternoon's shopping.

Still haven't had enough? Insatiable you?

281 LONDON ON A SCHEDULE ▼ 281

We love it! Get on the tube and go one more stop to Brent Cross, where you can work an entire shopping center that's a cross between Hong Kong and middle America.

Special Offer
Buy a Bantam Book
for only 50¢.

Now you can have Bantam's catalog filled with hundreds of titles plus take advantage of our unique and exciting bonus book offer. A special offer which gives you the opportunity to purchase a Bantam book for only 50¢. Here's how!

By ordering any five books at the regular price per order, you can also choose any other single book listed (up to a $4.95 value) for just 50¢. Some restrictions do apply, but for further details why not send for Bantam's catalog of titles today!

Just send us your name and address and we will send you a catalog!